Blueprint for Acti

Achieving Center-Based Change
Through Staff Development

Paula Jorde-Bloom

Marilyn Sheerer

Joan Britz

(with contributions from
Norma Richard)

NEW HORIZONS
EDUCATIONAL CONSULTANTS AND LEARNING RESOURCES

Distributed by
Gryphon House, Inc.
P.O. Box 275
Mt. Rainier, MD 20712
(301) 779-6200

Cover design: Graves Fowler Associates

Library of Congress Catalog Card Number 91-062329

Publisher's Cataloging in Publication
(Prepared by Quality Books, Inc.)

Bloom, Paula Jorde
  Blueprint for action : achieving center-based change through staff development / Paula Jorde Bloom, Marilyn Sheerer, Joan Britz.
  —
    p. cm.
    Includes bibliographical references and index.
    ISBN 0-9621894-2-1
    1. Day care centers — United States — Administration.
  2. Education, Preschool. 3. Organizational change.
  4. Employees — Training of. I. Sheerer, Marilyn. II. Britz, Joan. III. Title.

  HV854   372.21
                        QBI91-1106
                        MARC

Odcc 25088577
ISBN #0-9621894-2-1

Acknowledgments

The impetus for this book came from our work on a Head Start leadership training grant. The grant provided the opportunity for us to work collaboratively in developing training materials for Head Start personnel. It also provided the opportunity for us to formulate our ideas regarding change in early childhood settings. The experience convinced us that a comprehensive model of staff development was needed — one that would address the concerns of child care center directors in a variety of settings.

We are appreciative of the valuable insights we received from the graduate students in the Early Childhood Leadership and Advocacy Program at National-Louis University. These directors and teachers worked with us to test and refine the theoretical ideas upon which this staff development model rests.

Thanks, as well, to Barbara Willer of NAEYC whose helpful suggestions on earlier versions of the manuscript helped guide our understanding of how center-based staff development initiatives could enhance collective efforts to professionalize the field of early childhood.

We are particularly indebted to Karen Kelly, Director of the Gertrude Nielsen Child Care Center; Susan LoSavio, Director of the Busy Bee Children's Center; and Delores Herman, Director of the Dearhaven Child Care Center for their valuable feedback in pilot-testing the exercises and assessment tools included in this book.

Appreciation also goes to those who assisted in the production of the manuscript. Without the research, typing, and editorial assistance of Connie Lohman, Vanessa Payton, Linda Rohaly, and Jason Erb, this book certainly would not have been possible.

And finally, we are deeply grateful to our spouses and families for their continued encouragement and support for all our professional endeavors.

▶ Table of Contents ◀

Introduction

nyone who has chased the shadow of a center director for even a brief time knows that being an effective administrator means wearing many hats: budget analyst, building and grounds manager, staff supervisor, record-keeper, receptionist, community liaison, curriculum developer, instructional leader, public relations coordinator, program evaluator, fundraiser, nutritionist, nurse, and child advocate. The list is long and varied.

And the job seems to have gotten even more complex over the last decade. Indeed, when seasoned early childhood directors get together, one of the most common topics of discussion is how their administrative role has changed. Increased regulatory requirements, multiple funding sources, more complicated fiscal reporting procedures, a greater number of families with special needs, more complex networks of social services to coordinate with, and a host of societal changes have dramatically altered the scope of responsibility and the demands placed upon early childhood center directors.

The director stands center stage. Like the architect, engineer, and construction foreman all in one, the director is the individual responsible for designing and constructing a model program. It is indeed a prodigious task, one for which few program administrators feel their training and education have adequately prepared them.

From our discussions with center directors, we are convinced that a critical element is missing in the training and education of most early childhood program administrators — a theoretical framework for understanding child care centers as organizations. A theoretical framework is important because it serves as a blueprint guiding our actions and behavior. Without a perspective for interpreting the dynamics of center life, directors are apt to go on tackling problems in piecemeal fashion — scrambling to put out one fire at a time — without ever really making lasting changes that improve their programs.

We have found that even in those centers that regularly engage in a range of staff development activities, there seldom exists a coherent model or philosophy of professional development. In other words, when asked to explain why they engage in the practices they do, few directors can articulate a rationale for their approach. A philosophy of professional development is important because it gives substance to action.

Blueprint for Action is designed to help you move beyond a "quick fix" notion of staff development and center improvement by serving as a guide for program analysis and action. It details a comprehensive method for analyzing the different components of your program to increase its effectiveness. It will help you diagnose common organizational problems and select appropriate strategies for implementing change and evaluating progress. It will also help you change the "us" versus "them" atmosphere that permeates many child care centers. In its place will develop a collective sense that the responsibility for center change is a shared one.

Blueprint for Action will serve as a practical resource for directors engaged in improving the overall quality of their programs. The premise for this book rests on two basic assumptions. First, every center has both areas of strength and areas of weakness. The "quality" center is distinguished by its willingness to deal with its imperfections. Lightfoot (1983) used the term "consciousness of imperfection" to describe this organizational characteristic of the exemplary high schools she observed. We think the term is just as apropos to the early childhood setting. The role of the director is one of a catalyst, setting the climate that allows staff to reflect on how program practices might be improved.

The second assumption is that center change can come about only through change in individuals. That is why the emphasis in this book is on linking individual needs to organizational needs. The blueprint presented here will serve as a guide for enhancing the professional development of all who work together in a center to achieve a shared vision.

In this book, we use the terms professional development and staff development interchangeably. This use reflects common parlance in the literature. Technically, however, professional development refers to the growth and change of an individual while staff development refers to the collective professional development of teachers on a staff. It is appropriate in the context of this discussion to use the terms interchangeably because the model of staff development presented in these pages is one that is truly individualized.

A word about how this book is organized

The first three chapters of this book provide a global perspective on the issues. Chapter I presents a social systems model to help you better understand the significance of day-to-day life in your center. At first glance, this chapter may appear weighty, perhaps "too theoretical." We encourage you to read it carefully, though, because it will give you a perspective for better understanding how child care centers function. This chapter is also important because it introduces the terminology used throughout the book.

Chapter I introduces you to a case study featuring Martha, the director of the Children's Corner. Martha's experience of how she applied the ideas presented in this book will breathe life into the theoretical concepts that serve as the foundation for this approach to center improvement.

Chapter II addresses the nature of change and provides an overview of how change occurs in child care centers. Change, as discussed in this chapter, implies altering the people, structure, and processes of a center to achieve more desired outcomes. This chapter sets the stage for Chapter III which describes more specifically the director's role in the change process. In addition to the case study of the Children's Corner, throughout these first three overview chapters are scattered "real life" vignettes connecting the concepts presented to practical situations similar to those you may have encountered. As you read these examples, think of your own center. Jot notes in the margin. This will help you make that important link between theory and practice.

In the second half of this book we connect the theoretical concepts introduced in the first three chapters to a blueprint for action for you to implement at your own center. Chapter IV looks at how you can go about assessing the needs of your center as a whole. This chapter explores issues regarding communication, supervisory processes, goal consensus, leadership style, center climate, and a host of other organizational characteristics. A step by step process for collecting data about your center is presented with numerous assessment tools ready for you to adapt.

Chapter V looks more specifically at how you can assess the needs of the individuals who work at your center. It presents a framework from which you can develop individual profiles for each member of your staff. This information will serve as the springboard from which to implement the staff development model you will learn about as a result of reading Chapter VI.

Chapter VI takes you through a step by step process of designing an individualized model of staff development for your center. This model will serve as a template for putting your philosophy of center improvement into action. The model of staff development presented in this chapter is in sharp contrast to what we customarily call inservice education. Inservice is typically interpreted as something done "to" teachers to remedy some defect. These occasions are often nothing more than an indoor spectator sport where an inspirational speaker is invited, a smorgasbord of workshops offered, and, of course, gallons of coffee and dozens of donuts consumed.

Chapter VII links the notion of individualized staff development to the supportive organizational structures that will ensure its success. This chapter presents information that will help you design a comprehensive performance appraisal system and a career ladder for professional advancement. Chapter VIII, the final chapter of this book, talks about how you can mesh organizational needs and individual needs into a unified approach for achieving change. Collaboration, shared decision making, and team building are the driving forces that make such a vision of center-based change possible.

To help get you started in implementing the ideas proposed in this book, we have included an extensive appendix of assessment tools and sample forms that you can adopt or adapt to meet the specific needs of your program.

We are ardent believers that the blueprint for action detailed in this book works. Where the principles we have shared have been woven into the organizational life of a center, we have seen notable changes in staff morale and in overall program quality. We are confident you will experience the same degree of success at your center. Best of luck!

Paula, Marilyn, Joan
June, 1991

Chapter 1

Child Care Centers as Organizations: A Social Systems Perspective

There are many different ways of thinking about early childhood centers as organizations. Typically when directors are asked to "draw a picture of their organization," they respond by illustrating some version of an organizational chart. This kind of model reflects the formal reporting relationships among jobs and the formal work units that make up the center. While this is one way to think about child care centers, it is a very limited view. It only addresses one aspect of the structure of the center, and captures only a small part of what goes on.

With a limited view of how centers function as organizations, directors are apt to think of individual incidents that occur in the everyday life of their programs as isolated events. Such a narrow perspective can hamper their ability to respond to situations appropriately. The result is that they are more likely to deal with problems that arise in a piecemeal fashion, failing to see the interconnections between isolated problems.

We would like to propose another view of child care centers that takes a broader perspective of organizational life. This approach views centers as dynamic and open social systems. A social systems perspective draws on the literature of organizational theorists such as Beer (1980), Bronfenbrenner (1979), Getzels and Guba (1957), Hoy and Miskel (1987), Katz and Kahn (1978), Moos (1976), Nadler and Tushman (1983) and Owens (1981).

In this chapter we connect the observations of these well-known management theorists with our own experiences in the field of early childhood to construct a model of how child care centers function as organizations. This perspective is important because as directors consider the serious business of improving their programs, it is critical that they look at the "whole" as well as the "parts," viewing their center as a true ecosystem. This chapter provides the framework for that analysis.

What is a System?

The concept of social systems is a general one that applies to groups regardless of size or purpose. Thus we can also think of our family, club, or a corporation as a social system. In simplest terms, a system is a set of interrelated parts. A system is characterized by the interdependence of its parts, differentiation from its environment, a complex network of social relationships, and its own unique culture. When the organization interacts with its external environment, it is an open system.

Now let's take this abstract concept and see if we can come up with some concrete examples of how systems theory can be applied to early childhood programs. Central to a systems theory approach is the notion that the system is comprised of subsystems or components. On a very rudimentary level, for example, we could say a child care center is comprised of different classrooms, or even different groups within the classroom. This is just one way of thinking about programs as an integrated whole made up of interacting parts. It's analogous to an automobile. A car is made up of many different parts all interacting to perform a specific function. This conceptualization, however, is still too basic; it doesn't capture the complexity of the interacting components of child care centers. The remainder of this chapter will describe a more detailed model of child care centers when viewed from a social systems perspective. This model includes several components.

Components of the System

Each component or subsystem of the model described in the following pages is definable and separate but also interrelated and interdependent. These components consist of the external environment, people, structure, processes, culture, and outcomes. Table 1.1 will serve as a useful reference. It summarizes the key elements of each component. Figure 1.1 graphically presents the relationship between these components. As you read the description of each component, think of your own program and make marginal notes concerning the elements of your setting that seem to fit the description provided.

External Environment (the outside world)

Centers do not exist in a vacuum. Every organization exists within the context of a larger environment which includes individuals, groups, other organizations, and even social forces, all of which have a potentially powerful impact on how the organization performs (Nadler & Tushman, 1983).

Early childhood centers, for example, exist in an environment from which they receive inputs such as money, personnel, and clients (parents and children) and to which they produce outcomes. This environment also includes governmental and regulatory bodies, competitors, and special interest groups. It is critical to organizational functioning. The external environment makes demands on the center. For example, it may require a certain kind of service or a certain level of quality. The environment may also place constraints on organizational action. It may limit the types or kinds of activities in which the

center can engage. For example, many state licensing requirements put constraints on the child care center to conform to certain standards. In the mid 1980s, child care centers around the country were severely impacted by the insurance industry when it raised insurance rates for programs. Many programs had to shut down; others found they needed to raise tuition rates or adjust their expenses in order to cover the cost of increased insurance premiums. Finally, the environment provides opportunities which the organization can explore. For example, a program sponsored by a large social service agency may be able to tap other resources of the agency such as volunteers or expertise in program management.

Centers as social systems can be viewed as open systems because they interact with their external environment. The environment in which centers exist has certain values, desired goals, information, human resources, and financial resources. In many respects the external environment creates the context for the organization. It is the source of the inputs and in return receives the outputs.

The values of the broader society as well as the immediate community in which the program exists also influence the center. These are two other facets of the external environment that must be considered. Problems often occur when directors perceive their centers as closed systems disregarding their dependency on the broader environment. But centers are indisputably affected by the values of the community, by politics, and by history. Some examples of the external environment are:

▶ sponsoring agency — for example, Head Start grantee agency, church or synagogue, public school, YWCA, United Way, military command

▶ local community — the immediate neighborhood surrounding the center; mental health and family support services in the community

▶ professional community — professional associations, universities, and teachers' unions that impact the program; other child care centers

Table 1.1

Components of the System

External Environment	People	Structure	Processes	Culture	Outcomes
sponsoring agency	Individuals	legal governing structure	leadership style	shared values and beliefs	Organization
local community and	sex	size (student enrollment,	decision-making processes	norms	reputation of the center
immediate neighborhood	age	total number of staff)	problem-solving processes	history of the center	fiscal viability
professional community	ethnic/cultural heritage	program composition (type	communication networks	traditions of the center	internal efficiency
(prof. associations,	socio-economic group	of program, hours,	planning and goal setting	organizational climate	
other child care centers,	family history	services provided)	processes	ethics	Staff
universities, unions)	educational level	policies regarding children	group meeting processes		absenteeism
legislative bodies and	training	(enrollment, group size,	interpersonal relations		turnover
regulatory agencies	work experience	group composition,	conflict management		level of competence
economic, social, and	interests/skills/talents	ratios)	supervisory and training		job satisfaction
political climate	personal traits (level of	policies regarding parents	processes		commitment to center
business community	abstract thinking,	(roles/responsibilities)	performance appraisal		professional fulfillment
technological environment	temperament,	policies regarding staff	processes		
	learning style, degree	recruitment and training	center evaluation processes		Children
	of flexibility, general	division of labor (job title,	socialization practices		social competence
	dispositions, self-	roles and responsibilities)	child assessment practices		cognitive competence
	confidence, energy	supervisory and perform-	teaching practices		overall health
	level)	ance appraisal policies			
	needs and expectations	pay and promotion system			Parents
	adult development stage	accounting and financial			satisfaction with center
	career stage	management system			perceived support
	commitment	physical environment			
	motivation	(arrangement of space)			Community/society
	professional orientation	materials and equipment			service provided
	beliefs and values	size (square footage of			
	concomitant roles	indoor/outdoor space)			
		philosophy/mission/vision			
	Groups	(center goals/objectives)			
	dominant coalitions	written curriculum			

Figure 1.1

Child Care Centers As Organizations: A Social Systems Perspective

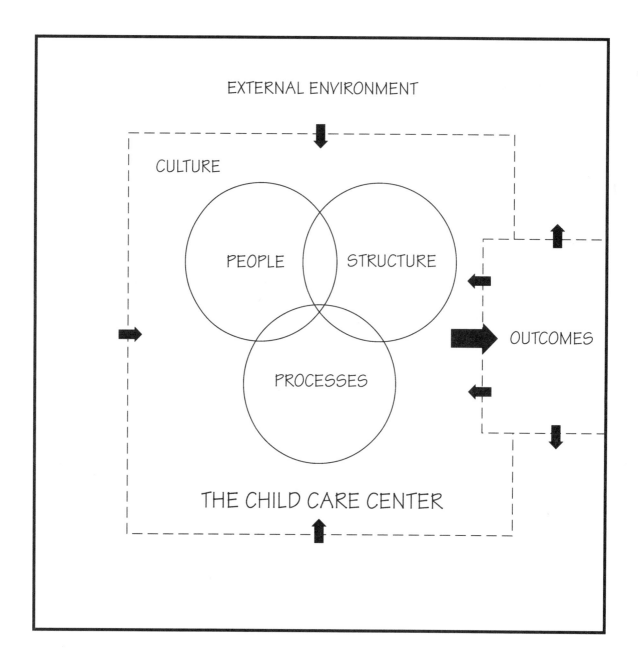

- legislative bodies and regulatory agencies that impact the program — for example, the state's Department of Children and Family Services or Department of Education

- society — social, economic, and political climate

- business community — support, expertise, resources

- technological environment — the availability of different technological resources to which the center has access such as computer support, duplicating, or fax services

Case Study: The Children's Corner

Martha is the director of a Head Start program in a large metropolitan area. Her program, the Children's Corner, is one of five Head Start programs operated by a large nonprofit social service agency. The agency also operates a nursing home and recreation center for senior citizens. Martha's program is housed in a small church.

Martha is keenly aware of the constraints as well as the benefits of the external environment in which her program operates. On the down side, she feels she is inundated with paper work both in meeting Head Start's Performance Standards and the administrative demands of the social service agency that sponsors her. She also has to accommodate the demands of the church which houses her program. That means putting away all her equipment and supplies on Friday afternoon so the church can use her classrooms for Sunday School.

On the positive side, Martha recognizes that she receives many benefits from her external environment. Her agency, for example, is able to get a discount on food, equipment, and supplies because it purchases products in bulk quantities for all its centers. Martha also doesn't have to worry about trying to recruit new teachers. Finding qualified candidates for teaching positions is taken care of by the central administrative office of her agency. Since the agency also operates a nursing home and recreation center for the elderly, Martha was able to tap into this resource for a pool of volunteers to start an intergenerational day care program at her center.

Because the context of each child care center is unique, so too will be the constraints posed by the external environment. Programs that are funded by the military, for example, have a very different set of issues to deal with than those we saw confronting Martha in her Head Start program. Likewise, the effects of the external environment will be quite different for programs in the for-profit proprietary or corporate sector.

Mark and Jennifer are co-owners of a large, for-profit proprietary day care center. Their goal is to provide high quality care at affordable rates. They believe that with cost-effective measures, they can still make a profit while providing a needed service for the community. Mark and Jennifer are fairly autonomous in their decision making, not hampered by having to get things approved by a board of directors. They also feel lucky that they are not burdened by an unending stream of paperwork for a sponsoring agency. This part of their arrangement they like. They find, however, that there are other aspects of the external environment that impact them adversely. These have to do with stereotypical perceptions held by the local community and the professional community about private, for-profit day care. Mark and Jennifer feel sometimes they are swimming upstream against the tide of public opinion and negative press regarding poor quality day care offered by some in the for-profit sector. They believe that parents enrolling children in their program are far more critical of the tuition even though their rates are competitive with nonprofit programs in the area. They even sense that the licensing agent is more critical of their program just because it is a private, for-profit day care. Reversing these impressions has consumed considerable time and energy. Mark and Jennifer are dedicated to doing a good job, but they often feel unappreciated.

People (the cast of characters)

 Organizational theorists refer to the people component of the system as the psychosocial subsystem. The psychosocial subsystem is made up of individuals (psycho) and groups of individuals (social) within the center. People are the raw material of any social system. This component includes the values, attitudes, motivation, morale, and personal behavior of each individual who works for the center. Also included are relationships with others and interpersonal issues such as trust, openness, and group dynamics which ultimately help or hinder the center in its effort to achieve a common goal (Kast & Rosenzweig, 1970).

The people subsystem is based on the idea that a set of individuals is more than an aggregate of persons. As people interact in a social setting, networks of social relations have important effects on behavior (Hoy & Miskel, 1987). Social systems are composed of personalities. Although people occupy roles and positions in the center, they are not simply actors devoid of unique needs. No two teachers or directors in the same situation behave exactly the same way. They have different person-alities, needs, and expectations that are reflected in their behavior. Thus individuals shape their roles with their own styles of behavior.

Beer (1980) reminds us that it is important to distinguish between the "can do" or abilities of an individual and the "will do" or motivational aspects of performance. Motivation ultimately is the ener-gizing force needed to coalesce people into action to meet organizational goals. Indeed, when individ-uals accept jobs at child care centers, they enter into what Schein (1985) calls a "psychological contract"; they expect certain rewards in return for meeting organizational expectations. For each indi-vidual this reciprocal relationship will be slightly different because of the unique motivational char-acteristics of each person.

Just how do people differ? The following describes some of the things that go into making every individual so unique. A more complete description of each of these characteristics will be offered in Chapter V.

- personal background — sex, age, ethnic/cultural heritage, socio-economic group, family history

- educational level/training

- work experience

- interests — our varying preferences

- skills and talents

- personal traits and characteristics — energy level, level of abstract thinking, temperament, learning style, flexibility, general dispositions (e.g. curiosity, nurturance), degree of self-confidence/self-efficacy

- needs — internal forces that determine the goal and the direction of behavior such as the need for achievement, security, or acceptance

- expectations — ideas about what we want and how we should be treated

- adult development stage

- career stage

- organizational commitment

- level of motivation

- professional orientation

- values — those core beliefs that guide our behavior

- concomitant roles — one's obligations outside of work

When individuals come together in groups, the group takes on a kind of collective personality that is the composite of the background character-istics, needs, values, interests, skills/talents, expectations, and dispositions of the individuals making up the group. Typically people seek inter-action with those they like and avoid interaction with those to whom they are not attracted. Some groups are actively sought out, and admired; others are not. And groups have their own person-ality evidenced by their degree of cohesiveness (Barker, Wahlers, Watson, & Kibler, 1987).

Groups can also be viewed as dominant coalitions. These may be formal coalitions (e.g. by role — administrators, teachers, support staff, parents) or informal coalitions (cliques). Some coalitions have more status, power, and influence than others. The different patterns of interaction among individuals and groups, and the status structure defined by them, shape the social structure of the group (Hoy & Miskel, 1987).

Case Study: The Children's Corner

Prior to accepting the directorship at the Children's Corner, Martha was the director of a parent cooperative nursery school. In that previous position, she was confronted daily with the realities of a very influential "dominant coalition," the parents who comprised her board of directors. After three years as director, Martha finally decided to leave her position because she felt that on too many occasions, she had to compromise her professional judgment in order to appease a very diverse group of parents. When she accepted the position at the Children's Corner, Martha had no idea how strongly the people dynamic in her new job would also influence her sense of professional fulfillment. At the first staff meeting she scheduled, she was struck by the level of resistance and defensiveness of three members of the staff. These three teachers were clearly a dominant coalition. They considered themselves the "old guard," having taught in this Head Start program since the early 1970s. Martha was determined not to be intimidated by them, but she also recognized that they were a force to be reckoned with. Whenever one of the other teachers would suggest a new idea or approach, Mary, Bea, or Georgia would snap back with, "We tried that years ago. It didn't work then, there's no reason to think it should now." Martha felt stymied. She knew she had to contend with this threesome or she would be frustrated in her efforts to make her staff work as a unified team.

Structure (formal and informal arrangements)

The structure of an organization is similar to the frame of a house. Like the supporting beams of a building, the structure is the skeleton or supporting framework that holds the center together. We can think of the structure of a child care center as including several elements: the actual physical arrangement of space; the size (number of students and staff); shape (legal structure, lines of authority and division of responsibility); and the formalized policies and procedures guiding behavior (usually detailed in a center's bylaws, or parent and employee handbooks).

The key feature of the formal structure is that the roles, goals, and division of labor are consciously designed to guide the activities of members (Hoy & Miskel, 1987). Implicit in this formal structure is the power and status relationships of individuals working at the center.

Not every center has formalized all the following elements of structure, nor can we assume that what is written is actually how practices are carried out. We will get to this later when we talk about organizational processes. The following are common structures of child care programs:

legal structure/size

▶ legal governing structure — for-profit/nonprofit; public/private

▶ size — student enrollment; total administrative, teaching, and support staff

policies and procedures

▶ program composition — type of program (e.g. half-day/full-day); hours; types of services provided (e.g. infant care, preschool, school-aged child care)

▶ policies regarding children — enrollment; teacher-child ratios; group size; group composition

▶ policies regarding parents' roles and responsibilities

▶ policies regarding staff recruitment and training — requisite qualifications; hiring guidelines (e.g. affirmative action)

▶ division of labor — job titles; roles; responsibilities

▶ supervisory structure — lines of authority, status

▶ performance appraisal policies

▶ pay/promotion system — salary scale; career ladder

- accounting, budgeting, and financial management system

physical structure

- physical environment for children and adults

- materials and equipment

- size — square footage of indoor and outdoor space

philosophical structure

- philosophy/mission — the center's written goals and objectives

- written curriculum

While there are numerous examples of the importance and impact of structural components of child care centers, the following vignette captures the relationship between aspects of a center's structure and the program's outcomes.

Connie had taught kindergarten in the public school system for 20 years. With a small inheritance from her uncle, she decided to leave the security of her job and open a preschool of her own. In starting her new school, Connie thought a lot about the structural elements of her program. Things like establishing the legal governing structure, deciding on program composition, and formalizing her financial management system all seemed fairly straightforward. When it came to making decisions about the supervisory and performance appraisal structure, however, or how she would go about delineating roles and responsibilities, Connie was less sure of how to proceed. She had previously worked for a district that she perceived was a bureaucratic straitjacket. It had so many rules and regulations that she had felt constricted in her every movement. Connie was intent on not creating the same kind of bureaucratic environment in her school. She also felt strongly that job descriptions, reporting relationships, supervisory and training policies, program philosophy, and educational objectives should

be developed once she had her staff in place. When Connie hired her first teachers and aides, she was disappointed to find that they floundered with the informal structure of her program. While they were excellent teachers in the classroom, they wanted and needed more definitive guidelines about center policies and practices. They complained that the lack of formal job descriptions and clearly delineated roles and responsibilities created confusion in knowing who was expected to do what, how, and when. Further, they complained that the lack of a formalized pay and promotion system bred competition between staff and intensified feelings of job insecurity. During the first year of operating her new school, Connie experienced a 50% turnover in staff. It really hurt her to see such able teachers leave her program. The experience convinced her she needed to take action to clarify the personnel policies and procedures of her school.

Processes (how things get done)

This component of the system includes all the behaviors and interactions that occur at the individual or group level. While the structure provides the framework, processes occur when individuals interact within a given structure. The processes of a center are the cement that holds it together. The processes tell us how things actually get done. In other words, often a center will have a stated policy, but the way that policy is carried out is very different than what appears in writing.

The following are some of the more common processes that characterize child care centers:

- leadership style — the type of leadership that characterizes the director's behavior in carrying out the center's mission

- decision-making processes — who is responsible for making what types of decisions, when, and where?

- problem-solving processes — how problems are solved (or not solved)

- communication processes — ways in which

oral and written information is communicated both formally and informally; the vertical and horizontal communication network of the center

▶ planning and goal setting processes — the ways in which a program's philosophy and objectives are translated into action

▶ group meeting processes — how often meetings take place, who is expected to attend, and the patterns of behavior that characterize meetings

▶ interpersonal relations — the type and quality of daily interactions between individuals; the degree of cohesiveness and esprit de corps that characterize human relations at the center

▶ conflict management — how differences in style, beliefs, and opinion are resolved

▶ supervisory/training processes — how day-to-day supervision is handled for the novice as well as the experienced teacher; the type and frequency of inservice staff development

▶ center evaluation processes — how the program as a whole is evaluated

▶ performance appraisal processes — how administrative, teaching, and support staff are evaluated, both formally and informally

▶ socialization practices — how new staff are socialized into the center; how the center molds the behavior of personnel to make individual beliefs and values correspond with those of the center

▶ child assessment practices — how children's progress is evaluated

▶ teaching practices — the behaviors that characterize teacher-child interactions in the classroom

Case Study: The Children's Corner

One of the things that impressed Martha when she was hired for the position as director of The Children's Corner was the written philosophy of the program. Martha was impressed with the well-articulated statement that appeared in the parents' handbook. It stressed the importance of developmentally appropriate experiences and a child-centered curriculum as well as a learning environment that encouraged exploration and experimentation. But Martha was hired during the summer months; she did not have an opportunity to see the program in action. She was horrified during the first week of school when she saw the teachers distributing dittoed worksheets to 3- and 4-year-old children. She witnessed children waiting in line to go to the bathroom, waiting at the table to get their snack, and waiting to be called on in large group activities that stretched their patience and attention span. When she questioned the teachers about what she saw, to her surprise they stated that they felt they were providing children with developmentally appropriate experiences. Martha realized that the incongruence in what she had read as the center's educational philosophy and what she actually saw as everyday teaching practices would provide a real challenge for her in the months ahead. She wasn't sure how she would accomplish it, but she knew she had to begin to reduce the discrepancy between the stated philosophy of the program (structure) and the everyday teaching practices (processes) that were in place. Martha knew she had her work cut out for her.

Culture (what makes it unique)

The culture of an organization describes the basic assumptions, shared beliefs, and orientations that emerge to unite members of a group (Schein, 1985). Firestone and Corbett (1988) define the culture of a school as the socially shared and transmitted knowledge of what is, and what ought to be, symbolized in act and artifact. The culture, they state, "provides points of order and stability in the blooming, buzzing confusion of everyday life. It helps to clarify what is important and what is not" (p. 335). In the early childhood setting, the culture of a center includes the following elements:

- ▶ shared values — the collective beliefs or principles about what is important in life (e.g. openness, trust, honesty, cooperation, teamwork)

- ▶ norms — expectations for what is appropriate and acceptable in everyday behavior

- ▶ history of the center

- ▶ traditions of the center

- ▶ climate — collective perceptions of staff about different organizational practices

- ▶ ethics — a shared system or code of morals guiding professional obligations and practice at the center

Some of these elements of the culture need further clarification. For example, the distinction between norms and values is sometimes a fuzzy one. Generally, values define the ends of human behavior, and social norms describe the legitimate and more explicit means for pursuing those ends (Hoy & Miskel, 1987). When we make a value judgment, we make a subjective estimate of quality. That estimate is based on our principles and beliefs of what we feel is important in life. Norms, on the other hand, are really the standards or codes of expected behavior. As people work together, implicit agreement develops about the ways in which they are expected to behave in a variety of situations. These patterns become stable over time and define what is appropriate and acceptable behavior (Jorde-Bloom, 1986a). We use the term norms to describe these rules about behavior. Most child care centers have norms about everyday demeanor, the use of space and materials, the appropriate use of time and expectations for workload, professional conduct with children and parents, collegiality, communication, decision making, and change and experimentation.

Jeff had never thought much before about the norms of a center until he happened to walk into the 3-year-old classroom at his center one morning to help orient a new assistant teacher who had just been hired. Jeff observed

a series of incidents that forced him to reflect on how subtle the norms of appropriate conduct are in each work setting. The new assistant teacher, Valarie, had worn an old pair of jeans and a sweatshirt to work that morning. She had just come out of the kitchen with a coffee cup in hand and was wandering around the classroom introducing herself to the children. "Hi Jason," she said from across the room in a loud voice to a child who had just entered the classroom and was getting his name tag from his cubbie. At that moment Jeff was called back to the office to attend to an administrative issue. It wasn't until the end of the week that he had a chance to revisit Valarie's classroom. When he walked into the classroom, he couldn't believe he was observing the same assistant teacher. Valarie was wearing a nice pair of pants and sweater. She was quietly making her way around the classroom assisting children with their projects. She did not have her coffee cup in hand. When a child entered the classroom, she quietly made her way over to the cubbies, knelt on her knees, and softly greeted the child with a friendly hello and pat on the head. Jeff was impressed. He talked to the head teacher to find out if she had taken Valarie aside and instructed her about the do's and don'ts of appropriate behavior and conduct at the center. "I didn't need to," she said. "Valarie just figured it out herself by watching the teachers and checking their reactions to her behavior. I guess we send a pretty clear message about what behavior is expected at this place."

The history of a center is also part of its culture. Centers are strongly influenced by events in the past. For example, a center that has had allegations of child abuse levied against it may feel the effects of the adverse publicity that the incident generated for many years to come.

Related to history are all the traditions that characterize a center. For example, some centers have an annual summer picnic for staff; other centers host a holiday party for staff and their families in

December. These traditions play an important role in helping to define the uniqueness of each center.

Culture is often used as a synonym for climate. The two concepts, organizational culture and organizational climate, though related, are conceptually distinct. Culture is the more inclusive concept, taking in values, norms, ethics, traditions, and the history of a center in addition to its climate. In the context of child care, we can think of organizational climate as a kind of global perception of the perceived quality of a center. These perceptions are subjective interpretations which vary between people. This is because people perceive reality differently depending on their role in the center, their value orientation, and the context of the situation. Organizational climate is thus the collective perceptions (shared beliefs) about the people, processes, and structure. It is akin to the personality of a center.

These perceptions about organizational practices can be viewed from several dimensions: degree of collegiality; opportunities for professional growth; degree of supervisor support; clarity of communication, policies, and procedures; the center's reward system; the center's decision-making structure; degree of goal consensus; task orientation; the center's physical setting; and the degree of innovativeness or creativity. While perceptions in each of these areas certainly are related, research has shown that they are distinct enough to warrant separate dimensions (Jorde-Bloom, 1988a).

One of the hallmarks of a true profession is that it has a code of ethics guiding the decision making of practitioners. While early childhood education has not yet achieved full professional status in society, individuals working in the field have a working set of assumptions that dictate their behavior when confronted with moral dilemmas. The ethics that undergird their behavior may or may not conform to the stated ethics of the early childhood profession (Feeney & Kipnis, 1989; Katz & Ward, 1978). An example of this discrepancy would be the director who knowingly enrolls more children in her program than is allowed by the licensing code for her state. The collective sense of ethics of teachers and administrators working for a particular program can be said to be part of its culture. To be

sure, the center's code of ethics is a powerful force shaping individual and collective behavior.

Outcomes (the effects of the program)

We can think of outcomes as resulting from the intersection of people, structure, and processes. Figure 1.1 on page 8 visually portrays this relationship. Outcomes can be conceptualized on several different levels: the organizational level; the group functioning or staff level; the client level (both parents and children); and the community or broader societal level.

▶ organization — professional reputation of the center; fiscal viability; internal efficiency and effectiveness; the center's professional orientation

▶ staff — absenteeism; turnover; level of competence; job satisfaction; degree of commitment to the center; sense of personal and professional fulfillment

▶ children — social and cognitive competence; overall health

▶ parents — overall satisfaction with the program; degree of perceived support from the center

▶ community/society — service provided

The outcomes of a center essentially serve as a barometer for organizational effectiveness. But as Hoy and Miskel (1987) remind us, organizational effectiveness is a multidimensional concept. No single criterion can capture the complex nature of organizational functioning. Some outcomes of a center are readily apparent and easy to measure; others, however, are more subtle and difficult to assess.

A problem arises in some situations when directors and boards have a lack of adequate data and base decisions about outcomes (center effectiveness) on inference. The following three examples illustrate this point and underscore the importance of using multiple sources of evidence to assess an organization's effectiveness.

▶ When enrollment at a center is full and a long waiting list exists, one might naturally infer that the program has a positive reputation in the community. But that inference may be presumptuous. Full enrollment could also be due to the lack of other viable options for parents in the community.

▶ A board of a center, in looking at its high turnover rate of staff, might be tempted to conclude that the quality of work life at the center was unacceptable or that the director was not doing a good job. This may or may not be the case, however. A high rate of turnover could be due to faulty hiring practices of the board. For example, the board could be hiring individuals who are overqualified for the position and who quickly become dissatisfied with the pay and lack of challenge in their jobs.

▶ Parents are generally quite vocal when they are dissatisfied with an aspect of a program. It is natural for directors to focus on only the negative feedback they hear and conclude they are not meeting parents' needs. This conclusion may be erroneous, though, because many parents who are pleased with a program often do not take the time to compliment the teaching or administrative staff. The director may be getting an unrepresentative sample of parents' true perceptions about program quality.

If we look back again at Figure 1.1 on page 8, we see the arrows extend outward from the outcomes component back to the external environment. This completes the loop of influences. Sometimes the effects of outcomes on the external environment are strong and direct as in the case of a higher demand for services when a program has achieved a strong reputation.

Other times the effect can have far-reaching consequences. We have seen, for example, how a few well-publicized cases of child abuse in child care centers have resulted in legislation in several states mandating fingerprinting of all child care

workers and new child abuse reporting procedures. On a more positive note, we have also seen how the highly publicized program outcomes of the Perry Preschool Project in Ypsilanti, Michigan (Berrueta-Clement, Schweinhart, Barnett, Epstein, & Weikart, 1984) have been used by child care advocates to increase funding for disadvantaged children.

Characteristics of Centers When Viewed as Social Systems

Now that we have looked at all of the components of the child care center as a social system, let us turn our attention to some of the common characteristics of centers when viewed as systems.

Change in One Component Will Have an Effect on Other Components

Central to a social systems perspective is the notion that change in one component of a center will have a rippling effect throughout the social system of the center. For example, the hiring of a new director or master teacher will clearly alter different processes at the center. Likewise, a change in the structure of a center (for example, a change in the size or the division of labor) will have a strong influence in shaping the attitudes, behavior, and expectations of individuals who work at the center. Changes in the external environment, as well, will impact a center in different ways. State and federally funded programs, for example, are keenly aware of how the external environment affects organizational practices, particularly when there are changes in funding levels or regulatory requirements.

Kagan (1990) argues that one of the shortcomings of our current care and education system for young children has been that it is "too fragmented," fostering competition and inequities. Kagan stresses the need within the external environment for greater collaboration and inter-agency working agreements that foster cross-agency staff training, common planning for new programs, and information and resource sharing. She states, "Providers are coming to understand that such creative planning can yield innovative use of limited dollars and result in programs that better meet children's needs and parents' schedules" (p. 20). In other words, changes in the external environment can facilitate smoother program functioning in the internal components of the center.

Organizational Equilibrium is a Desirable Goal

Most organizational theorists believe maintaining a sense of equilibrium is essential for the continued adequacy and viability of an organization's ability to carry out its functions. An example will help illustrate this point. People work in early childhood education in order to satisfy certain needs. And, presumably, the center where they work has needs of its own which are fulfilled by the participants who function in its various roles. Getzels and Guba (1957) describe this as the interplay between the nomothetic (the organization's needs) and the idiographic (the personal needs of the individuals who fill various roles). From this perspective, organizational equilibrium means maintaining that delicate balance between meeting the needs of the organization and those of the individual. As long as this state of equilibrium exists, the relationship presumably will be satisfactory, enduring, and relatively productive (Owens, 1981).

Organizations Must Change and Adapt

A social systems perspective gives us a dynamic view of the child care center. Social systems theory is not a static model of how organizations function. To the contrary, child care centers as organizations are dynamic in nature — always in flux, constantly adapting and changing. It goes without saying that to remain vital, thriving, and maintain a sense of equilibrium, centers must be flexible and adaptive. The ability to reexamine the current structure and processes of the program in light of changing trends is the key to this adaptation.

Sometimes these changes are abrupt and organizations must respond quickly. A tragic incident in 1989 in a wealthy suburb of Chicago illustrates the point. A young woman went on a shooting rampage in an elementary school. Within days, virtually every educational institution in the surrounding communities had instituted new security procedures. This single incident in the external environment had a strong and immediate impact on child care centers in the area. Directors of these programs knew they had to adapt and implement swift changes in order to calm the fears of parents and teachers about their children's safety.

Organizational Health is Related to the Congruence Between Components

Matthew Miles (1969) defines a healthy organization as one that "not only survives in its environment, but continues to cope adequately over the long haul, and continuously develops and extends its surviving and coping skills" (p. 390). Organizational health can be viewed as the relative degree of congruence or "fit" between different components of the system.

Organizational health, Beer (1980) states, is the capacity of an organization to engage in ongoing self-examination aimed at identifying incongruities between components. For example, one aspect of the center's structure is the division of labor and the tasks associated with each job. The individuals assigned to do these tasks have certain characteristics (e.g., skill, knowledge, motivation, interest). When the individual's knowledge and skill match the knowledge and skill demanded by the task, performance (an outcome) will be more effective. Likewise, when the physical environment (structure) and philosophy (structure) of a program support the teaching practices (processes), better outcomes in the way of staff satisfaction and fulfillment will be ensured.

From these two examples, it is possible to see how a web of connections between the people, structure, and process components directly affect outcomes. Nadler and Tushman (1983) state that just as each pair of elements within and between components has a high or low degree of congruence, so too does the aggregate model display a low or high level of system congruence. They believe that the greater the total degree of congruence or fit between the various components, the more effective will be the organization. The director's role in this assessment is central. In Chapter IV, we will discuss ways that directors can assess their programs to determine the degree of fit between various components.

A Final Word

A systems approach for describing early childhood centers can lead to a better understanding of the impact of change and a more accurate estimate of anticipated outcomes. Moreover, the incorporation of a systems view of organizations into planning center change can help directors see a broader view of expected outcomes. The systems view of organizations in itself is not a planning strategy nor does it predict outcomes or results. It is merely a way of looking at centers as an integrated whole that is made up of interrelated, interacting parts. By asking what impact a particular change may have on all components of the system (external environment, people, structure, processes, culture, and outcomes), it is possible to be more aware of, and thus be better prepared to manage, the negative aspects of change as well as to take advantage of the strengths inherent in the center.

A social systems model also helps us understand the potential sources of conflict and problems that are part of organizational life. Many problems of centers, for example, arise from the fundamental conflict between the needs and motives of an individual and the requirements of the organization. Individuals attempt to personalize their roles, that is to reshape bureaucratic roles, so that personal needs can be actualized. Conversely, the center attempts to mold and fit individuals into the prescribed roles in order to best achieve center goals. Thus it is natural that there will be an inherent tension between these two elements in the system (Hoy & Miskel, 1987). We can see, then, how this relates to center outcomes. High morale, for example, typically results when organizational goals and expectations are compatible with the collective needs of individuals.

One important implication of this model is that organizational improvement (change) involves first describing the system, then identifying (diagnosing) problems, and finally analyzing the degree of fit to determine the causes of problems. This model implies that different configurations of key components can be used to gain better outcomes. Therefore, it is not a question of finding the "one best way" of managing, but rather determining effective combinations of components that will lead to desired outcomes for a specific center.

Chapter 2

The Dynamics of Organizational Change

In today's world, the question of whether change will occur is no longer relevant. Instead, the issue is how can directors cope with the inevitable barrage of changes that confront them daily in an attempt to keep their centers viable and current? As Hersey and Blanchard (1982) state, "Although change is a fact of life, if managers are to be effective, they can no longer be content to let change occur as it will. They must be able to develop strategies to plan, direct, and control change" (p. 266).

This chapter will look at the nature of change in child care centers. This overview will set the stage for Chapter III which will look more specifically at the director's role in the change process. Two important points are central to this discussion. First, change is an integral part of thriving child care centers. It is not something to be avoided. To the contrary, change should be welcomed and to the extent possible, even anticipated. Second, directors who understand the nature of change will not be seduced by "quick fix" solutions to the complex problems that beset their programs. As Kilman (1984) stresses, it is time we stop perpetuating the myth of simplicity. Organizations generate complex problems that cannot be solved by simple solutions. The only viable alternative is to develop a truly integrated approach to organizational improvement.

Before proceeding, take a moment to complete Exercise #2.1. Reflect back on some change or innovation you have been involved in and recall why or why not that change or innovation was or was not successful in achieving its desired outcomes.

What is Change?

In many respects change is really an abstraction; it takes on personal meaning only when we can link it to specific examples that have some relevance. By definition, change is any significant alteration in the status quo that affects an individual or organization. Educational change, for example, is usually intended to improve school outcomes. Change usually entails some alteration in the roles and responsibilities of the people involved. For instance, in order to improve parent relations at a center, a director may decide to institute new policies in the way staff report children's progress or keep anecdotal records.

> *"Change —*
>
> *only babies like it."*
>
> *— Roberta Newman*

Although closely related to change, innovation has a slightly different meaning. Innovation refers to any proposed change or set of changes that are intentionally implemented that represent something new or novel to the people being changed. Innovations vary in type, in complexity, and in the values associated with them. It is important to stress, though, that it does not matter if the particular innovation under consideration is "new" by some objective standard; it is the perceived newness of the innovation by the potential adopter that counts. For example, even though microcomputers have been around for some time now, implementing a computer billing system at a center that has always invoiced parents by hand-

Attitudes and Experiences Regarding Educational Change

Many educational innovations have been implemented during the past decade resulting in changes in early childhood programs. Some of these innovations such as bilingual education, mainstreaming of special needs children, or providing for infant care have entailed major alterations in the way programs are run. Others, like incorporating mixed-aged groupings of children, adopting different curriculum packages, implementing new screening procedures, or introducing new audio-visual equipment may have required only minor adjustments.

Think back during the past three years and name one innovation or educational change that you implemented in your classroom or your center. This innovation could have been a procedural change in the way your classroom or program was run, or a structural innovation that changed the operation of your program.

Describe the innovation/change: _____

_____

What was the impetus for this change? Was it self-initiated or mandated?

_____

At the time you implemented this change, what was your degree of confidence that it would work?

I was _____% sure it would succeed

If you are still using this innovation, how successful would you rate your efforts at implementing this change?

_____ not successful   _____ somewhat successful   _____ successful   _____ very successful

Has your innovation been modified since you first initiated it? Describe how.

_____

_____

If you have abandoned the innovation/change, describe the reasons why. If this was an innovation/change that you initiated, what would you do differently if you were to make the implementation decision again? If this was a change that was mandated for you, what could have been done differently to ensure greater success?

_____

_____

written notes would be considered an innovation for this center. Likewise, implementing a new curriculum like High/Scope (Hohmann, Banet, & Weikart, 1979) or Math Their Way (Baratta-Lorton, 1976), or instituting new admission procedures to allow for the inclusion of special needs children would also be considered innovations.

The Impetus for Change

The impetus for change can come from many sources. Often change is mandated from our external environment. For example P.L. 94-142 and P. L. 99-457 are mandated rules and regulations that specify what shall or shall not be done with respect to children with special needs. The power of mandated changes is derived from the sanctions imposed if the center does not comply. For instance, funding may be taken away or a license may be revoked.

At other times, the impetus for change comes as the result of a crisis at the center. An uncontrollable case of head lice, for example, may prompt a director to institute procedures for sanitizing the children's toys and equipment daily. Parental complaints, as well, can also be the stimulus for change. Parents may be unhappy about the way behavioral problems are handled in the classroom or the lack of communication between home and school. Programs sensitive to parental needs and expectations will feel an obligation to make programmatic changes to accommodate parental wishes. Programs sensitive to children's needs will also institute changes when necessary. For example, an influx of newly immigrated Vietnamese families enrolling in a program may prompt the director to institute a variety of programmatic changes to meet their special needs.

Program outcomes, as well, are also a powerful impetus for change. A director faced with high turnover and staff dissatisfaction will probably feel the necessity to review her center's pay and promotion system and make some changes to improve staff stability. Other outcomes such as declining enrollment may prompt a director to expand enrollment options for the community. For instance, the decision might be made to expand services from half-day to full-day care or from serving just preschool-aged children to also serving infants and toddlers.

The Nature of Change

How can we take such an abstract concept as change and translate it into some fundamental principles that will serve to guide our center improvement efforts? The results of research in this area provide us with a convenient starting point. From the multitude of change efforts that have been studied in educational settings, researchers have extracted some basic principles that can help us be more successful in our change endeavors. The work of Fullan (1991), Hall and Loucks (1978), Havelock and Havelock (1973), and Berman and McLaughlin (1976) is particularly helpful in this regard.

Change is a Process, Not an Event

Perhaps the most grave mistake directors can make is to view change as a single event. To the contrary, change takes time and effort to enact. Change should really be thought of as evolutionary. It is an incremental process that is achieved in stages. Most organizational problems do not fit into the category of being solved in a short period of time. Indeed, most major educational changes take several years, not months, to implement. Many innovative educational programs fail not because they are poorly conceived, but because they are rushed.

Jorde-Bloom (1982) found that one of the characteristics of directors who experienced job burnout was their inability to accept change as an integral element of organizational life. They had a linear view of their jobs and treated change as a singular event. They viewed change as having a precise beginning and a definitive end. Thus, they tended to have unrealistic expectations for program stability following their change efforts. These directors viewed themselves as failures because they could not control change.

Directors who are successful in their administrative role view change as an integral component of a thriving center. They see it as a continuous and never-ending cycle of identifying problems, exploring change options, implementing new strategies, evaluating those changes to redefine the problem and then developing new strategies to improve their centers. Later in this chapter we will present a diagram of the change process. This diagram captures the cyclical, ongoing nature of change. Regardless of how successful a center is in one year, there is always a new year around the corner, one that will hold a new set of problems to be addressed.

What Works Well in One Setting May Not in Another

We have all heard stories of directors who implemented procedures that were highly successful in another center, only to find that they flopped in their own center. This should not come as a surprise. Teaching staffs vary considerably in years of experience, level of education, teaching style, instructional skills, and willingness to change. There are so many variations among centers, both in people's willingness to adopt new procedures and in their capability to implement new approaches. The conditions that support the adoption of a new innovation in one setting may not be present in another. This does not mean that the innovation is not worthwhile; it only means that it is not appropriate for all settings.

"Not everything that is faced can be changed; but nothing can be changed until it is faced."

— James Baldwin

On a broader scale, we can relate this principle to the early childhood program models approach promoted in the 1970s. The program models that were part of the Planned Variations study were designed to serve as exemplar prototypes. The inherent assumption, as Kagan (1990) explains, was that "what worked well in one locale would work equally well in another." Kagan goes on to say that "not only were there problems encountered because different settings had their own unique cultures, but numerous challenges emerged as programs attempted to move from small to large scale" (p. 18). The problem, of course, is that new models are often not incorporated into the life of the organization; they never become "institutionalized." The most successful educational experiments in the adoption of educational innovations have been those where models have not been adopted wholesale, but rather "adapted" to meet the unique needs of the school (Berman & McLaughlin, 1976; Fullan, 1991).

Success Depends on the Felt Need for Change

Change is more likely to occur and be successful when it relates to a felt need or resolves a problem that is important to those implementing the change. Teachers, for example, are more likely to try out a new approach to classroom management when they feel their current methods are not working well. The research on successful educational change consistently underscores the principle that individuals are more likely to change when they focus on problems significant to them and have input into how to best resolve those problems.

While this principle makes good common sense, it also presents a dilemma for directors. Often a director will have a clear idea of how a center should be organized to achieve desired changes in attitudes and behavior. But these ideas may not be shared by others. In fact, considerable evidence exists that directors' view of organizational practices is significantly different than their staff's view (Jorde-Bloom, 1988b).

Beer (1980) states that change will occur only when sufficient dissatisfaction exists with the status quo by those who must change. Sufficient dissatisfaction creates momentum for change. But even then, Beer adds, individuals may be reluctant to change unless they are convinced the proposed new approach will really solve their problem. Unilateral pressure to change can create resistance and hostility directed at the source of pressure. Sometimes all it takes is direct discussion between a director and teacher to provide an awareness of problems that will stimulate change. But other times the recognition of the need for change is more difficult to communicate.

All Change Isn't Necessarily Good

This principle can be summed up by the old adage, "If it ain't broke, don't fix it!" Some administrators think that there is no progress unless things are in turmoil. But change for the sake of change can be detrimental. When people are made to change for no apparent reason, they will develop resistance to the concept of change. Wu (1988) believes effective leadership is not characterized by either constant or radical change. If no valid reason for change exists, than chaos may result.

Change Has a Ripple Effect

Some of the most successful organizational changes have happened in small increments. A director may not be able to convince her whole staff to adopt a new curriculum or instructional technique, but she may be able to convince one teacher to try it out. Success experienced by that one teacher will often have an impact on others. Thus change in one person or one classroom may provide the impetus for change in another person or in another classroom.

Models of Change

Now that we know something about the nature of change, it is appropriate to look at the advantages and disadvantages to different approaches to change. The framework for this discussion is provided by Beer (1980) who defines three models of change that characterize organizations: top-down, bottom-up, and collaborative change.

Top-Down Change

Many decisions regarding center change are mandated by decree; they are essentially top-down directives of new procedures to be implemented. Sometimes these are decisions about new personnel, new organizational structures, or new ways of doing things. Top-down changes are typically introduced rapidly. Sometimes they are mandated by legislation and public policy makers or by central office administrators. Many of the change decisions that directors make are also implemented using a top-down model. A top-down model of change is essentially a directive model.

Top-down changes are usually unilateral. Only a few people make the decisions. For this reason, the changes can be introduced very rapidly. If the solution is appropriate to the problem that triggered the need for the change in the first place, the changes will probably obtain immediate results. A directive top-down model of change can work if people anticipate some positive outcomes of the change, will support it, and develop a commitment to it. It is the speed of the top-down approach that makes it attractive to directors under pressure to obtain immediate results.

One of the shortcomings of this approach, however, is that solutions are not always appropriate because people who know about the problems are not consulted. Top-down changes often do not reflect the needs of individuals affected unless the administration of a program is well attuned to their needs. Typically, staff are not as committed to the idea because they do not have sufficient information and have not been brought along. The likelihood that the top-down approach will produce a lot of psychological strain is strong. Staff will think of the change as a directive. Even when teachers agree that the changes may be necessary, top-down models risk having teachers feel manipulated and powerless. The result may be animosity, hostility, and overt behavior to undermine the proposed change.

Juanita is the director of a large for-profit day care program. She is also something of a technological whiz and has always used a personal computer to do her work. Juanita was appalled that Nancy, the office accountant, still did all the billing of parents by hand. She perceived this to be both too time consuming and tedious, so she purchased a computer for the office and wrote a program to keep track of the accounts receivable. Juanita assumed Nancy would enthusiastically embrace this new technology as being a labor-saving device. When Nancy arrived at work one morning, the computer was sitting on her desk. Next to it were elaborate instructions on how to use it. Nancy was angry. While she understood that the computer would make her job more efficient, she was hurt that she was not consulted about whether or not she even wanted to use the computer to do her job. She felt it was being jammed down her throat and that the least Juanita could have done was ask her if she wanted to learn how to use the computer. Fortunately Juanita was a seasoned director, sensitive to differing points of view. She apologized to Nancy for not consulting her and acknowledged that it was insensitive of her to think that Nancy would love technological gadgetry as much as she did. With this acknowledgement, Nancy began to open up. She confessed it wasn't so much the computer itself that she was opposed to, but the change in the relationships that she feared would happen with the parents. Nancy believed that her handwritten notes to parents each month with their tuition invoice provided a personal touch that conveyed that the center really cared about them as individuals and wasn't only concerned about their financial support. She feared that a computerized system might make the whole financial billing process too institutional and cold.

This incident was a clear case of making a hasty decision based on only partial information. Juanita perceived that the world viewed technological devices the same as she did. She did not take into consideration the anxiety level of Nancy, a first-time computer user. Fortunately, however, she was a sensitive administrator who took the time to understand the point of view of her subordinate.

Kevin was recently hired as the director of a state-funded prekindergarten program. He had always felt that accurate record keeping was the hallmark of a professional. One of his first directives in taking over the program was to send a memo to the teachers telling them about the importance of keeping anecdotal notes on each child. He indicated that all teachers would now be required to make one anecdotal note on each child each day. He stressed how this new procedure would improve the quality of parent conferencing at the center. The teachers at this center were a very experienced group of individuals. They did not feel there was a need for all this record keeping. They felt they had been conducting parent conferences just fine without reams of anecdotal notes. They followed the directive for about three weeks and then gradually stopped taking notes altogether.

Kevin's directive was destined for failure from the start. First, he did not anticipate that a group of seasoned teachers might interpret such a directive as a challenge to their professional autonomy. Second, his decree was communicated in a written memo. From the teacher's perspective, this made the directive very impersonal and easier to dismiss. Third, the teachers were simply not convinced of the need for more anecdotal notes. Finally, Kevin did not make any structural changes in the program such as allotting additional planning time for the teachers to write up their notes. This kind of structural change may have helped sustain the new procedures he proposed.

Despite the drawbacks of the top-down model, it appears it is the prevailing model for making organizational changes in child care programs. A top-down model can be effective in cases where circumstances dictate that quick action be taken. For example, the incidence of neighborhood vandalism may prompt a director to institute new security precautions for the center. Staff in this kind of situation are more apt to comply with the directive. They understand the urgent nature of the directive and the rationale for the decision.

A top-down model of change can also be effective when the focus of the change only tangentially concerns staff. For example, teachers may not be very interested in change decisions regarding routine managerial aspects of running the program. The decision to change janitorial services or landscape maintenance services may have little consequence for teachers. A top-down model of change may be quite appropriate for these kinds of decisions.

Bottom-Up Change

In bottom-up change, the responsibility for defining and developing a solution is left to the teaching or support staff of the center. This responsibility may be delegated or assumed. This kind of change model is often apparent in programs where directors assume a hands-off approach to management. Their non-directive leadership style assumes that people can implement changes that are necessary for them to do their jobs more efficiently. The problem with this approach, though, is that it often results in a clash over the goals or the direction of change. Also, because the director or board are not involved and sometimes not even aware of the change, they are not in a position to implement the administrative structures that can sustain the change assuming it is a positive one. The following example illustrates this point.

Gayle is a preschool teacher. At her local AEYC conference she heard some teachers from another center talk about the High/Scope curriculum. During her spring break, Gayle decided to enroll in a four-day High/Scope training program to find out for herself if the curriculum would be appropriate for her classroom. She was really excited about what she learned and came back from vacation enthusiastic to implement the new methods. But given the frenetic activity of the program and all the other demands tugging at her sleeve, Gayle just couldn't seem to find the time to get herself organized to launch her new curricular approach. After a month, Gayle decided the High/Scope curriculum just wasn't suited for her classroom and she abandoned all hopes of making her classroom a High/Scope showcase for the center.

Gayle's innovation did not fail because it was not well suited for her classroom. It failed because she lacked the appropriate incentives and administrative support to sustain her enthusiasm in it. Had Gayle been more actively encouraged to try out some new instructional strategies by her director or her peers, her level of interest in High/Scope may have been sustained. If she had worked at a center where supervision and performance appraisal processes were in place to ensure that she had the resources and technical support to adopt new ideas for her classroom, her

attempt at implementing the High/Scope curriculum would probably have been met with greater success.

The caregivers at a large urban day care center were discontent with their salaries, benefits, and lack of job security. They met with a group of caregivers from another center that had recently unionized to learn more about their labor rights. They decided they had nothing to lose by confronting their director with the possibility that they, too, wanted to unionize if their current conditions were not improved. Under pressure, the director convinced her board to implement a small salary increase. She also implemented new procedures for ensuring that the staff got a short break in the morning and the afternoon. The teachers were jubilant. They felt empowered by their success at changing the center's policies. What they hadn't anticipated, though, was the increased strain and tension with the director that would result from their actions. The director felt she had been coerced to take action. She viewed the whole incident as a direct challenge to her authority. What had been an amiable working relationship between the director and staff had now turned sour.

We see, then, that there are several shortcomings to the bottom-up model of change. If the administration of a center delegates completely to staff the right to define the change, it gives up its influence in the definition of problems and their solutions. Even if one classroom adopts a change, the likelihood that the whole center will change will be less. Second, there is a high potential for clash if the outcomes of the change are not valued or they conflict with the center's values. Finally, the likelihood that the change will not become institutionalized is high. Virtually all changes in a program in order to be sustained have to be supported from the top.

Collaborative Change

Top-down and bottom-up change represent extremes in the distribution of power in a center. For most kinds of changes, the most successful model is simultaneously top-down and bottom-up;

it is collaborative change. Here both the administration and the staff are involved in identifying problems and developing solutions.

The concept of collaboration as having power with, not over, colleagues is central to success in this approach. Parity in status and equal responsibility for work characterize the relationship between teachers and directors in centers where this model of change prevails. In such environments, teachers are active partners in some or all of the stages including clarifying the problem, collecting and analyzing the data, generating solutions, and evaluating results.

"Nothing endures but change."

—Herclitus

Behaving collaboratively does not mean that the director must relinquish the right and responsibility to provide expertise, however. Necessary technical assistance and support are clearly vital contributions of the director. What collaboration does imply is that the expertise of others is recognized and incorporated into the center's improvement efforts. Saxl (1989) states that a collaborative approach is focused and directed, but not directive in a controlling sense. It is similar to a "helping orientation" that induces cooperative learning, mutual growth, reciprocal openness, and shared problem solving. Collaboration rests on trusting relationships.

The drawback of collaborative change is that it takes longer to implement. Time for data collection to discern problems, time for meetings to help clarify the direction of change, and time to provide feedback during the change process itself can be painfully slow. Immediate turnaround of a problem is not likely to occur. For this reason, it is understandable that this approach is not used frequently. But these disadvantages appear to be outweighed by the positive benefits resulting from utilizing this model. In a collaborative model, staff tend to have a far clearer idea of expectations and what their roles and responsibilities will be in the change process. Most important, however, is that a collaborative model results in a higher level of trust and commitment and overall satisfaction with the direction of change.

A collaborative model tends to be appropriate for working with individuals and groups who are achievement motivated, seek responsibility, and have a degree of knowledge and experience that may be useful in solving problems. Indeed, as we saw in the example with Kevin earlier, a mature group of teachers may become rigid and opposed to change if it is implemented in a directive manner. A directive approach is inconsistent with their perceptions of themselves as mature, responsible, self-motivated people who should be consulted on issues that directly affect them. At the same time, a collaborative approach may not be productive when working with a group of inexperienced teachers who need a greater degree of guidance and structure. In Chapter VI, we will discuss how these models of change (top-down, bottom-up, and collaborative) relate to different supervisory styles.

In sum, there are no universal rules for implementing change in early childhood programs. Participation is useful sometimes, but its form will vary from center to center. One cannot assert that any particular change model is most effective; it depends on the situation and the nature of the problem being resolved.

The basic assumption of this book is that bringing about change is an important task of directors. But forcing changes — even "good" ones — endangers the goal of fostering human relations in a center. Further, forced change only rarely results in a lasting change in teachers' behavior or in the operation of the center. The role of the director, then, is to create the interpersonal context which frees, encourages, and helps people to experiment with change (Sergiovanni & Elliott, 1975).

Factors Influencing the Adoption of Innovations

There are many interrelating factors that can potentially influence one's behavior with respect to decisions about the adoption or rejection of educational innovations. These factors relate to the attributes of the innovation itself.

Attributes of the Innovation

Embodied in the decision-making process to adopt a specific innovation is the assumption that the individual or group responsible for the decision weighs alternatives in an effort to discern the relative advantages of a particular innovation over existing practices or other potential innovations. These alternatives generally center on various attributes of the innovation and thus serve as incentives for adopting or rejecting the innovation. The individual's perceptions of these attributes are of considerable importance because they help explain why some innovations enjoy rapid and widespread dissemination while others fade to obscurity. It also helps explain the rate and ease with which different innovations are implemented. Drawing predominantly on the work of Zaltman and Lin (1971), Rogers (1983), and Fliegel and Kivlin (1966), it is possible to develop a taxonomy of some of the characteristics used to classify a wide range of innovations. These eight criteria are not intended to be exhaustive, nor are they intended to be mutually exclusive. Considerable overlap exists among them. Nevertheless, taken together they represent a fairly comprehensive set of criteria for making decisions to adopt or reject an innovation.

Cost-effectiveness. Cost is clearly a critical factor for many innovations. But economic considerations also involve more than initial capital investment, particularly when supplies and ongoing maintenance may be an issue. In considering cost, a distinction must be made between initial costs and continuing costs (or operating costs). It must also be remembered that cost-effectiveness is a relative attribute and must be assessed in relation to other variables such as increased output, reduced production costs, or other economic or social factors deemed important. It is for this reason that microcomputers as an administrative tool are such a popular innovation. While their initial cost is high, the perceived benefits in terms of increased output and time savings generally make them an attractive innovation for early childhood directors to consider.

Social approval. This is a non-economic attribute associated with the status and prestige that different innovations confer. Social approval is clearly an important motivator with respect to adoption and rejection decisions. The social cost of an innovation may come in the form of ridicule, ostracism, or even exclusion from a group. Some educational innovations are clearly seen as conferring more status than others. The widespread appeal of NAEYC's center accreditation project (NAEYC, 1984), for example, is due in large part to the perceived professional status it confers on those centers that achieve accreditation.

Complexity. The degree of complexity associated with an innovation may also have an important bearing on acceptance or rejection. Complexity is the degree to which an innovation is perceived as difficult to understand and use. Some innovations are readily understood; others are more complicated. Innovations that are challenging yet have a high likelihood for success are more apt to find wider acceptance than those that are too simple or those that are highly complex. The success of the adoption of the Creative Curriculum (Dodge, 1988), for example, can be attributed to the fact that while the innovation requires some specialized training, the training is not perceived as complex.

Efficiency. This is a rather broad attribute and can be measured both in terms of time saved and the avoidance of discomfort. The saving of time clearly has direct economic implications. It is interesting to note that the efficiency attribute is one of the strongest motivators for directors contemplating the use of computers for managerial functions. Unfortunately, what is often not anticipated is the considerable time and patience required during the initial orientation phase. This proves to be a disappointment for many new users expecting quick results and immediate gratification.

Trialability. The degree to which an innovation may be experimented with on a limited basis before one decides on full-scale adoption also influences whether or not it is adopted. Trialability reduces the uncertainty associated with complex or costly innovations. The possibility of trying out the innovation on a limited scale allows one to minimize possible unanticipated negative consequences and to postpone decisions regarding large investments of educational resources. Many programs that implement mainstreaming, for example, first start out with just a small number of children in one classroom.

Observability. The degree to which the results of an innovation are visible to others also has an impact on adoption decisions. In other words, the easier it is for individuals to see the results of an innovation, the more likely it is that it will stimulate peer discussion. This may increase the likelihood of adoption. The enthusiasm generated for the whole-language approach to emergent literacy is a good example of this principle. Having the opportunity to observe a classroom where one can see first hand the results of this instructional strategy convinces many teachers it is a worthwhile innovation for their own classrooms.

Compatibility. The individual's or group's present values and past experiences have a considerable influence on adoption decisions. If an innovation is too incongruent with current practices, it may be perceived as too threatening and thus unacceptable.

Terminality. Terminality describes the ease with which a particular innovation or change can be ended if it isn't working out. Terminality can serve as a strong motivation to adopt or resist an innovation. Innovations that can be more easily reversed are more apt to be adopted. It is for this reason that many school districts have been slow in adopting a career ladder approach to professional advancement. Once implemented, a career ladder is difficult to terminate given the contractual agreements that it may have imposed.

It is important to underscore the salience of individual differences in people's perceptions with respect to these various attributes. What may appear to be a simple and easily understood innovation to one person may seem like a highly complex and intimidating one to another.

Steps in the Change Process

Implementing center-wide change is essentially a problem-solving process involving a series of steps to remedy an unsatisfactory situation. These steps move from initial problem identification to action based on an agreed-upon solution. The following diagram graphically highlights the different steps in this process.

The first step in the center-improvement process involves defining the most pressing organizational problems that need to be addressed. This step sounds fairly straightforward, but in reality involves careful analysis of present conditions and how these differ from ideal conditions. Change efforts, in other words, should focus on attempting to reduce the discrepancy between real (actual) and ideal (desired) conditions.

In order to form a clear, valid picture of the problems of a center, it is usually necessary to gather some data. Clear accurate data of the situation at hand helps the director and staff avoid the mistake of focusing on mere symptoms of the problem (e.g., high turnover, parental dissatisfaction, or low commitment to center goals) rather than on the core problems that need to be addressed. Chapter IV will provide guidelines for directors who would like to undertake a needs assessment of organizational problems.

The third step in the change process entails analyzing the situation. This step results in generating possible solutions and weighing alternative courses of action. From this analysis an action plan is developed to address problem areas in need of improvement. The final step in the process is evaluating the effectiveness of the change effort. The problem-solving process is essentially cyclical in nature since the information gleaned from evaluating the improvement efforts should result in reformulating and redefining new problems to be addressed.

A Final Word

This chapter has provided an overview of the change process in child care centers. It has also helped clarify why many organizational change

Figure 2.1

Steps in the Change Process

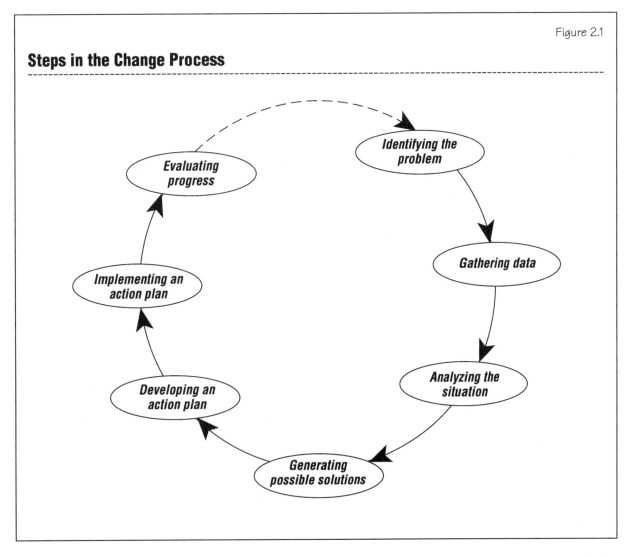

efforts fail to result in lasting improvements. In reviewing the research, Parkay and Damico (1989) conclude that failure to achieve the benefits we see from institutional changes are usually due to two reasons. First, there is typically a lack of staff input. This results in improvement efforts where the goals of the proposed change are not in keeping with the staff's needs and beliefs. Second, many change endeavors are viewed too narrowly; they do not take an ecological systems approach that considers the current prevailing political, social, demographic, economic, and technological forces in the surrounding environment.

So far we've looked at the broad issues surrounding center-based improvement. Now let's turn our attention to the role of the director in the change process and how a systems perspective of child care centers can help to achieve lasting change.

Chapter 3

The Director's Role in the Change Process

R are is the director who does not feel caught in a whirlwind of activity. With new staff to train, new procedures to implement, new curricula to evaluate — where is the calm, the expected, the anticipated? Change and child care administration go hand in hand.

How is it, though, that some directors are so successful in implementing substantial, significant changes in their centers? Who is it that initially senses the need for change and nurtures the change process? Where do the innovative ideas come from? And how can staff be motivated to support needed change? This chapter will explore these and other questions in an attempt to set the stage for how directors can take charge in implementing change that will improve center life and achieve program goals.

The perspective of change proposed in this chapter takes a systems view of centers as dynamic entities continually interacting with their external environment, changing and adapting to ensure greater congruence between people, structure, and processes. The underlying assumption of this model is that when these components are not congruent, the program cannot achieve its desired outcomes. When this condition does not exist, people in the center will perceive barriers to accomplishing their work and meeting their personal needs. The director's job, in a nutshell, is to maintain a sense of congruence within and between these components of the program.

The Director As Change Agent

The director's role is central in the change process. In a number of powerful ways, the director shapes the center as a workplace. The director as leader plays a pivotal role in both assessing the current situation and structuring change to improve conditions. More than anyone else, directors are the agents of change. This does not mean that they impose change, but rather encourage and support it by developing the interpersonal context which frees, encourages, and helps people to assess their program and become actively involved in the change process.

"What you leave behind is not what is engraved in stone monuments, but what is woven into the lives of others."

— Pericles

The important thing to remember is that directors are facilitators of change, not dictators. Mobilizing and empowering people means helping others create new behavioral expectations. But keeping change efforts on target is not easy. Managing change is not a haphazard process. It is a delicate balance of providing direction yet suppressing the urge to overmanage. Facilitating change is the fine art of providing sufficient assistance and leadership on the one hand, yet avoiding oversupervising on the other. Facilitating the process means helping to maintain the momentum, the pace, and the spirit.

Building a Vision for Change

Fundamental to successful change is directors' ability to have a clear, informed vision of what they want their centers to become. This sounds so basic, yet often directors can articulate what is wrong with their programs, but have difficulty articulating just how their ideal program would function. Further, directors need to know how to translate that vision into realistic goals and expectations for teachers and children. This means creating the climate that supports progress toward goals and expectations.

A vision statement provides the direction and driving power for change. It is not some elusive abstraction, but rather the heart and soul of what guides a strategic plan of what one's program will look like in three to five years. A vision statement helps directors develop a set of realistic goals that are both purposeful and achievable.

Before reading on, take a few moments to complete Exercise #3.1. Write a dozen or so words or phrases that would describe your ideal program. Now take those words and phrases and weave them into a short statement of your vision of what you would like to see your program become in three to five years. While your vision statement will have elements of your ideal, it will also be reality based. These thoughts will be incorporated into the organizational profile you will develop at the end of Chapter IV.

Serving as a Catalyst for Change

The director is the one who must sense the need for change and communicate that need to others. This means interpreting changes in the external environment that may influence organizational effectiveness and developing mechanisms for eliciting feedback so as to have as much information and data about what is going on as possible. In other words, an integral part of the director's role is assessing the pulse of the center. Chapter IV will present a variety of assessment tools to aid this process.

Serving as the catalyst for change also means the director must be able to take the initiative. This necessitates being proactive rather than passive or reactive. Taking the initiative some-times requires being a risk-taker, an uncomfortable role for many administrators.

Finally, if directors are to be effective change agents, they need to keep abreast of new methods, approaches, and current research in the field. Studies have shown a strong relationship between directors' professional orientation and their degree of innovativeness (Jorde-Bloom, 1986b; Jorde-Bloom & Ford, 1988). The extent to which child care programs change and are receptive to innovative ideas depends in large part upon the professional orientation of those in charge. It stands to reason that directors who regularly participate in professional organizations, subscribe to journals, visit other centers to get ideas about innovative practices, and attend conferences to enhance their expertise are more likely to be exposed to a wider variety of innovative methods. They are also more likely to develop a network of resources to help in the implementation of desired changes.

Acknowledging that the director is the one who serves as the primary catalyst for change does not mean that we should underestimate the ability of those around us to come up with innovative ideas. Many good suggestions for improving program quality come from staff, parents, and even the children we serve. The key is to manage in such a way that divergent thinking and creative problem solving are promoted at all levels.

Creating the Climate for Change

The director is the key figure in establishing organizational norms that support or inhibit change. By a combination of position and sheer persuasiveness, directors can initiate or inhibit, build or erode, expand or contract the norms that bear critically on center quality. Developing a sense of trust, openness to experiment, willingness to risk failure are all norms that will impact a center's ability to incorporate needed change. Further, the director must know how to deal with institutional cynicism (the "we've tried that before" syndrome) and be able to assess the underlying causes that breed cynicism and defensiveness. Sometimes the comments a director makes in either formal staff meetings or informal conversa-

Vision-Building: Clarifying the Ideal

Write a dozen or so words or phrases that describe your ideal program. Now take those words and phrases and weave them into a short statement of your vision of what you would like to see your program become in three to five years. While your vision statement will have elements of your ideal, it should also be reality based.

_____   _____

_____   _____

_____   _____

_____   _____

_____   _____

_____   _____

My vision of what the program could look like…

_____

_____

_____

_____

_____

_____

_____

_____

_____

_____

_____

_____

tions when talking to staff can reinforce or inhibit norms of experimentation and risk-taking.

The director also has a strong impact on institutionalizing norms of self reflection and looking for ways to do things better. These norms cannot be changed overnight, though. Many programs have a culture characterized by inertia. Coaxing the system to be less complacent is not easy, but it is essential if a program is to work on resolving problems. Thus, the director's role in creating a climate for change is essentially one of energizing the problem-solving process.

Case Study: The Children's Corner

Christine was the newest teacher to be hired by the Children's Corner. She was young, enthusiastic, and a recent graduate of the university's early childhood program. At one of the first staff meetings in the fall, a discussion ensued about the problems teachers were experiencing with tote bags getting mixed up and papers being sent home with the wrong children. "I have an idea," Christine chimed in. "At the lab school we color coded the tote bags. It really helped organize everything. We bought plain canvas tote bags, dyed each groups' bags a different color. Then we put the children's names on the bags in big bold letters. The parents paid for the cost of the bags." Bea immediately countered, "Well, that may have worked at the lab school, but it sure won't here. You forget what kind of background these Head Start kids come from. Their parents sure as heck don't have money to throw away on a new tote bag every year!"

Inside Martha was furious at the way Bea just dismissed Christine's suggestion. But she also realized there was much more going on in this brief exchange than met the eye. Martha knew that Bea actually felt a bit intimidated and perhaps even threatened by the youthful exuberance Christine exhibited. Her comments were really a defensive posture intended to put Christine "in her place." Calmly Martha intervened, "You're right on target, Bea. Our parents don't have the money to buy a new tote bag. But I think Christine has an innovative idea here that is worth exploring. How could we take this idea and turn it into a workable solution to our tote-bag problem? Think we might have a small fundraiser to cover the cost of the tote bags? Bea, you've had a lot of experience with fundraising. Do you have any suggestions on how we might proceed?"

Providing Resources, Support, and Recognition

Another vital function the director plays in the change process is that of resource provider. The director brings together a variety of needed resources. These can be financial resources such as money for substitutes, materials, trainers, travel, equipment, or evaluation. Resources may come from professional associations, publishers, vendors of new material, or outside consultants.

Another leadership task is providing encouragement and recognition to staff for their efforts. The importance of this task cannot be overstated. Reinforcing positive behaviors, listening, providing emotional support, and allowing people room to make mistakes are all part of the director's role in providing support for change. In a defensive climate, people do not have the time or emotional energy to be creative because their energies are dissipated in trying to protect themselves from critical feedback.

Beer (1980) states that in order for change to spread through the organization and become a permanent fixture, early successes are needed. It is desirable but not necessary for the results of a change to be able to be measured. But Beer believes feelings of success are more important than quantitative measures. When individuals or groups feel more competent than they did before a specific change was implemented, this increased sense of competence reinforces the new behavior and solidifies learning associated with the change. He cautions, however, that intrinsic feelings of success are not sufficient for patterns of organizational behavior to be changed permanently. Self-confidence will quickly erode if extrinsic rewards in the organization do not immediately follow the early indicators of improved performance. These rewards can include recognition by the director, the board, or peers. The structure and processes of the center such as personnel policies and practices, performance appraisal procedures, promotion guidelines, and budget allocations must also support the new behaviors being sought.

Managing (and Protecting) Time

Time is the biggest barrier to change. The press of everyday events typically requires teachers and directors to be more concerned with just maintaining the stability of the status quo than envisioning change. In fact, time is a central ingredient in the change process itself. Time is needed to share knowledge and information about the content of a planned change or innovation; time is needed to develop the skills necessary to ensure a smooth change process; and time is needed to make the coffee, order the donuts, and set up the chairs for the meeting to plan and carry out the proposed change.

Time can also be viewed as a kind of resource. As such it must be judiciously planned and jealously protected if change endeavors are to be successful. Unfortunately, it is the kind of resource that is typically neglected in the planning process. It is easy to underestimate the amount of time needed for information sharing, training, support group meetings, and administrative coordination. Change initiatives will make little progress without adequate time being allocated.

We know that carving out sufficient time to address organizational issues is a persistent problem for directors. Directors undertaking any change endeavor will ask themselves, "Where will I possibly find the time to do a proper diagnosis of center needs?" "How can I ensure that staff will actually devote the time needed for this change?" "Do I have the time to manage all the activities, locate appropriate resources, and follow through in a way that will ensure success?" "And how can I help my staff so they do not become impatient with the amount of time it takes to achieve workable long-range solutions?" An important part of the director's role in ensuring success in any change endeavor, then, is to assess how time is currently being used, set priorities for the judicious use of time, and eliminate time wasters whenever possible. In fact, the use of time in a center may well be the focus of change efforts.

The Challenge of Balancing Individual and Organizational Needs

Schein (1985) calls the interaction between the individual and organization a dynamic, two-way process. This interaction, he believes, consists of a mutual sense of obligation between the interacting parties. Schein calls this reciprocation. Centers employ individuals because their services are essential for the center to achieve its goals successfully. Individuals, in turn, relinquish some of their personal autonomy and independence to the center in order to fulfill their personal needs. This relationship is cooperative only when it offers both entities — the individual and the center — the opportunity to fulfill their respective needs.

If we could distill the essence of what leadership means in the context of early childhood program administration, perhaps it could best be summed up by the challenge directors face in balancing individual and organizational needs. The center must achieve a balance between helping individuals meet their personal needs and at the same time it must meet organizational goals. Successful directors acknowledge the importance of centers being goal-oriented, but they are also mindful that "people are not willing to sacrifice themselves at the altar of the organization" (Dyer, 1984, p. 123).

> "The well director doesn't work to make people love her, but makes people love to work for her."
>
> — Roger Neugebauer

The issue of how to best balance individual and organizational needs has caused many a sleepless night for Carlos. As the program administrator of a multi-site child care organization, he is keenly aware of the staff's dissatisfaction with their level of pay. He's heard their grievances and listened attentively to their complaints. Yet he struggles to come up with a satisfactory resolution to the problem. From the teachers' perspective, the solution to the problem seems clear; raise tuition rates and let the parents assume a greater share of the cost of providing a quality program. The teachers feel that for too long their low wages have subsidized the centers' low tuition rates. Carlos is sympathetic to their situation. He feels, however, that the teachers don't understand how difficult it is to balance the budget. He has worked very hard to have tuition rates structured so that he can assure a full enrollment. He feels certain if he raises the tuition, he will lose some families and cause dissatisfaction among others.

Leadership Style

The director is typically the individual who has the "big picture" of the organization. It is akin to being the only one who knows what the picture on the front of the jigsaw puzzle box looks like. Staff make up the individual pieces of the puzzle. And linking their individual needs together to achieve a unified whole is the challenge of effective center leadership. Often it comes down to achieving a balance between order and coordination (getting the job done) and respecting the individual's professional right to autonomy and individual expression.

The organizational management literature is replete with references to the effects of different leadership styles as they relate to organizational effectiveness. The work of Blake and Mouton (1969), Getzels and Guba (1957), Hersey and Blanchard (1982), and Reddin (1970) are particularly helpful in understanding how different leadership styles can help directors to balance organizational and individual needs. The following conceptualization is a synthesis of their work. It is characterized by three different styles.

The ***task-oriented style*** stresses institutional or organizational needs. Directors whose behavior is characterized by this style tend to emphasize the requirements of the center and the achievement of center-wide goals. They tend to go by the book and stress following appropriate procedures. Staff are expected to conform to organizational expectations. Directors employing this style try to be conscientious in applying the same rules and procedures to all staff. Conformity and control are emphasized. The director assumes that if roles are well developed, clearly articulated, and closely monitored, then center goals will be achieved. The message is clear; the center's needs come first. Job descriptions are precisely defined and staff are expected to conform to the demands of the role. While this style tends to promote efficiency, staff working in centers with this type of leadership may complain that it is too bureaucratic and neglects individual needs.

The ***people-oriented style*** is characterized by a director who focuses on people and their individual needs more than organizational requirements. This type of director puts a premium on human relations and believes a happy staff will be a productive staff. The director thus devotes considerable attention to maintaining comfortable, friendly, and satisfying relationships among staff. This leadership style stresses the importance of allowing staff to exercise control, allowing them to actualize their individual needs, and become more self-directed. Although acknowledging the necessity for some policies and procedures, the people-oriented director believes that rules and regulations should be tailored to fit the needs of individual staff. Job descriptions are designed with specific individuals in mind. While positive human relations are a desirable outcome of this style, staff working in centers with this style of leadership may complain about the lack of order and coordination.

The ***transactional style*** stresses an appropriate emphasis on the center's needs and the individual worker's needs. The transactional leadership style is situational in that it calls attention to the need for moving toward one style under one set of circumstances and toward another style under another set of circumstances.

Directors characterized by this leadership style understand the necessity of having explicit roles and expectations for staff, but also understand that roles and expectations are implemented by people who have needs that must be met. This style of leadership rests on the premise that the director should not simply steer a middle course between organizational and individual needs, but rather assess the correct balance for different situations. In other words, different situations require different leadership behaviors and the effectiveness of an approach will depend on the situation in which it is used. The transactional style stresses that the demands of the center need not clash with the needs that people have for satisfaction and recognition from their work. This leadership style is most likely to yield optimum results in a center.

Results, in this case, mean achieving center goals and maintaining a high level of morale among staff.

In many respects, achieving the appropriate balance between organizational needs and individual needs requires one to balance all the technical aspects of running a center (tasks) with the people aspects of the program. Directors who are too task-oriented may be viewed as being inflexible, uncaring, and too controlling. Directors who are too people-oriented may have centers that lack unified goals, seem uncoordinated, and foster role ambiguity and role conflict. Effectiveness in one's administrative role may be gauged, then, by the degree to which the director can develop relationships with employees so that they are motivated to accomplish organizational goals of their own volition.

Change Viewed from a Systems Perspective: Linking People, Structure, and Processes

There are different schools of thought about the best way to create change in child care centers. Some focus on changing individuals through staff training and educational programs; others emphasize direct intervention in the processes of the center (e.g., changing decision-making processes); still others focus on changing the structures of the organization (e.g., pay and promotion policies). The central point of this book, though, is that lasting change must consider all three components of the center: people, structure, and processes. Centers need a variety of interventions to effect change and these changes may need to happen concurrently.

People, structure, and processes are noted here as the most important components to target if we want to effect change. That is not to say, though, that we ignore the external environment and the culture, but our strategies with these two components are slightly different. Yes, it is true that impacting the external environment through different advocacy efforts will produce change, but our control over most elements in the external environment is limited. Because of this, the external environment is much slower to respond to our

change efforts. Those efforts are important, but they are not the focus of this book.

We can only change the culture of a center by changing people, structure, and processes. For example, there may be a strong prevailing norm at a center that divergent points of view are not welcomed and that the board and director make all key decisions. But by changing decision-making processes at the center to those that are more participatory in nature, this norm will change. Likewise, if there is a norm at a center that staff do not talk about their rate of pay or the benefits they receive, this could be changed quite quickly if a center adopted a career ladder and salary schedule that detailed rates of pay and benefits for positions with differing qualifications and experience. We see, then, that the culture will change as a result of our efforts to change people, structure, and processes.

Kathleen is the kindergarten teacher at a private school serving children three through six years of age. She received a flyer from her principal suggesting that she attend a Math Their Way workshop at the local university. Kathleen resented the implication that her math program was inadequate, but since the school offered to pay her workshop fee and provide a substitute teacher to cover her classroom during the two-day workshop, she agreed to go. Much to her surprise, she was amazed at how the workshop expanded her awareness of important math concepts. She realized how much more she could be doing in her class-room. Kathleen came back to the school energized and very much a convert to the Math Their Way approach. She offered to share what she had learned at a staff meeting, but she was told the meetings for the next several months were already scheduled with other more important business. Still, Kathleen was eager to try out the Math Their Way approach in her class-room. She submitted a purchase requisition to her principal for $80 to purchase some new manipulatives for the Math Their Way activities. She also asked if she might be able have $20 to pay the school's high school student aide to *help her make the games on a Saturday. The principal wrote back a note explaining that the budget was very tight and all the school could afford was $15 toward supplies. Further, the principal felt it would be too much of an imposition to ask the aide to work on a Saturday. She reminded Kathleen that the school had already paid her workshop fee and the substitute. If she wanted to make some new games, she would have to schedule it into her free time. Kathleen was hurt and disappointed. Gradually her enthusiasm for Math Their Way disappeared. Somehow, she never did find the free time to make all the new games.*

The above scenario is not atypical. There are no villains in this story, only miscommunication about expectations. The training did achieve its objective in increasing Kathleen's awareness, but the lack of school resources to support her after the training meant that real change in behavior never really occurred.

We believe change will be more successful if it takes a total systems approach. Changes in one component of the system will be more successful if they are supported by changes in other components of the system. For example, if teachers are trained to use new procedures for assessing children's progress, their use of these new procedures will be short-lived unless accompanied by structural and process changes in the program such as changes in teachers' work schedules, the center's reward system, or the center's performance appraisal processes.

People Strategies

Educational change is fundamentally dependent upon change in people's knowledge, attitudes, and behavior. The changes which occur in terms of utilization of space, delineation of roles, curriculum content, and all the processes of the center cannot happen without changes in the people responsible for those elements of the program. The importance of changing people to effect organizational change is essential. People's needs, expectations, beliefs, and abilities strongly influence all other components of the social system.

Changes in knowledge tend to be the easiest to make; they can occur as a result of reading an article or hearing something new from another person. Attitude changes are typically more difficult to make than knowledge changes. This is because attitudes are so closely related to one's values. This means they may be emotionally charged in a positive or negative way. Changes in people's behavior are even more difficult and time-consuming. Most people who smoke, for example, are well aware of the health risks associated with smoking (knowledge). They may even want to stop smoking (attitude). But to stop smoking (behavior) is just too difficult a step to accomplish. Likewise, merely telling a teacher that a new approach will make classroom routines smoother will not ensure the teacher will actually follow through and use the approach. We often assume as directors that just because we provide the knowledge about something that teachers will see the benefits and change their behavior. This can be an erroneous assumption.

Allison is the director of a small half-day nursery school. Recently, she attended a workshop on emergent literacy at the annual state conference of nursery school directors. She was really inspired by the presentation and later visited the presenter's preschool. Allison was quite impressed with what she saw — teachers actively engaged in taking student dictations, words and phrases displayed around the classroom, and handmade books of children's stories displayed in the library corner. The whole language approach these teachers used obviously worked. Allison asked the presenter if she would come do a workshop at her center. She paid her teachers to attend the workshop on a Saturday morning. The teachers reluctantly attended, but afterward complimented Allison on her choice of presenters. They were equally impressed with the presentation. Given this level of enthusiasm about emergent literacy, Allison was disappointed to see that over the next several months virtually nothing changed in the way the teachers taught in the classroom. She was perplexed. They had obviously learned a lot from the workshop and thought the whole language approach was good. Why hadn't they changed their instructional methods to incorporate this new approach?

What Allison didn't appreciate was that she was actually quite successful in changing the teachers' knowledge and even their attitudes about emergent literacy. But changing their behavior by exposing them to one workshop was not a realistic goal. Behavior change is so difficult because it usually entails unlearning old behaviors and substituting new ones. This is not something that can be accomplished easily with many individuals. There is an undeniable comfort in the status quo. The teachers at Allison's center were clearly impressed with the possibilities of a whole language approach, but they were obviously not dissatisfied enough with their present techniques to want to change. Remember the principle of change presented earlier in Chapter II, "success in change is related to the felt need for change." The teachers in Allison's center didn't internalize the need to change. Indeed, they may have even resisted this kind of change because of the perceived additional work they thought this approach would entail.

Hall and Loucks (1978) remind us that change is a highly personal experience. Too often directors and administrators involved in staff development ignore the perceptions and feelings of people experiencing the change process. The personal dimension may be more critical to the success or failure of the change effort than the actual innovation or change being implemented. Since change is incumbent on individuals, their personal satisfactions, frustrations, concerns, and motivations, and perceptions must be taken into consideration.

Particularly when individuals have limited ability, flexibility, and confidence, they may become frustrated with changes which they have not had an active part in planning. This is why staff development and change go hand in hand. The intention of staff development is to create the right set of conditions to enable change to occur. The process begins with self-diagnosis — the indi-

vidual's perceived problems and needs. Chapter VI will provide a framework for helping individuals structure their own professional change. The director's job is to help ensure that this individual change supports center goals.

Wu (1988) cites research showing that the most crucial learning for teachers occurs in their first two years. Beyond that point, inservice education becomes a matter of unlearning as well as learning. That is why change is so difficult with staff who have been teaching for many years. The process of unlearning old behaviors may be more difficult than learning new skills. Recall, for example, the last time you drove a friend's car. Think of how awkward it felt when you reached to turn on the lights or windshield wiper and ended up grabbing the wrong knob.

What happens if individual change is not forthcoming and an individual is not willing to adapt behavior to be consistent with center goals? Often in joint planning, it will become clear that the needs and expectations of the individual do not match those of the organization. If this is the case, directors are faced with decisions about replacement or termination. There may be problems with personal style, philosophy, lack of flexibility, skill, or ability. While making decisions about termination is painful for any director, successful leaders understand that the replacement of key individuals can speed up changes in a group's performance and in achieving desired outcomes. The goal in the termination process is not to assign blame, but rather to help the individual understand that there is a mismatch between the individual's needs and the center's needs. Such an awareness conveys respect and allows the individual to be terminated with integrity intact. A systems perspective can help an individual realize the fit is not right. With an open, direct, and supportive approach, it is possible to turn the termination process into an opportunity for personal growth.

Structural Strategies

Early childhood educators have long regarded people strategies as fundamental to achieving center-based change. Staff development, after all, is central to the director's job. But a systems view of centers as organizations supports the proposition that change at the individual or group level is not as likely to be sustained unless it is supported by structural changes in the way a center operates. For example, increased competence in the classroom as the result of staff development is not likely to be sustained unless there are changes in the reward and promotion system or the performance appraisal system of a program.

Structural changes tend to be highly visible and can often be implemented relatively quickly. But structural changes alone cannot create permanent change. The educational experiments of the early 1970s with respect to open classrooms provide a case in point. Many districts knocked out walls, regrouped teachers, and changed teaching assignments. To the casual observer, it would have appeared that these programs had implemented open classrooms. But while the physical structure of the schools changed, teachers, in many cases, had not. They still treated children in the same way and taught under the same assumptions as before. The teachers, it seems, had either not really bought into or fully understood the philosophy of open education. It is not surprising, then, that many open classroom experiments were considered a failure. Within a year or two, the walls went back up and the schools took on a more traditional look. The lesson learned from these failures is that changes cannot be adopted wholesale; they must be modified and tailored to the unique conditions of each context and each group of teachers. Making a few structural changes in the program will not achieve lasting impact unless the people implementing the changes also adopt new attitudes and behaviors that support the structural changes.

Process Strategies

Directors recognize that many of the processes in their programs are neither efficient nor effective. These may be decision-making processes, communication processes, supervisory processes, or any of the other processes detailed in Chapter I. Recall the case study of Martha at the Children's Corner.

Clearly the processes that characterized her staff meetings were preventing her from achieving her goals for the center. The processes of an organization as they relate to supporting structures and the people who carry them out certainly have a direct effect on center outcomes.

We have seen that a director who wants to improve center outcomes can do so by changing or redesigning organizational structures, or by changing the behavior of key individuals. But often, direct intervention is required in modifying center processes that may be blocking center effectiveness. Effective working relationships between people and groups depend on their capacity to communicate feelings and perceptions. This can only be achieved by getting people together to listen to each other, negotiate, problem solve, and work through feelings. In a sense, many of the process interventions center on helping people learn new behaviors and develop new relationships.

Janet and Maria both work part-time for a church-sponsored nursery school. They share a classroom, with Janet teaching in the morning and Maria teaching in the afternoon. For the past year they have felt they have not been able to carry out their tasks effectively because they have conflicting ideas about how the learning environment should be arranged. They also have a very different tolerance level for clutter. Their interpersonal relationship is characterized by tension and hostility. In the past, their director has essentially ignored the situation. Her philosophy is that people should be allowed to resolve their own differences without interference from her. Neither Janet or Maria is willing to confront the situation directly. Instead, they have made critical remarks to the other teachers and to parents about each other's style. The interpersonal relationship processes that characterize the interactions between these two teachers are clearly blocking their ability to carry out their roles effectively. Their interpersonal friction is also having some negative consequences on other aspects of the program.

Janet and Maria need help. The hands-off leadership style that characterizes their director's behavior is not helping the situation. Clearly a process intervention is needed to support a change in the attitudes and behavior of these two teachers. Their inability to appreciate their differing styles is having a negative impact on the program.

Sometimes process changes are best facilitated by an objective third party. Depending on the severity of the problem, outside support may be needed to improve interpersonal relations and communication processes at the program. Sometimes all that is needed is for the director to take a more active role in structuring and supporting needed changes. Process interventions are critical because they are most likely to have a strong impact in modifying the culture of a center.

In most centers, an assessment of group meeting processes and decision making processes is a good place to start. Virtually all organizations experience some problems in communication, trust, and relationships which block organizational efficiency and effectiveness. Process interventions can help deal with these problems directly. Chapter IV provides assessment tools to evaluate the effectiveness of these and other center processes.

Tuning Into Staff's Levels of Concern

Hall and Loucks (1978) underscore the point that change is a personal experience for each individual involved. This means that each person will have somewhat different concerns about any particular change or innovation being considered. If the implementation of an innovation is to be successful, it is critical that directors tap into staff's level of concern.

Many teachers, for example, are well aware of the importance of individualizing instruction for children, but they may resist approaches to individualize because they fear they will lose control of the group. Other teachers may have a fear of failure that may prevent them from embracing new educational ideas. These concerns need to be addressed up front. Often the most important information we need to generate before initiating any

new change has to do with the staff's feelings, assumptions, fears, values, defenses, and worries about the specific change being considered.

Directors can approach this in a couple of ways depending on the type of change or innovation being considered. Certainly the most informal and direct approach is to simply ask each staff person, "When you think about this innovation, what concerns do you have?" Such an open-ended approach can be used at any time a new change is being proposed.

Another approach would be to solicit feedback by way of an informal survey. Assessment Tool #1 adapted from the work of Reddin (1970) is an example of such an informal survey. The approach has the ancillary effect of moving individuals from a vague global feeling of concern to being able to pinpoint those specific areas that may be important to them. With this feedback, the director is in a better position to counter any potential negative impact. An analysis of the feedback generated from such a survey can help directors address those initial informational needs and personal concerns. These may be issues having to do with planning, time, or organization,

Hall and Loucks (1978) have developed another approach for soliciting information about staff's concerns that is appropriate for curricular innovations or new instructional techniques. Their instrument measures the individual's stages of concern about an innovation. Hall and Loucks believe that an individual's concerns move from self, to task, to the innovation's impact. Table 3.1 summarizes seven stages of concern.

Hall and Loucks (1978) have also developed a questionnaire to assess an individual's level of concern. Assessment Tool #2 is an abbreviated version of their instrument using the High/Scope curriculum as an example of an innovation. The data generated from the administration of this questionnaire can be interpreted in a variety of ways. It is possible to simply note the stage that received the highest percentile score for the individual (or for the entire staff if scores are combined). This indicates the kinds of concerns that are most intense for the individual or group at

Typical Expressions of Concern About an Innovation

Table 3.1

Stages of Concern		Expressions of Concern
I **M** **P** **A** **C** **T**	REFOCUSING	I have some ideas about something that would work even better.
	COLLABORATION	How can I relate what I am doing to what others are doing?
	CONSEQUENCE	How is my use of this innovation affecting the children? How can I refine it to have a greater impact?
T **A** **S** **K**	MANAGEMENT	I seem to be spending all my time getting materials ready.
S **E** **L** **F**	PERSONAL	How will using this innovation affect me?
	INFORMATIONAL	I would like to know more about this innovation.
	AWARENESS	I am not concerned about this innovation.

Adapted from Hord, S., Rutherford, W., Huling-Austin, L., & Hall, G. (1987). *Taking charge of change.* Alexandria, VA: ASCD, p. 31. Reprinted with permission.

that particular point in time. The implications of this profile for planning staff development are seen in the following example.

Margo attended a conference where the High/Scope curriculum was being showcased. She did some additional reading about the curriculum and talked to several directors in her community who had gone through the High/Scope training themselves. Margo was convinced she needed to implement the curriculum in her center. She took a proposal to her board asking that the center allocate money to pay for three Saturday inservice staff development days to train her staff in High/Scope techniques. Margo met with the trainer to ensure that the inservice sessions would be well designed to include intensive training in both materials and techniques. Before embarking on this training, however, Margo followed the suggestion of one of her board members who thought it would be a good idea if she administered the Stages of Concern inventory to her staff prior to the training. Margo was sure glad she did. She discovered that her staff was primarily concerned about how much time this new approach was going to take (management concerns). Further, several noted comments at the end of the question-

naire that they weren't sure if this innovation was even needed at all. It seems they were really quite content using the eclectic theme-based curriculum they had been using for years. She also noted their concern about having to give up a weekend day to attend training. Realizing her enthusiasm for this innovation might be met with a wall of resistance, Margo quickly changed her plans. Based on the results she got from administering the Stages of Concern questionnaire about the High/Scope curriculum, a decision was made to address information and personal concerns first. She decided to spend only a portion of the money she had allocated for training and have the trainer provide a half-day overview of the curriculum. Staff could elect to attend or not. Those that did would be paid at their regular hourly rate. After the overview, staff would be given the option to decide if the High/Scope approach was an innovation that would be worthwhile implementing at the center. If so, additional staff development days would be scheduled for those who wanted to participate.

Had Margo not assessed her staff's level of concern about this particular innovation, there is a high probability that her attempts at implementing change in her program would surely not have succeeded. By tapping into staff's concerns, she was able to redesign the staff development program to address the issues that were most pressing to them. Nonusers, for example, are typically less concerned about the implications of an educational innovation for students than they are about what the innovation means to them (e.g. added time planning, etc.). Hall and Loucks (1978) believe that by using such an assessment tool, guesswork is removed from the planning process. "Gut feelings" about training needs are replaced by a reliable yardstick of concerns. Research on their instrument shows that the individual and group data generated can be used in various ways: to plan interventions, to evaluate progress, and to spot individual problems (Colette & Russell, 1988; Hall & Loucks, 1978; Hord et al., 1987).

A Final Word

Wu (1988) underscores the importance of linking what we know about change to what we know about staff development. "If staff developers apply the research with common sense, we will have a notably better chance to effect change in people and in programs" (p. 13). This chapter has stressed that one of the factors involved in improving child care programs is empowering the people engaged in the day to day life of the center and supporting their change efforts. The remaining chapters in this book will provide the tools necessary to help you, the director, make collaborative change possible.

Chapter 4

Assessing Organizational Needs

irectors often have a kind of global impression that things are either going well or not so well at their centers, but they lack specific information on just what areas of the program's operation contribute to these impressions. Without a clear sense of how the people, structure, and processes of a center interact to produce desired outcomes, directors lack the knowledge of how to ensure that their program will be as effective as possible. The information gleaned from assessing organizational needs helps directors turn those vague or amorphous feelings into more precise data about what aspects of the program can be improved. Assessing organizational needs helps directors identify the issues that are most pressing so they can prioritize their time and resources to address these concerns. When used properly, organizational assessment provides a sound basis for determining the objectives, content, and emphasis of staff development programs. It is the first step in linking organizational goals to individual goals.

This chapter will present a systematic approach to assessing the external environment, people, structure, processes, culture, and outcomes of a program in order to improve a center's effectiveness in solving its problems and achieving desired goals. The focus in this chapter will be on tools for assessment at the organizational level. Chapter V will address issues pertaining to the assessment of individual needs. Later chapters will discuss how to mesh organizational and individual needs. The approach is issue oriented focusing on existing and anticipated prob-

lems and generating possible strategies to neutralize the forces that create the problems.

The Importance of Assessment

Ongoing assessment is important at the organizational level not only because it gives structure to center improvement efforts, but because it also conveys respect for staff and encourages a team approach to problem solving. Staff can be incredibly resourceful at generating solutions to center-wide problems if provided the opportunity to participate in a meaningful way. The nonverbal message that is conveyed through assessment is a powerful one — the responsibility for improving the center is a shared responsibility. Indeed, the most effective early childhood programs are those where teachers, students, administrators, and parents together engage in problem solving, decision making, and implementation of program improvement plans. Clearly, the more perspectives that can be obtained on any relevant issue will ensure that fewer obstacles will be encountered in the change process.

The two-way communication that can emerge from assessing organizational issues can lead to a collaborative approach to problem solving and establish a precedent for future change. Since change is more likely to occur in work settings in which individuals feel that new ideas are welcome, such data can be used to "unfreeze" existing norms and attitudes. When the information is perceived as valid, accurate, and unbiased, the description of organizational conditions arrived at through the assessment process can be a potent force in helping bring about needed change (Bowditch & Buono, 1982).

Even when a center director is not aware of any immediate problems, it can be helpful to conduct periodic assessment of different aspects of the center's functioning. Monitoring center outcomes, in particular, is one way to ensure the center stays healthy. When used in this way, assessment is preventative in nature. It helps direct people's energies from potential griping to coming up with solutions before issues develop into unsolvable problems.

Diagnosing a Center's Need for Change

When we feel sick and go to our doctor to find relief, we expect that our doctor will do some kind of diagnostic assessment of our condition before prescribing a remedy for our illness. Doctors generally ask us to describe the symptoms we are experiencing. They may listen to our heart with a stethoscope, take x-rays, and even run a series of blood tests. All these diagnostic assessments provide the data our doctor needs to make an accurate diagnosis of our condition.

Directors of early childhood programs, as well, need diagnostic data to help them improve their centers. Unfortunately, most directors lack a systematic way to diagnose and monitor center effectiveness. They may sense their program has a low grade fever or a few minor aches and pains, but lack the specific diagnostic skills to identify the problem or problems that may be contributing to these symptoms. Without concrete tools to focus their assessment, directors may end up misdiagnosing the situation or merely treating the symptoms of problems. Worse yet, a haphazard approach to organizational assessment may even end up aggravating the ailment.

"Looking back, I think it was more difficult to see what the problems were than to solve them."

— Charles Darwin

Pinpointing Problems

In the diagram presented on page 29, we noted that the first step in the change process begins with the identification of a condition that someone feels needs to be improved. The success of the change plan will be affected by the degree to which everyone involved realizes that a problem exists, defines the problem in the same way, and agrees that improving the condition is desirable (Dyer, 1984). Change is bound to get off track if some people see the problem one way but others either do not admit there is a problem or see it differently. Identifying the problem means achieving some kind of general consensus as to why there is a problem as well as what the problem is. This sounds rather straightforward; in reality, problem identification is very difficult to achieve.

A problem is the discrepancy between current and ideal conditions. Hersey and Blanchard (1982) state that a problem exists when there is a discrepancy between what is actually happening (the real) and what you or someone else would like to be happening (the ideal). They stress that unless you can explain precisely what you would like to be occurring and unless that set of conditions is different from the present situation, no problem exists. "Change efforts involve attempting to reduce the discrepancy between the real (actual) and the ideal" (p. 267).

Hersey and Blanchard caution, however, that change efforts should not always involve attempting to move the real closer to the ideal. Sometimes after diagnosis, you might realize that your ideal is too unrealistic and should be brought more in line with what is actually happening. In other words, the director and staff need to ask themselves: Where are we now and where would we like to be? The problem is essentially the gap between where you are now and where you would like to be.

Problems should not be confused with symptoms. Most problems manifest themselves in a variety of symptoms. For example, students may be disruptive, teachers may be apathetic, or parents may not follow through on their obligations. These situations imply the possibility of a problem, but such behavior is usually only symptomatic of the problem rather than the problem itself. Even so, symptoms should be noted because they signal where to search for the cause of the problem. Remember, a problem is defined as a difference between the present situation and the ideal situation.

Recall the vignette in Chapter I where Connie was experiencing high turnover among her employees. This turnover, while very troublesome, was really only a symptom of a far deeper problem — the lack of role definition and role clarity in personnel policies. Recall, also, the case study of Martha who encountered cynicism and overt hostility by several teachers at the first staff meeting she conducted in her role as director of the Children's Corner. This unproductive staff meeting was only symptomatic of a far deeper problem at Martha's center — the lack of collegiality, trust, and cooperation among the teachers.

A problem is more than a frustration. Schmuck and Runkel (1985) caution that we should not mistake frustrations for real organizational problems. Some frustrations, they state, go away by themselves; others may remain as minor irritations. When we listen to teachers discuss their frustrations, we hear them say or imply that they would prefer something to be different. Often, however, they are not able to specify the features of that improved state of affairs. Schmuck and Runkel state that teachers who complain about the present without conceiving a better alternative have not yet conceived a problem and are therefore not ready to solve a problem. "A problem is a discrepancy between a present state of affairs and a more preferred state — sufficiently more preferred that one is ready to spend some energy to get there. Without the two parts — the current situation and the more desirable one — no problem has been specified. Frustration, irritation, anger, or confusion is often a feature of a problem — part of the present state of affairs — but it is not in itself a problem" (pp. 200-201). Frustrations are usually only symptoms of underlying problems.

A problem depends on one's point of view. We know that directors and teachers often have differing perceptions of organizational practices. Research has provided convincing evidence that directors uniformly rate organizational conditions far rosier than their staff (Jorde-Bloom, 1988b). Moreover, teachers typically look at issues from a fairly narrow perspective; directors hold a broader perspective of organizational issues. Whether the perspective is narrow or broad is of secondary importance in problem identification, however, because individual behavior is guided by one's own perceptions regardless of how "accurate" those perceptions are in some objective sense.

An understanding of point of view is critical to accurate diagnosis in center assessment. Because point of view is one's frame of reference for assessing a given situation, it is important to determine through whose eyes the situation is being described or observed — your own, those of the board, the parents, or the staff. Ideally, to get a full picture of the situation, you should get as many points of view as possible — particularly those people who will be affected by any proposed changes.

Schmuck and Runkel (1985) also point out that problems lie in people's heads, not in the real world. In other words, when a person says a center has problems, what that means is that person believes things should be different. But different individuals may have very different images in their heads of the present situation. The implication is obvious; one of the first steps in problem solving is to ascertain with some precision the different images the people concerned have of the present state of affairs. Achieving clarity about differences in perceptions of any situation is critical for effective group action. The goal of problem identification is thus to build a shared vision of what the center should be like and be able to articulate in meaningful images how the center will get there.

A problem usually involves more than one component in the system. One way to approach problem identification is to ask yourself a series of questions about each component of the system (external environment, people, structure, processes, culture, and outcomes). This preliminary diagnosis can help you identify problems in congruence within and between components. Looking at program outcomes is particularly useful. For example, you can ask yourself if there is a discrepancy between what you want or expect you should be achieving and what you actually have achieved? In this kind of analysis we can view a problem as the difference between actual and ideal outcomes. A problem exists when a meaningful difference is observed between outcomes at the organizational, staff, child, parent, or community level and what is desired. Remember, however, this information only tells you that a problem exists; it does not specify what the causes are.

We have seen in this section that agreeing on the problem isn't quite as easy as it might appear to be, but that should not dampen your desire to move forward. Picking the right problems and finding the right solutions to those problems is at the heart of center-based improvement. Exercise #4.1 provides a number of questions to get you started on the road to identifying the most important problem areas for your center that may need to be addressed. As you read through the series of questions, jot some notes to yourself in the margins of the exercise. When you have finished, write two or three problems as you presently view them.

Pinpointing Organizational Problems

External Environment

▸ How have changes in federal or state regulations affected the center in recent years?

▸ How have mandated requirements from the center's sponsoring agency helped or hindered it from achieving its mission?

▸ How does the physical location of the center affect center performance?

▸ Does the community support the center? How does the immediate neighborhood react to the presence of the center?

▸ How does the presence of other early childhood programs in the community impact the center? How would you characterize your professional relationship with other centers in the community?

▸ What experiences has the center had with respect to the vendors it uses for materials and equipment, food service, landscape maintenance, and other goods and services?

▸ How does the current political, social, and economic climate affect the program?

▸ Have their been any significant technological changes impacting the center over the past few years?

▸ Has the center been able to utilize the resources of local universities, colleges, and professional associations effectively?

People

▶ Do employees possess the knowledge, skills, and attitudes needed to carry out their jobs effectively? Are any employees overqualified for their assignments?

▶ What do employees say they like or dislike about their work? To what extent do their positions allow them to improve and grow personally and professionally?

▶ Who are the dominant coalitions? How have they changed over time? Do they help or hinder the program from achieving its goals?

▶ Have there been any noticeable changes in the clientele (parents and children) over the past few years? How have these changes impacted the program?

▶ Are the current members of the Board of Directors supportive or critical of the program's functioning? Why?

▶ Do supervisory staff set the tone for the center providing good role models for new or less-qualified staff?

Structure

▶ What is the philosophy of the center? How has it changed over time?

▶ Are the center's goals clearly defined? Are they understood and accepted by the Board and staff?

▶ Does the written curriculum accurately reflect the philosophy and goals of the center?

▶ How are teaching roles and responsibilities defined and communicated?

▶ Are reporting, supervising, and evaluating relationships clearly defined? Are interdependence and collaboration supported by job descriptions and reporting relationships?

▶ Is there a sound rationale for each level in the decision-making hierarchy of the center? Is the decision-making structure adaptable to change?

▶ Does the division of labor facilitate or hinder communication and problem solving?

▶ Are parents' roles clearly defined and communicated when children enroll in the program?

▶ Does the physical environment support program goals and desired teaching practices? Does the physical environment facilitate team behavior?

▶ Are space and materials allocated on the basis of task and need or on the basis of status?

▶ How equitable is the pay and promotion system?

▶ Do budgeting priorities reflect the goals of the center?

Processes

- ▶ How would staff characterize interpersonal relations at the center — warm and supportive or tense and competitive? Do staff appear at ease? Do they laugh with one another and appear to enjoy one another's company?

- ▶ How are interpersonal differences handled?

- ▶ Are personnel recruitment practices effective in attracting staff with the right knowledge, skills, and attitudes to do an effective job?

- ▶ How are new teachers and substitutes treated? How are employees oriented to their new positions?

- ▶ Do supervisory practices match the career level and professional needs of individuals?

- ▶ How are staff evaluated? Do they perceive evaluation practices as fair? Do they perceive evaluation practices as being supportive in helping them grow in professional competence?

- ▶ Are meetings productive? How are they conducted (who speaks most and to whom)?

- ▶ How are organizational problems solved?

- ▶ Are teaching practices consistent with the stated goals and educational objectives of the center?

- ▶ Do leadership practices provide a clear vision for the center?

Culture

- ▶ What are the center's shared values and beliefs?

- ▶ What are the critical events in the history of the center?

- ▶ What norms describe the culture of the center with respect to everyday demeanor, communication, risktaking, and how employees are valued?

- ▶ How would you characterize the general organizational climate of the program?

- ▶ Do individual and group behavior reflect a shared code of ethics?

Outcomes

- ▶ What is the general reputation of the center in the community?

- ▶ Does the center have full enrollment? Is the program fiscally healthy?

- ▶ Does the center seem to be running efficiently; is it able to anticipate and prepare for change or does it operate in a crisis orientation?

► How would you rate general employee satisfaction and overall staff morale? Do they appear to be personally and professionally fulfilled?

► How would you evaluate overall employee competence in performing their respective roles and responsibilities?

► Do employees appear to be committed to the center? Is there high absenteeism and turnover among staff? Are there indications of undue stress or work overload?

► Are children achieving at expected levels? Do indicators of social and cognitive competence allow one to conclude they are thriving in the environment?

► How would you characterize the general health of the children enrolled? Is there excessive absenteeism due to illness? Are there any indications of child abuse or neglect?

► How satisfied are parents with the program? Do they communicate positive feedback when they are pleased or do they tend to focus feedback on only negative impressions of the program?

Perceived Problem: (Describe what is actually happening now in a particular situation)

_____

_____

_____

_____

_____

Describe what is likely to happen in the future if no change takes place.

_____

_____

_____

_____

_____

_____

Collecting Accurate Data

 In most cases your first attempts at stating a problem will be incomplete. Additional data is usually needed to define the problem more clearly and ascertain underlying causes for the problem. The goal of data collection is to form a valid picture of the needs and problems of a center as a basis for action. Valid information is fundamental to understanding and dealing with problems which staff face. The instruments used to collect data should allow staff the opportunity to both describe the factors which contribute to their perceived problems and their feelings associated with these problems. Collecting accurate data is integral to center-based improvement. It is part of the change process described in Chapter II. Before proceeding with the actual data collection, however, several questions need to be addressed.

When should data be collected? It should be clear from the preceding section that center assessment is not a one-time process — assessing center-wide conditions needs to be ongoing. After all, situations and people change and centers must respond. Directors will definitely want to collect data when a problem seems to have surfaced to which there may be multiple perspectives or when additional information is necessary to clarify the problem situation. In most cases, an annual assessment of conditions will be sufficient. Many directors feel that the late spring is the best time to do this. Even if a center operates year around, there is a typical school-year pattern of enrollments and staffing that seems to exist with changes being made during the summer months. If data is collected in the May or June, it can be summarized during the summer months and shared with staff as they prepare for the new school term.

Data should also be collected before undertaking any kind of major organizational improvement process, even if it occurs mid-year. This is important because such data can serve as baseline information on progress toward achieving goals. Centers will sometimes implement exciting organizational changes but have no benchmarks to measure their progress. Initial baseline data provides a starting point for directors to chart their progress in improving organizational functioning. Virtually all of the assessment tools described in this book can be used as a pre and post measure. In this way, both directors and staff can see the incremental progress they are making in achieving desired outcomes.

How much data should be collected? Data collection begins with an assessment of an existing state of affairs. Diagnosis can be simple and straightforward or complex and very involved. It can include a few people or many. But in any case, it should give sufficient information about the existing situation so that plans for the future can be made with confidence. Diagnosis of any situation should provide sufficient data so that the director can find out:

1. What is actually happening now in a particular situation?

2. What is likely to happen in the future if no change takes place?

3. What would people ideally like to happen in this situation?

4. What are the blocks or restraints from achieving the ideal?

One caution, however. In their zest to get an accurate pulse on organizational conditions, some directors end up over-diagnosing. This can unwittingly have a negative effect on staff who will sense a kind of "paralysis of analysis" setting in. Too much time spent on diagnosis can convey to staff the impression that the center isn't really interested in moving forward with constructive change.

Who should collect the data? This is a difficult question to answer because each situation will be different. In most cases, the director or administrator of a center will be in charge of overseeing the assessment process. However, in some instances, it may be wise for an impartial outside party to collect the data. The key is to make people feel comfortable in stating problems without blaming anyone or arousing defensiveness. They need to be convinced that their perceptions are valued and important and that the data generated from assessment will help the center develop realistic goals that address key issues.

Regardless of who collects the data, it is critical to assure staff of the confidentiality of their responses. They need to feel confident that they can be as open as possible about sharing all positive and negative feedback and that the results of assessment will in no way be used against them. They need to be told up front who will have access to the data, how it will be summarized, and the extent to which the results will be shared with those who participated in the assessment process.

Because confidentiality is the most essential prerequisite for obtaining accurate information, any doubts respondents have about where the information will go and who will be identified can cloud the accuracy of data. If staff do not feel that their responses and their identity will be safeguarded during the assessment process, they may choose not to be completely truthful about some questions.

This presents a problem for administrators wishing to develop a questionnaire and tally the results themselves. Workers may not be totally candid if they know that someone directly associated with the center will be collecting and analyzing the results. The data generated from surveys conducted in this manner may be biased and of limited value.

In some cases it may be important to assure anonymity in addition to confidentiality. This can be done by having an agreed-upon third party collect the data and summarize it. Sometimes those in supervisory positions may be perceived by the staff to be the source of the problem. Under such circumstances, it is essential to have an impartial outside person conduct and analyze the data collected from surveys or interviews.

Should the results be shared? Unless the issue facing the center is highly sensitive, it is important to be as open as possible about sharing all positive and negative feedback. This process builds trust and confidence that staff do indeed have an important role to play in improving the center and that it is the collective responsibility of all concerned to both identify strengths of the program and come up with possible solutions to problem areas.

As an expression of administrative concern for their welfare, this step is what conveys to staff the director's intent to be open and supportive of needed changes. This demonstration of concern can in itself contribute to healthy staff relations. It can also open channels of communication and stimulate group problem solving. As feedback is translated into follow-up activities, staff will feel a greater sense of shared responsibility for implementing change and incorporating new practices.

Different Approaches for Data Collection

There are many different ways of gathering data. The assessment tools in this book provide several examples of different data collection techniques. It will be up to you to decide which assessments should be used to collect data about the problems you have described as a result of doing Exercise #4.1. The five most popular approaches to data collection include: questionnaires, interviews, observations, records and documents, and standardized tests.

Questionnaires. Survey questionnaires are probably the most widely used data gathering technique in educational settings. Questionnaires are particularly useful when one is interested is assessing the attitudes, beliefs, and values of a particular group of people. Moreover, they can provide useful information on changes in attitudes over a period of time.

The main strength of using questionnaires for data collection is that the approach is quick and, if the instrument is constructed well, the results are fairly easy to summarize. There are, however, some inherent limitations to using surveys. Questionnaires tend to be impersonal. Moreover, the questions may not adequately tap the desired information. Staff can also misinterpret a question, or skip over a question (or even a whole block of questions). Since most surveys are conducted anonymously, there is usually no way that missing information can be updated or probed more fully. This could be a problem because nonresponses may pose a threat to the validity of the data collected.

The primary issue with respect to questionnaires has to do with their validity and reliability — does the questionnaire measure what it purports to measure, and does it do so reliably and consistently. For this reason, it is probably wisest to use established validated instruments when they meet your purposes. The successful use of questionnaires rests in large part on the trust of the respondent. If individuals suspect the data will not be kept confidential or not used in ways intended, they may give socially-desired answers instead of truthful responses.

The questionnaires included in this book include several different types of response formats. There are both open-ended response formats (where the respondent is required to construct the response) and forced-response items (where the respondent is required to select their preferred choice from two or more alternatives). Forced-choice formats include multiple choice, yes/no, or rating scale questions. Table 4.1 provides a list of ten questions to guide you in selecting a questionnaire for your center-based assessment or in constructing your own questionnaire.

Interviews. Personal interviews are another approach to collecting data about your center. This approach is more direct and can lend deeper insight into the actual meanings of the issues addressed. Face-to-face interview methods provide greater flexibility to probe more fully certain issues that would be too difficult to elicit in a questionnaire. Like questionnaires, though, interviews can be open-ended or highly structured. Successful interviews, however, require considerably more time to administer. Scheduling staff for interviews, transcribing interview notes, and summarizing the results of interviews, even for a small staff, is enormously time consuming.

Observations. Perhaps the most effective way to tap what is actually happening in a given situation is to watch people's behavior as they work or interact with others. Such observations can be casual with anecdotal notes taken, or highly structured using checklists to code precise behaviors. Most directors are familiar with using observational techniques to code children's behavior and teachers' behavior in the classroom. But observational techniques can also be used to provide greater insight into organi-

zational processes other than just teaching practices. For example, observing organizational processes such as group meeting behavior and providing that feedback to participants can help group members increase their understanding of how to improve their methods of working together.

There are, of course, shortcomings to using observational techniques for collecting data. The most obvious is that observational methods are open to our perceptual biases. Since what we view is influenced by our own subjective feelings and experiences, it is possible to distort reality. We have all been in a situation where we have witnessed an event with others only to hear later multiple versions of the event being told. Objective reality varies with the lens one is using to view any situation. This underscores the importance of using observers who are highly trained and skilled in observational techniques. Saying that observers should be highly skilled does not necessarily mean that the observational tools need to be elaborate. Sometimes it is helpful to just have a frequency tabulation on how many people said what or how many times a behavior or an event occurred in a given situation.

Records/documents. Records and artifacts are another source of rich data for directors that can be collected to document certain patterns in organizational performance. Attendance records, staff memos, and parent notes are all examples of documents that may provide clues to problem areas that need attention. Analyzing staff absenteeism records or assessing annual turnover for the center may provide clues as to staff's level of commitment to the center.

Standardized tests. While the use of standardized tests with preschool-aged children is generally discouraged, they can serve a useful role in helping staff assess areas of the curriculum or instructional methodologies that may need to be improved. Children's scores on the Peabody Picture Vocabulary Test, for example, may provide useful clues for the staff on ways to improve instructional strategies to enhance language development. With staff who have limited training, the director may also want to use some kind of stan-

Table 4.1

Some Things to Think About in Selecting or Designing a Questionnaire

1. Are the directions on how to complete the questionnaire written in a manner that is easy for staff to understand? Are directions concise, clear, and complete?

2. Is the purpose of the questionnaire clearly explained in the cover letter or the directions?

3. Does the title of the questionnaire clearly tell you what the questionnaire is about?

4. Is each question worded clearly and concisely and does it address only one issue?

5. Are any questions too personal?

6. Is the response format appropriate for the questions being asked?

7. Is the questionnaire too long?

8. Are staff provided with clear directions as to what to do with the questionnaire when they are finished?

9. Is the instrument clearly reproduced?

10. Overall, is the layout and design attractive?

dardized knowledge base test to assess level of knowledge in child development or specific areas of the curriculum. Such a test may be useful as a pre and post measure of changes in knowledge if a staff development program is implemented that addresses staff's training needs in specific child development or curriculum content areas.

Tools for Assessing Organizational Needs

Collecting adequate data to assess the many elements of center effectiveness will undoubtedly necessitate using several different types of instruments, each with a different focus. Using multiple sources of evidence is important because no single instrument can capture the complex nature of organizational functioning with respect to people, structure, processes, culture, and outcomes.

In the appendix of this book are a number of tools (instruments) for gathering data about your child care center. There are times when you will want to use the tools from this book in the form in which they are presented. At other times, only a part of an instrument will meet your needs. It is hoped that the many examples presented in this book will assist you in gathering data about your center, diagnosing existing problems, and measuring your progress in achieving your objectives. The following provides a brief description of the range of organizational issues addressed in the instruments. More detailed information about administering and scoring these assessments is included with each instrument in the appendix.

One word of caution. It should be underscored that many of these assessments measure staff's perceptions about different organizational practices. These perceptions may or may not mirror objective reality. Objective reality is not as important, however, as what people perceive to be the case. For it is these internalized filtered perceptions that will guide and shape their behavior.

Organizational Climate

Organizational climate describes the collective perceptions of staff regarding the overall quality of work life at the center. Assessment Tool #3 is the short form of the *Early Childhood Work Environment Survey* (Jorde-Bloom, 1988a, 1989a) which can be used to assess the organizational climate of a program. This instrument measures staff's perceptions about a wide range of organizational practices. It is short and can be administered to the staff annually to take a quick pulse of organizational functioning.

Leadership Style

The first part of Assessment Tool #4 was adapted from the work of Blake and Mouton (1969), Getzels and Guba (1957), Giammatteo (1975), Hersey and Blanchard (1982), and Reddin (1970). It assesses three different leadership styles: the task-oriented style which emphasizes organizational needs; the people-oriented style which focuses on people and their individual needs; and the transactional style which stresses an appropriate emphasis on both the center's needs and the individual worker's needs depending on the situation. The second part of this assessment is an overall evaluation of the director's management and administrative behavior. It was developed by Exchange Press (Neugebauer, 1990). This instrument is designed to be completed by all staff who work at the center. The composite results summarize the staff's perceptions of the director's leadership style.

Goal Consensus and Communication

Peters and Waterman (1982) state that the hallmark of any successful organization is a shared sense among its members about what they are trying to accomplish. Agreed-upon goals and ways to attain them provide the foundation for rational planning and action. When the goals of a program are broken into attainable short-term targets, they

are called objectives. These constitute the tasks individuals must accomplish in order to meet the organizational goals. They are important because they help prioritize activities. One cannot assume, however, that just because a center's goals and objectives are committed to paper there is uniform agreement about those goals and objectives. Indeed, consensus on program goals and objectives is often lacking. This is because the goals of the center may not be truly embraced by individual members. Assessment Tool #5 assesses staff's rankings of various educational goals and objectives. From this information, you will be able to determine the degree of agreement that exists among your staff regarding various educational objectives.

Goal consensus rests in large measure on the effectiveness of communication in the center. Communication is the degree to which information is transmitted among the members of an organization. This transmission assumes many forms in child care centers; it can be written or oral, formal or informal, and personal or impersonal. Communication networks also vary in centers. They may be vertical (from supervisor to teacher) or horizontal (between teachers). Assessment Tool #5 assesses staff's perceptions of the effectiveness of communication at the center. The questions on this assessment tool were adapted from the work of Bean and Clemes (1978), Jorde-Bloom (1989a), and Rosenholtz (1989).

Collegiality and Collaboration

Assessment Tool #6 assesses staff's perceptions regarding their overall co-worker relations, particularly the extent to which they feel teaching at the center is a team effort. Whether or not teachers work collaboratively depends in large part on the harmony of their interests within the center — the degree to which they share similar goals and objectives. As Rosenholtz states, "Communal goals, problems, and values offer common substance from which to share" (p. 44). It should not be surprising, then, if the results of this assessment are similar to those of the goal consensus assessment tool described earlier. The questions on this assessment tool were adapted from the work of Rosenholtz (1989).

Decision-making Processes

The opportunity to participate in center-wide decision making is an important factor in the morale of teachers. We know from previous research, however, that the degree of desired decision-making influence by teachers varies from situation to situation. We cannot assume, for example, that all teachers want the same degree of decision-making influence in all areas of program functioning. Thus the roles that teachers and director play in decision making needs to vary according to the nature of the issue being considered and the background and interests of the parties affected. Assessment Tool #7 was designed to assess staff's perceptions of their current and desired levels of decision-making influence in five areas: ordering materials and supplies; interviewing and hiring new staff; determining program objectives; training new aides and teachers; and planning and scheduling activities. The purpose of this assessment is to measure the discrepancy between current and desired levels of decision-making influence. Assessment Tool #7 also includes questions about how the staff perceives the decision-making processes of the center. The information yielded from this instrument will give you a clearer picture of the areas in which staff desire a greater role in decision making. The questions on this assessment tool were adapted from the decision-making subscale on the *Early Childhood Work Environment Survey* (Jorde-Bloom, 1989a).

Supervision and Performance Appraisal Processes

The cornerstone of a center's capacity for self-renewal rests on the ability of staff to grow and adapt to change. It is the supervisory and performance appraisal practices in place at the center that allow this to happen. Assessment Tool #8 measures staff's perceptions of the extent to which the supervisory and performance appraisal processes of the center pose restraints or opportunities for professional growth. Using this assessment to tap staff's perceptions can provide important clues as to how to better motivate them to higher levels of performance. This assessment tool can also serve as a useful pre and post measure of the center's attempt to improve super-visory and performance appraisal processes. The questions on this assessment tool were adapted from the work of Bean and Clemes (1978), Jorde-Bloom, (1989a), and Neugebauer (1990).

Organizational Norms

Norms are the standards or codes of expected behavior at our centers. Although the existence of a norm is neither good nor bad per se, certain norms can facilitate or inhibit behavior. This in turn may have a positive or negative impact on the effectiveness of how group members carry out their respective roles. Norms can be both prescriptive (do's) and proscriptive (don'ts). Assessing staff's perceptions about the prevailing norms can serve as a starting point for understanding those norms and how we can best implement needed changes that will impact those norms. Assessment Tool #9 assesses the prevailing norms at the center in seven areas: everyday demeanor; use of space and materials; time and task orientation; professional conduct regarding children and parents; collegiality; communication and decision making; and change and experimentation. This assessment tool was adapted from the work of Fox and Schmuck (1973), Jorde-Bloom (1986a), and Schmuck and Runkel (1985).

Group Meeting Processes

In most organizations, workers spend considerable time in group meetings of one kind or another. Yet despite their importance to organizational functioning, few workers speak favorably about meetings. They usually view them as a burden and waste of time. In child care centers, staff meetings are typically the primary vehicle for decision making and problem solving. It would seem important, therefore, to regularly assess the effectiveness of how meetings are conducted. Assessment Tool #10 assesses staff's perceptions of the effectiveness of the staff meetings conducted at the center. The questions on this instrument are adapted from the work of Schmuck and Runkel (1985) and Jorde-Bloom (1982). The information generated from this assessment should provide a wealth of data from which to improve group meeting processes in the future.

Parent Satisfaction

Meeting the needs of parents is central to our mission of educating young children. It is incumbent that centers, therefore, regularly assess parental satisfaction regarding the range and quality of services provided. Assessing parental perceptions about program functioning communicates to parents a sense that they are important and that their opinions are taken seriously. The information gleaned from Assessment Tool #11 will provide the director and staff with parents' perceptions of overall center effectiveness. It is probably best administered in the late spring of each year.

Moving Forward: Considering Different Strategies for Change

We've stressed in the previous section that diagnosis is the cornerstone of adequate problem solving in child care centers. Without complete and accurate data, problems tend to multiply. Problem identification and data collection naturally flow into data analysis. Once a discrepancy (problem) has been identified, the goal of analysis is to determine why the problem exists. Analysis consists of identifying aspects of people, structure, and processes that can be altered or changed to reduce the problem.

Now that you have collected additional data regarding the initial problem you identified as a result of completing Exercise #4.1 on pages 48-51, you are ready to restate the problem, identify the symptoms, and summarize the results of the data you collected. This can be done on the Exercise #4.2 worksheet. The result of this exercise will yield a clear, succinct goal statement. This is nothing more than a precise description of the ideal situation you want to achieve. Bean and Clemes (1978) state, "When a group defines goals it gives substance to what people feel is important. People's feelings, attitudes, and expectations are critical to the success of achieving goals. They provide the energy and commitment that are necessary to do the work required to fulfill goals; motivation to action arises from feelings" (p. 74).

Some examples of goal statements might be:

- ▶ The center will achieve NAEYC center accreditation.

- ▶ Teachers will engage in collaborative planning and positive interactions with one another.

- ▶ The spatial arrangement of the physical environment will encourage children to engage in cooperative play.

- ▶ Parents will play an active role in center activities.

Having goals that are explicitly stated and focus on the future helps you and your staff direct your energies and encourages cohesiveness within the center. In sum, the purpose of this step is to generate a shared image of what the center will become. The importance of having a clear and shared vision for the change process cannot be overemphasized. All staff should be able to visualize a picture of what the center will be when the effort has been achieved.

Analyzing the Situation:
Assessing Helping and Hindering Forces

In the early 1950s, Kurt Lewin introduced a useful model for analyzing problem situations. His Force-Field Analysis Model is helpful in understanding the pressures and counterpressures of various forces that act to block or bring about change. He called these driving forces and restraining forces. He believed that organizational life could be characterized by a dynamic balance of forces working in opposite directions. The approach is useful because it helps us to think about any problem situation in terms of factors that encourage and facilitate change (helping forces) and factors that work against change (hindering forces). These forces may originate inside the organization (people, structure, processes, or culture) or outside the organization in the external environment.

Using this model as a framework for problem analysis helps us think of the present state of the problem as a balance between opposing forces.

Restating the Problem, Identifying Symptoms, and Summarizing the Results of the Data Collection

Problem: _____

_____

Symptoms: _____

_____

_____

Results of Data Collection: _____

_____

_____

_____

_____

_____

_____

_____

_____

_____

Goal: (ideal situation) _____

_____

_____

The task, then, becomes one of enumerating all the forces that are on either side. The helping forces are those that support change efforts in moving toward an ideal; hindering forces are those that are blocking movement toward the ideal. Lewin's Force-Field Analysis is a useful technique because it identifies the positive and negative factors affecting change, targeting the cause rather than the effects of a problem. Exercise #4.3 is a worksheet adapted from the work of Schmuck and Runkel (1985), Storm (1985), and Saxl (1989) to help you identify the helping and hindering forces as they relate to the present situation and your conception of the ideal you would like to achieve.

Generating Possible Solutions: Weighing Alternatives

The next step in the problem-solving process is to determine how the helping or positive forces can be strengthened or increased and how the hindering or negative forces can be reduced or decreased. It is usually recommended that a program's first priority be given to reducing negative forces since these usually have a stronger effect in achieving a desired ideal state than trying to increase the helping forces.

The solutions that are generated will probably involve all components of the system: changing people (through staff development or supervisory practices); changing structures (by implementing new policies or redefining roles); or changing organizational processes (by altering the way business is done). The internal components of the system are typically easier to change than the external environment. That is not to say, however, that some of the strategies might not entail changing aspects of the external environment that the center may have control over. Changing the culture of the program will probably not appear as an immediate solution. That is because the culture changes as a by-product of changes in people, structure, and processes. In other words, it will automatically change as a result of our efforts to modify other components of the program.

The next step is to determine the viability of each proposed solution. Some solutions will simply be impractical. Others will be too costly or take too long to put in place. In determining the viability of each solution, think, as well, of the possible effects that each solution will have on other aspects of people, structure, and processes. This involves anticipating the probable consequences of using each alternative strategy. The process implies trade offs. Exercise #4.4 provides a worksheet to guide your analysis. At the top of this worksheet state your goal. This will describe the ideal state you hope to achieve. Then proceed to list all possible solutions. Do not begin to assess the merits of each until you have noted all the possible solutions to your problem. Next jot down the possible consequences of each. After doing so, you will be able to assess which solutions are the most viable.

Developing an Action Plan

Once viable solutions have been generated and alternative strategies for change have been carefully considered in terms of their intended and unintended consequences, it is then possible to develop a concrete plan of action. A written plan serves not only to avoid ambiguity about who is to do what by when, but also serves as a tool for reminding individuals of the progress that is being made. Exercise #4.5 provides a worksheet to guide this planning process. The process is essentially one of translating the solutions generated from the previous exercise into objectives that will achieve the goal. This is the heart of your action plan because it provides the quantitative description of the goal you are striving to achieve.

Objectives are statements that define measurable, observable behavior that lead toward a goal. Objectives are typically stated in phrases that begin with the word "to," and they precisely define time limits. When writing objectives, think of what observable behavior will tell you that you are making progress toward achieving a goal. While goals are often quite broad statements of what we hope to accomplish, objectives are precise statements of what needs to be done to achieve a specific goal. Bean and Clemes (1978) state that well-written objectives should contain four elements:

Analyzing the Situation: Assessing Helping and Hindering Forces

----

Goal: (ideal situation) _____

_____

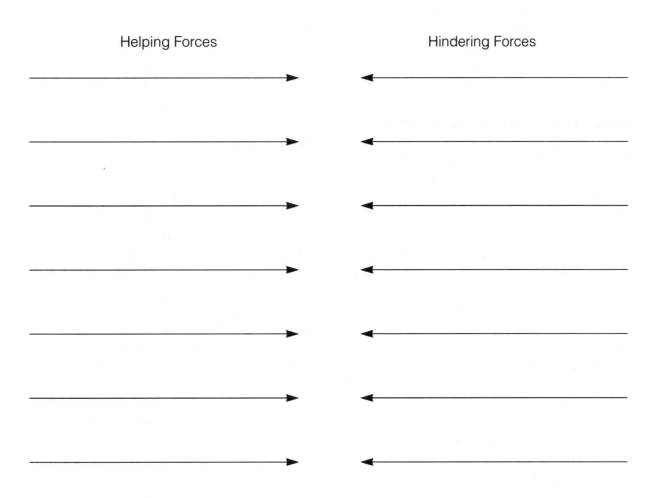

Helping Forces　　　　　　　　　　　　　Hindering Forces

Present Situation

Generating Possible Solutions: Weighing Alternatives

Goal: (Ideal situation) _____

_____

_____

Proposed Solution	Possible Consequences
_____	_____
_____	_____
_____	_____
_____	_____
_____	_____
_____	_____
_____	_____
_____	_____
_____	_____
_____	_____
_____	_____
_____	_____
_____	_____

Action Plan

Goal: _____

Objectives	Action Steps	Who Responsible	Time	Resources Needed (people, materials, $$$)	Evaluation Checkpoints

WHAT will be accomplished.

► the presence of new behavior

► the absence of a previously observed behavior

► the performance of a particular task

► the completion of a concrete product

WHO the persons are whose behavior will be measured.

► everyone

► a part of a group

► a person

WHEN the specific behavior will be measured.

► a specific date

► a contingent date (e.g. three months after a test is given)

► a general period of time (e.g. within one year)

HOW MUCH of the behavior will show that some standard has been reached.

► a score on a test

► a relative reduction in something (e.g. half as many...)

► a relative increase in something (twice as many...)

► an absolute number of something (10 instructional units completed)

The next step is to note all the activities that will be necessary to accomplish each of the objectives. Next to each activity should be noted the individual or individuals responsible for carrying out the specific activities delineated, the total amount of time necessary to accomplish the task, a proposed timeline, and additional resources needed (noting costs).

Finally, the action plan should include checkpoints for evaluation. In other words, how will you know you have accomplished your objectives?

These may be actual products if your objective is to produce something tangible, or it may be points in time where you will assess your progress. This last category is important because it will help you know how to measure progress in achieving your goal.

While we have shown the planning process in worksheet form here, it may be easier in group planning to make a separate task card for each activity. Each card should detail the task, who is responsible for carrying out the task, and how long the task should take to accomplish. These cards can then be arranged on a wall in the appropriate sequence to make a visual timeline in which they should be done. This process is recommended for undertaking goal setting which involves several objectives that entail multiple activities over an extended period of time. The process is useful because it provides all parties involved with a very visual blueprint of the scope of the change process to be undertaken.

On the following page we see how Martha, the director of the Children's Corner, defined her problem and detailed a plan of action. At the end of this chapter are the exercises that Martha completed for her program. These examples of completed exercises will be helpful as you identify problem areas that you want to improve in your own program.

Implementing the Action Plan

Picking the right problems and finding the right solutions only points you in the right direction. Implementing the plan is what actually leads to center improvement. If goals and objectives are important to the individuals involved and if they are "doable," then implementing the action plan should be a fairly straightforward process. In a top-down model of change, the director has control over this process. In a collaborative model of change, however, the director's role becomes a delicate balance of providing sufficient supervision to ensure that tasks actually get done, while at the same time providing sufficient leeway so that individuals will internalize a sense of ownership of the change process.

In Chapter III we discussed the vital role that the director plays in providing resources, protecting time, and giving staff the support and recognition they need during the change process to ensure feelings of success. It is critical that the change process not be viewed as a linear event. All kinds of circumstances can arise that will necessitate a modification in action plans and the timeline in which to carry out activities. Being flexible and viewing the action plan as a blueprint that may have to be revised from time to time will help you keep staff motivated to achieve desired goals.

Evaluating Progress

The final step in the change cycle is to evaluate progress in achieving desired goals and objectives (outcomes). Without evaluation, the actions implemented toward change would not be understood. Thus, evaluation should not be seen as the end of the process, but rather as a stepping stone to further identify new areas in need of change. This is a cyclical process, one which addresses the needs of a complex social system in action. What is the purpose of evaluating change? And what is the best way to pursue prac-

Case Study: The Children's Corner

Given the newness of her position and the gravity of the situation, Martha decided that time was scarce. The first couple of weeks on the job had convinced her that she would have to take the initiative to implement some changes. She would start out with a top-down model of change and gradually increase staff involvement as they were ready and willing. She knew that certain norms had set in over the years and that patterns of behavior would be difficult to change. But she had one thing going for her; she sensed that the teachers were also dissatisfied with the present situation. If she could implement a few structural changes and work on modifying some of the processes of the center, she might be able to establish the norms of collegiality and collaboration that would lead staff to begin to examine their own teaching practices.

Martha's first step was to clarify her problem. At first blush, she thought her problem was the hostility exhibited toward her at staff meetings. But after she pondered the issue for a while, she realized this might only be a symptom of a far deeper problem. She decided to collect some data regarding the staff's perceptions of center policies and practices. Martha was encouraged by how open and candid the staff were in completing the assessment tools. She saw how the process of asking their opinions signaled her interest and respect for them.

When Martha analyzed the data from the assessments, she realized that staff were generally distrustful of one another. Because of their lack of influence in decision-making processes and staff meeting processes over the past years, they had reacted by becoming very protective of their own turf. Martha knew that if she was to make any impact on this program, she first needed to improve the cooperative nature of relationships and establish an environment that encouraged collaboration. This became her goal.

Martha's objectives for accomplishing this goal were ambitious. First, she would try to increase staff's knowledge of different learning and teaching styles. Her hope was that this would lead to a greater appreciation of individual differences. At the same time, she would develop an individual profile on each staff person highlighting their teaching strengths. This information would be used to encourage collaboration between teachers. Second, she would work to modify some of the structures of the center that seemed to discourage collaboration. Staff work and planning schedules, in particular, seemed to be a real problem. Martha knew that meaningful interactions between teachers were often difficult given their overlapping and conflicting schedules. Even getting everyone together for staff meetings was almost impossible. She wanted to free up time to allow staff to plan activities together, observe other centers together, and go to conferences and workshops together. Finally, she would make some bold changes in the way staff meetings were conducted. She realized that valuable time was being wasted talking about trivial details that could have been covered in a memo. Meetings did not start on time and people did not have a stake in the agenda or in supporting productive interaction processes. Martha decided she would involve teachers in setting the agenda and facilitating discussions. She would also work to help the staff begin to examine the roles that each of them played in meetings. She believed that increasing their knowledge of group dynamics would have the ancillary benefit of actually improving group functioning.

tical and useful evaluation procedures? Perhaps a good way to begin is to define what evaluation means in this context.

During the implementation process, the director plays a monitoring role. The easiest way to determine how things are going is what Peters and Waterman (1982) call "management by wandering around," talking informally with staff involved in the change process. For example, the director may ask staff questions such as: "How is the new literacy program working?" "What was accomplished at the staff committee meeting on multicultural curriculum?" "Is our professional library for staff up-to-date?" "Have you noticed a change in the children's behavior since you rearranged your learning centers?" This informal "sensing the pulse" is a critical element in keeping change on target. This kind of formative evaluation serves to provide information on how the action plan might be improved.

At a designated point in the change process, however, the director will also want to gather data in a more formal, systematic way. This type of summative evaluation will assess the degree of success of the change endeavor in achieving desired outcomes. Formal evaluation occurs when the outcomes of these investigations are described in terms that can be measured. If the goals and objectives on the evaluation plan are described precisely, then this process is a fairly straightforward one. It may be done using some of the assessment tools discussed earlier as a posttest measure of the degree of improvement made in a specific area. This kind of evaluation provides useful data about the success of the change endeavor and any alteration in resources that may need to be made to make it more successful in the future.

Loucks-Horsley (1987) believes that the most important evaluation question to ask is whether the new changes are thought of as an improvement by those most affected by them. To assure objectivity in the formal evaluation process (particularly when the results of the evaluation will be used to document the need for additional funds from a sponsoring agency or external funding source), it is best to use an impartial third party to collect the

evaluation data and summarize the results of the change efforts. In sum, evaluation is both a basis for assessing whether intended outcomes have been achieved and pinpointing alterations in the action plan that should be made in subsequent change endeavors.

A Final Word

We have seen in this chapter that picking the right problems and finding the right solutions to them is the heart of center-based improvement efforts. We have also seen that a systems model can serve as a viable framework for center analysis and problem solving. Effective directors collect information on the quality of their center, compare the information with desired outcomes, identify discrepancies, and search for causes to problems. From this information it is then possible to develop a plan to alleviate the problems.

The director's role is to act as a catalyst to move the center toward its goals. Data analysis is the step that links the present to the future. If teachers can have an active role in analyzing the situation and generating alternatives, they will feel a greater sense of shared responsibility for implementing change and incorporating new practices. Examining the changes the staff would like to see leads naturally to developing objectives and designing appropriate strategies for change. The goal in the change process is to turn problem solutions into goal statements that clearly state what will be done in a specific, realistic, observable, and measurable way.

In sum, the assessment process is essentially a self-renewing process — it is dynamic rather than static. It is concerned with both outcomes and processes. It is a means for developing organizational teamwork and building collaborative action to bring about an understanding and acceptance of changes necessary to reach center objectives, and the responsibility for implementing those changes. Ongoing assessment should be an integral tool for creating, designing, improving, and maintaining effective early childhood programs.

Restating the Problem, Identifying Symptoms, and Summarizing the Results of the Data Collection

Problem: _Lack of cooperation among teachers. Inability (willingness) to collaborate._

Symptoms: _Low involvement in staff meetings. Mistrust, competition. Very little teacher sharing of ideas and resources. Teacher isolation._

Results of Data Collection: _Assessment Tool #10: Staff perceptions of staff meetings show they believe meetings are boring and a waste of time. Assessment Tool #6: Staff perceptions of collegiality and collaboration show that staff feel alienated from one another but want to find ways to reduce tension in their interpersonal relations. Assessment Tool #3: Organizational climate score = 65 Assessment Tool #7: Staff desire greater decision-making influence in all areas of center functioning, particularly in determining the content of staff meetings and in determining work schedules._

Goal: (ideal situation) _Staff will engage in collaborative planning and in more cooperative, supportive interactions with one another._

Analyzing the Situation: Assessing Helping and Hindering Forces

Goal: (ideal situation) *Staff will engage in collaborative planning and in more cooperative, supportive interactions with one another.*

Helping Forces	Hindering Forces
isolated instances of some teachers helping each other →	← protecting classroom "turf"
director willing to support collaboration →	← time
teachers' interest in greater involvement in staff meetings →	← some staff are afraid or unwilling to share ideas
staff willing to give honest feedback when asked →	← distrust of others
staff aware of tension →	← physical arrangement of space promotes isolation in classrooms
low staff turnover →	← conflicting work schedules
some new teachers have lots of enthusiasm and interest in sharing →	← history (norm) of lack of sharing and collaboration

Present Situation

Generating Possible Solutions: Weighing Alternatives

Goal: (Ideal situation) _Staff will engage in collaborative planning and in more cooperative, supportive interactions with one another._

Proposed Solution	Possible Consequences
1. create resource sharing bulletin board	some staff may not use
2. change work schedules to encourage joint planning and time to visit other centers together	more opportunities to work together but may result in cliques forming
3. involve staff in planning staff meetings	greater sense of involvement in decisions
4. conduct training on learning styles and psychological types	may increase understanding and appreciation of individual differences
5. director model cooperative behaviors	some staff may perceive as disingenuous
6. hire subs so teachers can observe one another's classrooms	will be expensive. Some staff may resist

Action Plan

Goal: Staff will engage in collaborative planning and more cooperative supportive interactions

Objectives	Action Steps	Who Responsible	Time	Resources Needed (people, materials, $$$)	Evaluation Checkpoints
To increase staff's knowledge of different teaching and learning styles	- invite speaker for fall workshop - have staff take assessment tools #16 and #17 - xerox handouts - purchase books on learning styles	director	- 2 hrs to plan workshop + write letter to speaker - 1 hr to score assessments	- guest speaker $100 - teachers $25 each for attending workshop - $40 xeroxing for handouts and books for staff library - $20 food for workshop	- feedback from workshop - see if reference is made to different styles during the year
To change center structure to encourage staff sharing of resources and ideas	- set up bulletin board and resource table - rearrange schedules to encourage joint planning time and opportunities to visit other centers together	director and teachers	3 hrs to set up resource center 16 hrs for individual conference time with teachers	- $150 supplies for resource center - substitute teachers for staff who want to observe approx 40 hrs total @ $8/hr = $320	- see how staff utilize the resource center - Administer Tool #6 as a posttest in May
To increase staff involvement in planning and conducting weekly staff meetings	- ask for volunteers to help plan and lead meetings - provide staff with handouts on group dynamics and how to conduct effective meetings	director and teachers	approx. 40 hrs released time for staff to plan meetings between Sept and May	- subs to cover planning time, 40 hrs @ $8/hr = $320 - misc. xeroxing of handouts for meetings $8 per meeting - $10 food per meeting - $75 for books on group dynamics	- Administer Tools #3, 7 as a posttest in May to see if change in perceptions - Administer Tool #10 after 6 meetings; share results

Chapter 5

Assessing Individual Needs

Over the past 15 years, increased emphasis has been placed on child development as providing the underpinnings of early childhood education. Specifically, teachers focus not only on developmental stages of young children, but also on unique developmental patterns, experiences, abilities, and backgrounds of individual children. Yet in our preservice and inservice programs for the professional development of early childhood teachers, we seem to have forgotten this developmental focus. Instead, training programs continue to be designed for an entire staff, as if all teachers had the same backgrounds, interests, and needs. It is the intent of this chapter to present teacher development from an individualized perspective.

Adults as Individuals

Assessing individual teachers in light of their developmental patterns, experiences, abilities, and backgrounds should provide a realistic analysis from which to design meaningful professional development approaches. It is our belief that knowledge and understanding of how teachers can achieve optimal growth rests on accurate assessment of individuals. This section looks at those areas that seem important in identifying strengths and needs of teachers. While there is some overlap among these areas, they also represent, to some degree, separate aspects of the developing adult.

Personal Background

The gathering of basic background information on individuals appears to be a relatively simple process on the surface. Often there is personal data gathered during the hiring process. To address family history or background variables in more depth, however, it is necessary for a supervisor to devote more time to the process; but the resultant information can provide greater insight from a developmental perspective. Information on family background, for example, may help illuminate why a teacher behaves in a particular way. Knowing, for instance, that a certain teacher was the product of a strict, religious upbringing can help the director understand why that teacher is a strong advocate of structured experiences for children. In the same way, knowing that a particular teacher is experiencing some turmoil going through a separation or divorce can allow the director to be sensitive to the side effects of such an experience which may impact job performance. Recognizing a teacher's lack of exposure to different ethnic groups can assist the director in understanding why the teacher is having difficulty with parents and children of different cultures.

Often a director may not have a clue to understanding a teacher's behavior until this kind of interpersonal communication occurs. In the following

> "Treat prople as though they were what they ought to be and you will help them become what they are capable of being."
>
> — Goethe

two examples, Martha talks about the connection between personal history and job performance:

Case Study: The Children's Corner

"Margaret seemed extremely nervous when I observed in her classroom. And although I had encouraged her to call me by my first name, she continued to use 'Mrs.' After one particular observation, Margaret and I met to discuss a child. I took the risk and told her she seemed bothered by my presence in her room. The conversation then wound its way to Margaret's relationship with her mother, who was my same age. Margaret described her mother as very demanding, critical, and a real perfectionist. She explained that she disliked having her mother attend any event where she performed for fear of a harsh assessment. Once Margaret could express her feelings about me as representative of her mother, we were able to establish a better relationship as supervisor and teacher."

"Scott had been late for work many mornings over the past two weeks. He apologized readily to me and to his classroom aide who had handled the children on her own. But he made no effort to offer an explanation. He appeared rushed and preoccupied and left the classroom at night right after the last child was gone. I invited Scott to have lunch with me and talked with him about his lateness. Reluctantly, he opened up and shared his personal situation. His wife was having some medical problems, and the care of his two school-aged children was falling on his shoulders. Since he worked in child care, he was even more guarded about sharing his dilemma. After all, he should be able to deal with his children and still get to work on time! Scott and I talked about his situation and I think I was able to make some helpful suggestions. Even though his lateness was the surface problem that had to be dealt with, I felt confident Scott benefitted from my having listened to all of the problems centering around his wife's illness."

Obviously, such information cannot be obtained through data sheets or written profiles. Rather it is elicited through many open, supportive conversations with staff. Just as the early childhood teacher seeks to know each child, his family, his cultural heritage, and his particular experiences, so, too, does the successful supervisor or director seek to know his/her staff. From such a knowledge base, understanding and meaningful support can be generated.

Educational Level/Training/Experience

It is necessary under most licensing regulations to document the staff's education, training, and experience. Well-maintained personnel records reflect specific educational degrees, the completion of special training programs, and the years and type of teaching or volunteer experience. For directors to provide appropriate professional development opportunities for individual staff members, they must be keenly aware of this data, as well as more informal information that staff members might not record about themselves. For example, through a conversation in the lounge, one director became aware that a particular teacher had completed two courses in sign language. With encouragement from the director, this teacher began exposing her 5-year-olds to signing through the singing of simple songs. Feedback was very positive from the parents concerning this curricular innovation.

With respect to experience, it is important for the director to be aware of the many and varied roles teachers may have performed over the years. Some may have worked in home day care or parent cooperatives while their children were young. Others may have volunteered in different capacities within the public school sector. Such experiences can provide a broad knowledge base from which the preschool teacher can interact effectively with parents and the community. Taking time during the initial interviewing and hiring process and at ongoing intervals throughout the year to discern the many and varied experiences of individual staff members contributes to their effective utilization and involvement and enhances the center's program.

Interests/Skills/Talents

Also important to note is specific information related to special interests, skills, and talents of staff. Often teachers have talents, particular skills, or abilities that can be integrated nicely into the early childhood program. Frequently, teachers have musical training or special artistic abilities that can enhance the program as well as the teachers' sense of their own worth. Sometimes teachers have very unusual or unique talents that are not readily apparent. One director told of a teacher who was an avid cook and baker. She was pleased when the director talked to her about using these special talents within the early childhood program. Menu planning and classroom cooking projects were woven into this teacher's role. Another teacher had a special talent for graphic design; the monthly newsletter became her special project. Through the scheduling efforts of a director, a teacher aide who spoke fluent Spanish and had a strong interest in bilingualism was able to spend some time in each classroom working with small groups of children. A Nigerian man working part-time in a university preschool program had an interest in enhancing the multicultural aspect of the curriculum. And one teacher who traveled extensively during the summers with her husband had a wonderful photo collection which the director encouraged her to build into the curriculum.

Acquiring and utilizing personal background data in a constructive manner requires that the director be able to establish a sense of trust with her staff. The director who is sincerely interested in the unique needs of individuals and is able to communicate a commitment to individual growth will be able to elicit that trust. Often it takes gentle probing by the director to find out about particular interests and talents. Staff members may not see their attributes as vehicles for contributing to the overall program. The director is in a position to take a supervisory role which emphasizes this kind of holistic approach.

Personal Traits and Characteristics

Adults, just as children, have very unique personalities and characteristics. To view supervision from a developmental, individualized perspective, it is necessary to consider such uniqueness.

Energy level. First, from a physiological standpoint, adults have very different energy and drive levels. Two teachers who seemingly have the same family demands, responsibilities, and outside interests may come to the work site in very different states. One complains constantly of being tired and worn out; the other seems to possess unlimited "bounce" and stamina. In conversations with these two adults, we find that one is able to go on very little sleep each night; while the other says she can't make it without her eight hours! Granted, such states may be related to psychological stress; but physically there are also legitimate differences among people.

Level of abstract thinking. An additional personal characteristic identified by Glickman (1985) is the level of abstraction demonstrated by individual teachers. Abstract thought, using Glickman's definition, is "the ability to determine relationships, to make comparisons and contrasts between information and experience to be used to generate multiple possibilities in formulating a decision" (p. 57).

Glickman classifies the abstract thinking of teachers as low, moderate, or high. Teachers who reflect a low level have trouble determining how to begin making changes in their classroom. Or, they don't seem to see the relationship of their own behavior to a problem they've identified. They often want quick answers or direction from a supervisor. Such a perspective is apparent in one teacher's plea to her director.

"These kids won't sit in a group for more than five minutes! All the boys want to do is play in the block area; and they all come to me constantly for help or to tell about somebody. What should I do — throw this developmentally appropriate stuff out the window? This approach just doesn't work with this group!"

Teachers with moderate levels of abstract thinking, according to Glickman, realize that the problems relate in some way to what they are doing. However, they are unable to adequately define the problem and find an appropriate remedy, as the following example illustrates:

"Some children want to spend all their time in art or blocks. So, I've decided to move small groups through each interest area for 20 minutes

"Everyone has peak performance potential — you just need to know where they are coming from and meet them there."

— Kenneth Blanchard

at a time. That way everyone will experience each area, and I won't have to be fighting with children to get them to try new things!"

Finally, highly abstract teachers use a rational process of problem solving by incorporating several sources of information and applying their own knowledge and experience. Before making a final decision about changing something, these teachers consider all available data and reflect on past experience in order to arrive at the best solution. In the following scenario, a teacher discusses her problems with her director concerning Peter, one of her students:

"I've been trying to find some new strategies to use with Peter when he becomes so frustrated and angry. I talked yesterday with his mother to see if we could come up with a consistent approach. It may be that excluding him from certain activities is warranted. I've resisted removing him from the block area, but I'm beginning to think this is necessary. His behavior is threatening the safety of others. I think it's important, however, for Peter to be involved in constructive things after he has been removed. In other words, I don't think he should just remain alone, unattended. He seems so vulnerable emotionally, and he needs my support."

Table 5.1 summarizes Glickman's delineation of levels of abstract thinking and can be used as a quick reference for determining where a particular teacher might be functioning.

Temperament/Psychological type. Many of the differences between people are reflected in various aspects of their personality and behavior. Some

---

Table 5.1

Levels of Abstract Thinking

Low	Moderate	High
Confusion about situation	Can define situation by focusing on one dimension	Can define the situation by drawing relationships between several sources of information
Doesn't know what can be done	Can think of several responses	Can relate the information to change in classroom practice
Asks to be shown	Has difficulty in thinking of consequences of changing the situation	Can generate many alternative responses
Has habitual responses to varying situations		Can evaluate the consequences of each response and choose the one most likely to succeed

From Glickman, C. D. (1985). *Supervision of instruction: A developmental approach.* Boston: Allyn & Bacon, p. 59. Reprinted with permission.

---

adults, for example, thrive on constant interaction and communication with their colleagues, while others need and want more alone time and may recoil from constant chatter and exchange. Some people respond in very flexible ways to unexpected demands and changing situations, while others may react quite negatively when routine and order are disrupted. The latter personality type wants everything planned carefully and exactly; the former is more of a situational decision maker and can thrive with a flexible, less-structured approach.

Carl Jung (1923) believed these similarities and differences in personality are not random, but rather predictable. In studying patterns of human behavior, particularly the way people perceive information and interpret reality, Jung concluded that people are born with a predisposition for certain personality preferences. In Jungian theory, behavior relates to basic functions involved in gathering information about one's world and making decisions based on that information. Jung's theory of psychological types was expanded by Katharine Briggs and her daughter, Isabel Briggs Myers, who developed the Myers-Briggs Type Indicator (MBTI) (Myers, 1980).

The MBTI assesses preferences for how we function along four continua: extraversion/ introversion; sensing/intuition; thinking/ feeling; judging/ perceiving. Table 5.2 summarizes the key characteristics of each dimension as they relate to preferences in different work situations. The extravert sees people as a source of energy, while the introvert prefers solitude to recover energy. The sensing type is more practical and concerned with the here and now, while the intuitive type tends to be more visionary and innovative. Thinking types base decisions on logic, data, and facts; feeling types base their decisions on their personal gut feeling of what is right. People who have a strong need for closure are likely to be judging types, while people preferring to keep things open and fluid are perceiving types. Use of the MBTI yields one of 16 psychological typologies.

Keirsey and Bates (1978) have taken the work of Jung and Myers and adapted it to educational settings. They refer to differing personality preferences as one's temperament. Temperament, they state, is a somewhat broader concept than "function type." As such, they believe it is a better explainer of behavior. Keirsey and Bates define temperament as "that which places a signature or thumbprint on each of one's actions, making it recognizably one's own" (p. 27). Keirsey and Bates state that because people have a preferred style or temperament, they are often baffled by others who do not see the world as they do. An awareness of similarities and differences in personalities can help foster interpersonal understanding.

Learning style. Styles and approaches to learning vary among any group of teachers. Dunn and Dunn (1978) state that each individual has an innate learning style that is modified with experience. Some adults are very self-directed, while some are other-directed. Self-directed teachers have the motivation to learn and the skills to choose the means to accomplish the learning. Other-directed learners may lack the necessary motivation and the skills to accomplish their goals.

According to McCarthy (1980), teachers' learning styles will also influence the selection of activities and learning situations. Some teachers learn best by reflecting, others learn by observing, and still others acquire new skills only by doing. While some teachers relish the idea of using the group setting to discuss problems and situations at length, others see this approach as time-consuming and cumbersome.

Even more specifically, adults have preferences in terms of perceptual mode of presentation. Some of us are visual learners, while others are mainly auditory. The lecture format with detailed charts and graphs may be the choice of visual teachers while auditory learners may enjoy brainstorming, debate, and group collaboration.

Wonder and Donovan (1984) discuss the split-brain theory as providing insights into our thinking and learning preferences. They propose that individuals have a tendency to prefer one side of the brain over the other, which affects their approach to life and work. It is possible for individuals to develop the skills of the less-preferred hemisphere, but they cannot change dominance or preference. Rather,

Table 5.2

Effects of Each Preference in Work Situations

EXTRAVERTS	INTROVERTS
Like variety and action.	Like quiet for concentration.
Tend to be faster, dislike complicated procedures.	Are careful with details, dislike sweeping statements.
Are often good at greeting people.	Have trouble remembering names and faces.
Are often impatient with long slow jobs.	Tend not to mind working on one project for a long time uninterrupted.
Are interested in the results of their job, in getting it done and in how other people do it.	Are interested in the idea behind their job.
Often do not mind interruption of answering the telephone.	Dislike telephone intrusions and interruptions.
Often act quickly, sometimes without thinking.	Like to think a lot before they act, sometimes without acting.
Like to have people around.	Work contentedly alone.
Usually communicate freely.	Have some problems communicating.

SENSING TYPES	INTUITIVE TYPES
Dislike new problems unless standard ways to solve	Like solving new problems.
Like an established way of doing things.	Dislike doing the same thing repeatedly.
Enjoy using skills already learned more than learning new ones.	Enjoy learning a new skill more than using it.
Work steadily with realistic idea of how long it takes.	Work in bursts of energy powered by enthusiasm, with slack periods in between.
Usually reach a conclusion step by step.	Reach a conclusion quickly.
Are patient with routine details.	Are impatient with routine details.
Are impatient when the details get complicated.	Are patient with complicated situations.
Are not often inspired.	Follow their inspirations, good or bad.
Seldom make errors of fact.	Frequently make errors of fact.
Tend to be good at precise work.	Dislike taking time for precision.

THINKING TYPES	FEELING TYPES
Do not show emotion readily and are often uncomfortable dealing with people's feelings.	Tend to be very aware of other people and their feelings.
May hurt people's feelings without knowing it.	Enjoy pleasing people, even in unimportant things.
Like analysis and putting things into logical order.	Like harmony. Efficiency may be badly disturbed by office feuds.
Can get along without harmony.	Often let decisions be influenced by their own or other people's personal likes and wishes.
Tend to decide impersonally, sometimes paying insufficient attention to people's wishes.	Need occasional praise.
Need to be treated fairly.	Dislike telling people unpleasant things.
Are able to reprimand people or fire when necessary.	Are more people-oriented—respond more easily to people's values.
Are analytically oriented—respond easily to people's thoughts.	Tend to be sympathetic.
Tend to be firm-minded.	

JUDGING TYPES	PERCEIVING TYPES
Work best when they can plan their work and follow the plan.	Adapt well to changing situations.
Like to get things settled and finished.	Do not mind leaving things open for alterations.
May decide things too quickly.	May have trouble making decisions.
May dislike to interrupt the project they are on for a more urgent one.	May start too many projects and have difficulty in finishing them.
May not notice new things that need to be done.	May postpone unpleasant jobs.
Want only the essentials needed to begin their work.	Want to know all about a new job.
Tend to be satisfied once they reach a judgment on a thing, situation, or person.	Tend to be curious and welcome new light on a thing, situation, or person.

they tend to have a thought style that results in a consistent pattern of behavior in all areas of their lives. For example, the left-brain dominant person is more apt to solve a problem by following a logical, sequential, and organized approach, while the right-brain dominant person will wait to see what happens and be more intuitive in solving problems. Wonder and Donovan stress that there is nothing inherently good or bad about a particular preference; but identifying one's preference may lead to a greater understanding of why some learning environments are more conducive than others.

Hunsaker and Alessandra (1980) offer a framework for assessing learning style types and identifying their characteristics. They describe the four learning modes as feeling, watching, thinking, and doing. "Feelers" learn best by involving themselves in experiences. They rely on intuition and feelings to make decisions in each situation. "Thinkers" are most comfortable with abstract conceptualization; they use rational logic when making decisions. "Doers" learn best through active experimentation and use the results of their tests to make future decisions. And "watchers" take a reflective, tentative, uninvolved approach to learning; they use careful observation and analysis.

The insightful director can discern linkages between individuals' learning preferences and their expectations of the director. Some teachers prefer a supervisory style that promotes self-directed learning, independent decision making, and indirect guidance. Others, however, look for clearly delineated curriculum guides, specific directions, and director-initiated decisions and answers. The following examples illustrate two different learning styles:

Belinda complained to her director, Sandra, that the role-playing sessions being used by the consultant who was presenting conflict resolution strategies to the staff were time-consuming and tiresome to her. She asked Sandra if she could just read the material on the subject and try implementing the approach on her own. The group sessions, as Belinda described them, were too "touchy-

feely;" she did not like being observed while trying new ideas and strategies.

Another staff member at the same center, Constance, mentioned at a staff meeting that she didn't feel the conflict resolution training was being tied closely enough to the actual classroom situations. She asked if the consultant could observe her as she taught in her classroom and give her specific feedback and suggestions. She stated that teachers needed to be given more support and direction in trying to implement something new.

These two teachers probably represent the two learning modes identified by Hunsaker and Alessandra of thinking and doing. Belinda would prefer to get the ideas from written material and try them out on her own. Thinkers usually learn best in impersonal learning situations, guided by theory and their own analyses. On the other hand, Constance would like to carry out the suggested theories and have someone observe her doing so. Doers thrive on active involvement in projects or innovations.

Degree of flexibility/Openness to change. Individual variance is great with respect to flexibility. Some teachers are firm believers in routine, order, "tried and true" solutions, and stability. Others seem to thrive on change, risk taking, and exploration of alternatives. Having both extremes on a staff can be a definite challenge to a director! Most people fall somewhere in between on a continuum; and, in providing individualized supervision, it is important for the director to have an idea of a particular teacher's orientation. Knowing how resistant or receptive to change a teacher might be can be very important when new curriculum ideas or practices are being promoted. If a director knows ahead of time that several teachers tend to be cautious and skeptical of change, she can work to offset potential resistance. For example, the director might allow these teachers to observe a particular curriculum idea in operation at another program before it is presented in the staff meeting. Presenting new ideas carefully and slowly while allowing discussion is another strategy a director can use to introduce an innovation. Less flexible individuals do not like new approaches thrown at them without lots of preparatory work on the part of the supervisor.

The degree of flexibility reflected by a particular staff member can also be described by the dichotomous terms of adaptor and innovator coined by Kirton (1976). Kirton conceptualizes the trait of innovativeness as a behavior preference related to two contrasting cognitive styles. He sees people as adaptors or innovators based on their preference to "do things better" or to "do things differently." Adaptors are characterized by precision and conformity; innovators prefer to approach tasks in unusual and different ways. Knowing where staff fall on this continuum allows the director to gain an insight into the diverse thinking and functioning preferences of individuals. Such knowledge can allow a director to understand why one teacher is so resistant to changing the physical environment of her classroom, while another teacher is constantly rearranging furniture and equipment to conduct experiments on the effects of different arrangements on children's behavior.

When one moves from theoretical constructs to practical application, Kirton's conceptualization of innovativeness is particularly appealing because it may assist in promoting collaboration in an organizational setting, especially in times of change. The approach emphasizes that a balanced staff is needed in order to be prepared for all contingencies. Thus we should not treat the noninnovative person in pejorative terms. Under pressure, adaptive personalities and innovative personalities usually disagree on what steps are appropriate to take, and they often hold negative viewpoints of each other when collaboration would be a more fruitful strategy. Innovators perceive adaptive individuals as dogmatic, stodgy, timid, inflexible, and compliant to authority. Adaptive people tend to see innovators as being unsound and unreasonable. Kirton states that an organization needs to allow for mutual appreciation of those with different modes of problem solving.

General dispositions. Quite often directors or other administrators refer to particular traits of staff that don't fit into the categories of skills or attitudes.

They speak of individuals having characteristics ranging from supportive, accepting, and enthusiastic to rejecting, impatient, and dull. Katz and Raths (1986) identify these characteristics as dispositions. They define a disposition as an attribution which summarizes the trend of a teacher's actions across similar contexts. The construct is descriptive; for example, a teacher who uses praise in specific contexts and on many occasions might be attributed a "supportive disposition." Katz and Raths argue that dispositions thought to be related to effective teaching can constitute goals for teacher development. For instance, a director might find herself in the position of talking with a teacher about the lack of a supportive environment in the classroom. Such a discussion would be more abstract in nature than one focusing on a particular skill. Yet, as many directors are aware, and as Katz and Raths propose, positive dispositions are essential to teacher effectiveness. It is important that supervisors addressing staff development issues from an individualized perspective be aware of the importance of particular dispositions.

"I am a person. Do not bend, fold, spindle, or mutilate."
— picket sign at Berkeley, 1964

Self-confidence/Self-efficacy. The issue of self-confidence or self-efficacy is a central factor in assessing why some teachers approach their own development in positive, assertive ways while others seem reticent about doing so. According to Bandura (1982), self-efficacy is the conviction that one can successfully execute the behaviors required to produce a desired outcome. Such judgments are important since they affect the decisions individuals make, how much effort they will expend on a particular task, and how persistent they will be to master that task. In other words, those teachers who have a strong sense of efficacy will usually exert greater effort to master new challenges.

According to self-efficacy theory (Bandura, 1982), there are four principal sources from which people form estimates of themselves:

▶ **Past performance accomplishments.** A teacher who has been able to design and implement an effective classroom in which students and parents are comfortable and students achieve and grow has a strong sense of her own worth and efficacy. She is able to use such an experience as a base to go forward and continue to grow and improve. Likewise, teachers who have had very negative classroom experiences, who are left with the feeling of inadequacy and ineffectiveness, have difficulty approaching subsequent experiences with any sense of confidence. They may be very reluctant to tackle new approaches or have someone observe in their classrooms.

▶ **Vicarious experiences.** Teachers who have the opportunity to observe other teachers in different settings often come away with a renewed sense of confidence (i.e., "I do a lot of those same things which someone else is saying are wonderful! I must be good, too!") Vicarious experiences rely on judgments of how similar one is to the person modeling a particular behavior. Observing others who are seen as being similar in ability carry out teaching practices which are successful can raise self-efficacy expectations.

▶ **Verbal persuasion.** When a director tells a teacher she is doing something well, it does not mean that the teacher will necessarily believe it. Verbal persuasion is not as strong a source of efficacy information. Yet if the teacher perceives the verbal reinforcement as sincere, specific, and supportive, it may also enhance the teacher's sense of self-confidence.

▶ **Emotional arousal.** The teacher's state of emotional arousal is another source by which self-efficacy expectations are acquired and/or altered. High arousal generally inhibits performance because teachers are less likely to expect success when they are tense or anxious. Thus, feelings of self-efficacy can be context specific in that a teacher may feel very confident in one area of her teaching and less so in another.

According to some researchers (Bandura, 1982; Hackett & Betz, 1981), self-efficacy also relates to gender differences. Females are typically more cautious of taking risks and tend to view themselves as less efficacious than males at certain activities. In the early childhood arena where we deal most frequently with females, this information is important to consider.

The following examples illustrate different perceptions of self-confidence/self-efficacy which appear to have come from particular experiences of the teachers presented:

Sharon was pleased when she was asked to help prepare a state presentation on infant and toddler curriculum with the director of her program. She had been refining her infant/toddler curriculum for the last five years and knew she had done a good job. Her ideas for the physical environment, sleeping arrangements, supervision of students in the setting, and parent feedback had met with praise from different sources. At her last state conference, she had attended sessions on infant/toddler curriculum and felt that, in many cases, she had better ideas than the presenters. She left the director a note the next day: "Thanks so much for inviting me to join you at OAEYC. I think I can do a good job with this, and I appreciate your thinking of me. One thing I know at this point is good programming for infants and toddlers!"

The staff met to discuss the parent open house scheduled for the fall. It was decided that each teacher would conduct an information/discussion session in her classroom on developmentally appropriate curriculum relative to the particular age group. After the meeting, Janet came into the director's office to express her anxiety. "I don't think I can do this talk to the parents. I know what developmentally appropriate is, I think, but I'm not ready to try to explain it to the parents. It gets too confusing with all of this Piaget stuff and questions about academic and reading readiness. We never talked about this approach when I was in school. And anyway, I hate talking to big groups; you would be a much better person to do this!"

Obviously, these two teachers reflect very different perceptions of their own self-efficacy. Sharon has had experiences and observations which have confirmed her feelings that she knows a lot about infant/toddler programming and can articulate that knowledge. Janet, on the other hand, implies that the new curriculum emphasis is overwhelming to her, especially with respect to articulating it to a group of parents. Most likely, she has had very little experience in presenting things to groups of people; and she apparently has not had sufficient experience with developmentally appropriate practice to give herself a sense of confidence about promoting the approach to others.

It becomes the director's task to understand that the lack of self-confidence can impede the performance and growth of an individual staff member. Sometimes it takes verbal persuasion on the part of the director to help the teacher begin moving in the direction of having more confidence in herself. And just as we attempt to plan experiences for children which build on their previous experiences in order to enhance self-efficacy, we need to do the same for the adults with whom we are working.

Needs and Expectations

The staff of an early childhood program is comprised of individuals with many different needs and expectations relative to themselves and the center. It is important for the director to be aware of a particular teacher's perceived needs and specific expectations of the workplace. At the same time, the director must also be aware of her own expectations relative to staff performance and be able to honestly communicate them.

Expectations are the assumptions — whether conscious or unconscious — that we have for our own or another person's behavior. In other words, we predict that the other person will act in a manner consistent with our expectations. Concurrently, however, the other person also has expectations for his or her own behavior. If an honest feedback process does not exist between the two individuals, confusion and disorientation can result. Consider the following interaction between a director, Marcy, and a teacher, John.

Marcy: "You don't seem to be taking as much initiative as I thought you would in keeping and organizing anecdotal records on the children. In your initial interview, I can remember your saying that this was a priority of yours."

John: "Yes, but I thought someone would provide me with some guidance on doing it. It seems like part of your job as director should be to assist teachers in setting up record keeping."

Marcy: "I guess my assumption is that you've had practice doing this type of thing in your teacher training program. Wasn't observation a key focus of one of your curriculum courses?"

John: "Not where I went to school. Anecdotal records were discussed, but we never had real experience using them. The concept behind using them makes sense to me, but part of the problem is finding the time to do them! How do you suggest I work them in?"

In this example, both players had different expectations relative to roles. John expects that Marcy, as a supervisor, should provide a lot of direction in an area that she sets as a priority. Marcy, on the other hand, assumes that John has the training and is proficient in carrying out such a process on his own. Without communication on this issue, both John and Marcy would tend to blame the other for the unmet goal. Consequently, both would cast the other as inadequate and tend to lower their expectations for desired behavior, or they might become hostile and discouraged.

Staff members of a center also represent a variety of needs, some of which are quite unconscious. The need for equity is clearly an issue for Pat at the Children's Corner whereas recognition seems to be a strong need for Shelly.

It is important for the director to address individual needs and expectations regularly so that honest, informed interactions can result. Once such issues are out in the open, they will appear far less insurmountable.

Case Study: The Children's Corner

Pat is a very seasoned, talented teacher at the Children's Corner. The competitive climate of the center in recent years, however, has heightened Pat's basic need for equity and fairness. During the first month of school Martha became conscious of how important equity and fairness were to Pat. This need first came to Martha's attention in late August when classroom art supplies were being distributed. Pat made a big fuss about how important it was that every teacher receive a fair and equitable portion. Equity issues for Pat also carried over into space, lunch hours, and expense reimbursement. Martha surmised that in a more collaborative, cooperative environment, these equity issues might not be quite so important to Pat. Unfortunately, the negative climate of the program tended to bring out the worst, even in this excellent teacher.

Case Study: The Children's Corner

Shelly, a young, new teacher at the Children's Corner seems to have a strong need for recognition. As soon as Shelly was hired, Martha quickly became aware of Shelly's need to be recognized for any extra time she put into the center. If this recognition wasn't forthcoming, Shelly tended to pout or make snide remarks about how early she was coming in each morning to prepare her classroom. But if Martha made comments on a regular basis relative to Shelly's overtime work, Shelly seemed quite content.

Adult Development Stages

Research in human development has found that we, as adults, continue to develop and change in adulthood just as children grow and change during their childhood. The literature in this area focuses on two aspects of development — the study of adults' capabilities to improve over time and research on life span stages and transitions. One major finding is that cognitive, social, and language development do not solidify at adolescence or early adulthood but continue to develop throughout life (Glickman, 1985). Unlike in children, these changes are usually more subtle, but move in the direction of greater complexity and higher levels of understanding.

The literature in the area of adult development has expanded greatly over the past twenty years.

Many different theories have been proposed to account for changes in people over their life span. In this section, we look at three key theorists whose work relates to issues of professional development.

Loevinger. Loevinger's (1976) research on ego and personality development identifies ten developmental stages from self-protective to integrated. At the lower levels, people may be characterized as more impulsive and symbiotic in their thinking. In other words, they are more dependent on others for decisions. At the middle of the continuum, individuals tend to conform in terms of socially approved codes but will also begin to develop self-evaluation standards. At higher levels, people show more autonomous and integrated thinking and respect for individuality.

Just what does this mean in terms of behavior? A person in the self-protective stage tends to blame others, circumstances, or parts of herself for which she does not feel responsibility. At the conscientious-conformist level, rules remain very important, but there is a growing awareness of self. In place of one right way, multiple right ways can be more easily understood and tolerated. At the highest level, the integrated stage, conflicts and polarities are transcended. Individuals have high respect for themselves and others.

Loevinger's theory underscores the fact that interpersonal relations are altered as people move through the ego stages. In the cognitive area, the same general trends are apparent. While our nervous systems decline with age and our reaction capabilities become slower, our abilities to process and understand information increase. Horn and Cattell (1967) label the latter as crystallized intelligence. Older people have more experience and knowledge to draw on. Thus, the problem-solving process becomes a slower but more thorough process with age.

Erikson. Research in the area of life stages and transitions offers additional insights when addressing individuals. In Erikson's (1968) theory of psychosocial development, each stage evolves into a new strata of social interactions establishing many new possibilities for building relationships between

Blueprint for Action **81**

oneself and others. Erikson believed that the decisions a person makes during a lifetime continuously mold and shape the tenor of an individual's relationships with other people. Each dimension of interaction can be viewed from the perspective of the two extremes of a continuum (e.g., trust and mistrust, intimacy and isolation). Growth and development occur when a balance is achieved. For example, too much trust can be as problematic as no trust at all. Overall, according to Erikson, there is a continuous search for identity because adulthood is not a static phase. Interactive experiences designed to meet the psychological needs of adults in different phases will promote growth throughout the life cycle. Such experiences will allow adults to continue to interact with others and to feel productive, to guide the less experienced, and to consolidate their life experiences.

How can an awareness of Erikson's life stages help directors and teachers better understand themselves and their particular stage of development? Directors and teachers can gain insight into interactive experiences by stepping back and assessing their reactions to different situations. For example, does working at the center promote feelings of safety and security? Do daily interactions give workers a sense of control over their environment and promote feelings of support and belonging?

As director of a small nursery school, Sonja worked hard to develop a strong esprit de corps among her staff. She frequently planned social activities in addition to professional development sessions and tried to promote open communication and a sense of community. One teacher, Anna, however, did not seem to appreciate Sonja's efforts. Although she attended staff meetings and training sessions, Anna never came early to chat or stayed afterward to enjoy a snack and coffee. She always seemed in a deliberate hurry to get away. Moreover, she usually made excuses for her lack of attendance at social gatherings.

Sonja was concerned about Anna's pronounced isolation and decided to have a talk with her. The initial interaction felt awkward

and strained; Anna indicated in many ways that she did not wish to share information about herself. Finally, Sonja asserted herself and told Anna that she really wanted (and expected) her to be more involved with the staff. This appeal seemed to open a floodgate of emotions for Anna and she shared with Sonja her reasons for withdrawing so frequently. It seemed that over the past six years she had suffered many losses — the death of her husband and her sister; a relationship with a man who later left her for someone else; and the breaking of a confidence by a very close friend whose support she had counted on. Consequently, Anna was fearful of forming close ties with anyone. She openly admitted she did not want to be vulnerable again. She stated that she would rather not be dependent on anyone any more. She would carry out all her responsibilities, but she didn't wish to be part of the "family" Sonja seemed to want to create.

Levine. Levine (1989) describes the three stages of adulthood (early, middle, and late) as characterized by different orientations and outlooks. Young adults are still experimenting with a variety of roles and relationships. They are dominated by life dreams, idealism, and feelings of omnipotence. In middle adulthood, people become more aware of their limitations. Becoming established in the workplace is the main objective along with the realization of possibilities in regard to marriage and home. In late adulthood, the focus becomes the reassessment of priorities and a consequent reallocation of their energies.

As adults move through these phases, they appear to go through periods of transition (Levine, 1989). We are all familiar with the commonly referred to transition, "midlife crisis." These times may be characterized by questioning, confusion, discouragement, or apparent burnout. Transitional periods take up almost half of our adult lives. Working with individuals at such points in their lives can be particularly challenging for supervisors and peers.

Adult development theorists consistently emphasize that adults need to take an active role in helping to define their own developmental stage and needs. The challenge for the director is to listen closely to individuals on the staff in order to be able to assist in this process of self-definition. This is done in the same way that we observe young children to determine what experiences and approaches are needed to mesh with their developmental levels.

Committing to a model of staff development that addresses individual differences requires an understanding of the many ways in which adults change over the life cycle. Overall, adult learning theorists believe that adults become increasingly self-directed if they are stimulated by real life tasks and problems that fit their developmental levels.

Career Stages

The idea of stages in people's careers is intricately related to adult development. Lilian Katz (1972) identifies four stages in teachers' profes-

sional growth patterns. Table 5.3 summarizes Katz's developmental stages of teachers' careers and their corresponding concerns. In Stage I, **survival**, the teacher's main concern is coping — whether or not she can just survive. A new teacher is frequently overwhelmed by all the new tasks and responsibilities required of her. This stage may last a full year; it is dominated by feelings of self-doubt and a strong need for acceptance.

In Stage II, **consolidation**, teachers move beyond an egocentric focus and begin to focus on individual children and problem situations. They begin to develop a knowledge base about children's behavior. In Stage III, **renewal**, which often occurs during the third or fourth year of teaching, teachers seem to tire of doing the same things. Recent research has shown that the third year of teaching is a critical time; many teachers leave the profession at that point. Gehreke (1988) notes that teachers in the third year begin to perceive the job as basically unchanging. They grow bored and unchallenged.

Teachers who decide to remain in the field may

Table 5.3

Developmental Stages of Teachers' Concerns

Developmental Stage	Concerns
Stage IV Maturity	Finding new perspectives and insights Sharing knowledge and expertise
Stage III Renewal	Sustaining enthusiasm Maintaining interest in new developments
Stage II Consolidation	Handling individual problem children Solving problem situations
Stage I Survival	Surviving on the job Being accepted by colleagues

permanently remain in Stage III and continue to battle "professional fatigue," or they may internalize a renewed spirit for their work and move on to Stage IV, **maturity**. These teachers now ask deeper, more abstract questions. They begin to integrate their knowledge and experiences and take on more responsibility in the center and in the field.

It is important to note, however, that not all teachers move on to Stage IV. As many directors are aware, some teachers remain stagnant and unmotivated, no matter what kind of energy and time are invested in them. Jorde-Bloom (1982) in writing about teacher burnout, calls these teachers the "rustouts." These individuals present real dilemmas for the director. The director is forced to make the decision of whether to terminate them or continue to deal with their diminished enthusiasm and less than adequate performance.

VanderVen (1988) describes a five-stage sequence in her model of professional development which extends the work of Katz. The formulation examines each stage in terms of level of professionalism, roles and functions, variables in adult and career development, adult cognition and affect, the concept of life long careers, male and female differences, guidance of practice, and educational preparation.

▶ **Stage I — Novice.** Novices work directly with children. They practice as nonprofessionals and usually enter the field without prior commitment as reflected by acquiring educational preparation. Often they reflect the lowest permissible legal level of education to be hired in a caregiving or aide position.

▶ **Stage II — Initial.** Initial stage practitioners also work directly with children. They are differentiated from novices in that they have shown some formal commitment to developing a career in early childhood education, often through participation in training at a preprofessional level.

▶ **Stage III — Informed.** Informed stage practitioners work directly with children, but may work with parents and other professionals as well. They

hold a minimum of a baccalaureate degree as the first level of professional preparation.

▶ **Stage IV — Complex.** Complex stage practitioners at this stage usually hold an advanced degree. There are two career path options that they follow: a direct practice path involving more advanced and specialized work on behalf of preschool children and families; and an indirect practice path involving work with the system (e.g., administration, supervision, program development, training).

▶ **Stage V — Influential.** Influential stage practitioners may hold a doctoral degree or similar advanced credentials. They are the leaders, and hopefully, the movers and shakers in the field with adequate preparation and experience to transform the entrenched systems, particularly the economic and political systems, that are detrimental to the advancement of the field.

Burden (1987) also identifies career stages for teachers which support Katz's model. He describes the beginning stage as one in which the new teacher is struggling for survival; the middle stage as a time in which the teacher is adjusting, growing, and exploring; and the final stage in which the teacher functions as a mature professional.

Fuller (1969) found that teachers with different stages of professional experience show different concerns. Like Katz, she found that beginning teachers were concerned mainly about their own survival. Adequacy, classroom control, and others' perceptions of their capabilities are the main issues. Older teachers are more concerned with the impact that they have on students. And highly experienced teachers always focus on pupil progress. Fuller states that when concerns are 'mature' (i.e., characteristic of experienced teachers), they seem to focus on pupil gain and self evaluation as opposed to personal gain and evaluation by others (p. 221).

McDonnell, Christensen, and Price (1989) identify eight stages of the career cycle — preservice, induction, competency building, enthusiastic and growing, career frustration, stable and stagnant, career wind-down, and career exit. The research conducted by these authors indicates that appropriate incentives need to be linked to respective career stages of teachers. The difference in teachers' career stages points to the need to consider models that advocate personalized, individualized support systems.

The complexities of human behavior do not allow for an oversimplified use of the career stage model. And often, with the move to a new classroom, a teacher may temporarily regress to an earlier stage as she takes on a different age group or works at a different center. Burke, Christensen, and Fessler (1984) suggest that teachers may experience many reoccurring cycles or professional career loops within their adult life. Teachers may work in the profession for several years, drop out to raise their families and then re-enter at a later point. Others may decide to enter a teacher training program for the first time in their late thirties or early forties. Thus, the interface between adult stages of development and career stages is not necessarily parallel. The director must draw on information about the individual teacher from both perspectives when looking at personal and professional development.

The case examples that follow present portraits of two different teachers employed at the Children's Corner whose career and adult development stages appear to overlap.

Case Study: The Children's Corner

Shelly is 22 years old and in her first year of teaching. She has come from a teacher training program that emphasized developmentally appropriate curriculum and practices. In her conversations with Martha, she expressed her frustrations with her job. "This group just doesn't respond to all the things I learned. They don't listen! They're always fighting and calling for my assistance. Maybe it's because there are so many aggressive boys in there! I'm not sure. But it would probably be better if we had more help. It's really a zoo! I thought 4-year-olds would be delightful and that I would be great with them! But I'm beginning to think I chose the wrong field. I worry all the time that parents will complain to you. But honestly, they've allowed their kids to be so disrespectful to people. And then we're supposed to straighten them out!"

Case Study: The Children's Corner

Georgia has taught different age groups at the Children's Corner and at another preschool for over twelve years. She always appears prepared and has a good attendance record, but her comments to Martha show an underlying lack of enthusiasm. "I'm not sure where I go from here. I like the kids, but I'm so tired of hearing the same old complaints from the parents. And I know you try to get us more money, but still the pay is low and the hours are so long. And, quite frankly, I hate all these training sessions we've been having. If I hear one more person tell me how to manage a classroom or interact with parents, I'll scream! I know how to teach; I just need better conditions to do it in! I guess I really don't know where I go from here. I'm drained! My husband says I shouldn't take it so seriously. In fact, he probably wouldn't mind if I quit so I could give him more time. Maybe that's not such a bad idea."

Shelly's remarks reflect several points identified in adult and career stage theory. First, she seems to be in a self-protective stage as evidenced by her tendency to blame others and circumstances for her problems. Secondly, she alludes to her "dream" of what teaching 4-year-olds would be like. She is not comfortable with her identity as a teacher but feels the need to commit to a profession.

Shelly seems to clearly represent the new teacher in the survival stage. Her responsibilities seem somewhat overwhelming to her. She has feelings of self-doubt and is striving for acceptance by students, peers, and supervisors; and she appears to be trying to achieve a security level in dealing with everyday problems and issues.

Georgia seems to be trying to reconcile some inner conflicts in relation to teaching in the field. She has a good sense of her worth and effectiveness, but she appears to need a "lift." She seems to be in the process of reassessing herself and reallocating her energies. As Levine (1989) suggests, she seems to be trying to redetermine her priorities.

Georgia appears to be in Katz's Stage III, in which teachers tire of doing the same things. They perceive their jobs as basically static and grow bored and unchallenged. Georgia in her maturity, is reflecting upon why she is doing this work. She recognizes that she may need to be re-energized, but her job description doesn't seem to give her avenues to do so.

Organizational Commitment

Organizational commitment is the relative strength of the staff's identification with and involvement in a particular center (Jorde-Bloom,1988c). It can be characterized by at least three related factors: a strong belief in and acceptance of the organization's goals and values; a willingness to exert effort on behalf of the program; and a strong desire to remain working at the center (Mowday, Steers, & Porter, 1979). To a large extent, organizational change depends on the degree to which individuals can integrate the goals of the center into their own structure of needs and values. This sense of belongingness represents the anticipation that one will be able to achieve personal satisfaction within the organizational framework. It is the essence of organizational commitment. Interdependence through achieving a common goal leads to relationships of trust and respect.

Hall (1988) defines commitment as "the soul of work." He states, "It is the sense of purpose that guides one's activities; it is the meaning that justifies one's investment of self; it is the feeling of responsibility that defines one's role and reason for being; and when shared, it is a common bond which holds people together in ways that transcend differences and personal gratification" (p. 100). Commitment is a personal desire to contribute to the success of the center. The goal of directors is thus to develop a strong sense of personal ownership and responsibility. According to Hall, three conditions are essential in order to achieve this: impact, relevance, and community.

> ▶ **Impact.** People need to know that what they are doing makes a difference. Teachers, in particular, may feel they make a difference in the lives of young children and may derive a great deal of personal satisfaction from their work each day, but they also need feedback that the work they do has a positive impact on what happens in the center. Impact relates to our

personal feelings of importance. For feelings of importance to be enhanced and sustained, people must receive affirmation of the important role they play in achieving center-wide goals. This affirmation supports a sense of purpose and commitment to something larger than one's own personal satisfaction.

> ▶ **Relevance.** Particularly in early childhood work settings, people need to expect their talents are being used appropriately and the time they spend on important tasks helps move the center to achieving its objectives. Many times staff will perceive they are stuck with irrelevant tasks which take time and seem meaningless. Hall states that irrelevant tasks undermine the sense of purpose so critical to commitment; they spawn frustration, resistance, and stifle motivation. Listen to the words of Twanya, a head teacher at a state-funded prekindergarten program.

"I've been teaching for 15 years in this district and have consistently been evaluated as an exemplary teacher. Last year the program administrator decided it would be a good idea if we turned in our plan books showing our detailed lesson plans with educational objectives for each activity. I wouldn't mind doing this activity if I felt somebody cared. My sense is that these lesson plans just get filed anyway. Nobody even looks at them. If the purpose of this exercise is accountability, then somebody ought to use the information. All this added paperwork takes so much time away from other activities that I feel are so much more important."

How widespread irrelevant work has become! It not only diverts energy, it undercuts commitment. When people are asked to spend their time doing mindless paperwork or sitting in on meetings that have little relevance to what they are doing, a sense of frustration and indifference cannot help but surface. The director's task, then, is to ensure that people spend time on "core" activities. People need to perceive they are supported in doing activities which they see as germane to their work.

▶ **Community.** Hall states that for relevance to become a shared experience, and for the sense of personal challenge and contribution to become a collective feature of the organization, there must be a norm of interdependence and mutual reliance. Little (1982) calls these norms of collegiality. Collegiality and interdependence foster mutual respect and a sense of shared responsibility for each other's well being. Community refers to the sense of oneness or a spirit of belonging. It is the belief that people can depend on one another. Striking the balance is difficult. In supporting individuality, some directors end up encouraging too much independence and unwittingly foster competition. Other directors are so task-oriented, they end up eroding collegiality. The goal is to try to focus on people and their needs and try to create conditions in which they can work together to achieve common goals.

Directors of programs are keenly aware of differences in individuals' levels of commitment. The teacher with a strong sense of commitment demonstrates active involvement in the center and in the field of early childhood. She usually arrives early to prepare her classroom, she turns in requested lesson plans or parent forms on time, and she takes an active role in professional activities.

Conversely, the teacher who does not demonstrate a strong commitment will not be eager to initiate or participate in opportunities for development. It becomes the director's task, therefore, to address this lack of commitment and decide to what degree it is interfering with the teacher's performance. Perhaps there are basic unmet needs; or perhaps the teacher is not clear about expectations and goals. The director may be able to assist the individual in making a personal assessment. If it is the case that commitment is so low that the teacher is lax about many aspects of her teaching role, the director may need to decide not to renew the teacher's contract.

Level of Motivation

Commitment to a center is directly related to the level of motivation an individual exhibits. Directors frequently find themselves asking why some people show a lot of initiative and desire to contribute to the organization, while others do not. Moreover, directors also wonder why certain incentives increase the motivation of some employees and not others. In other words, some people may be quite capable of assuming different roles and responsibilities, but they are not willing to do so. The "willing" part of the equation rests squarely on their level of motivation.

According to Weiner (1980), motivation is defined as the complex forces, drives, needs, tension states, or other mechanisms that start and maintain voluntary activity directed toward the achievement of personal goals. Motivation, according to Porter and Lawler (1968), results from the expectation that one's efforts will lead to anticipated outcomes.

Numerous theories of motivation have been proposed over the years, but perhaps the most well-known in the field of education is Maslow's hierarchy of needs (1954). The fundamental premise of Maslow's theory is that higher-level needs become activated as lower-level needs are satisfied. For example, if children come to a preschool program not having had breakfast in the morning, hunger presents itself as the prime motivator. It will be difficult for them to attend to other higher-level needs like achievement. Likewise, if teachers feel there is little job security where they work, they may be unable to focus on other goals or plans. A director reported that one of her most enthusiastic and dedicated teachers resisted attending staff meetings held after program hours. Upon looking closer, the director discovered that this teacher, a single parent, did not have the finances to cover the extended child care costs that resulted from her attendance. Lower-level needs must be largely satisfied before higher-level needs can be felt and pursued. An understanding of Maslow's theory may assist a director in considering whether an individual's basic needs are met and, therefore, whether that person is able to focus on higher-level goals.

Herzberg's (1966) research on motivation supports Maslow's hierarchy of needs. Herzberg distinguishes between the positive aspects of an individual's job that are "satisfiers" and the negative aspects of the job that are "dissatisfiers." The two categories, Herzberg asserts, are quite distinct as they relate to issues of motivation. Dissatisfiers include such things as salary, working conditions, status, job security, technical supervision, and organizational policies. Satisfiers, on the other hand, include the nature of the work itself, the individual's degree of responsibility, opportunities for growth and advancement, and a sense of achievement. Herzberg believes that eliminating dissatisfiers seldom improves an individual's performance; it merely reduces the irritations and frustrations in doing one's job. To motivate individuals to higher levels of performance, changes in the structure and nature of the work itself (the "satisfiers") need to be addressed.

While the available theories may not explain exactly why individuals demonstrate so much variance in motivation, they may be helpful in assessing adults and designing appropriate staff development strategies. The following example shows the relationship between one teacher's personal situation and her lack of motivation in addressing her work situation.

Maureen, an infant/toddler teacher, came in to discuss her annual evaluation with her supervisor. Maureen didn't disagree when they reviewed the low ratings in a number of areas — disorderly storage area, late lesson plans, cluttered classroom shelves, and inconsistency in keeping high chairs and equipment clean. But the reason for the disorganized aspects of the classroom operation related to something very personal. Maureen stated that she was having marital problems. Her perceived lack of stability in her personal life seemed to be keeping her from approaching her job responsibilities with the enthusiasm she knew she should have. She seemed unable to keep her professional life in good order when her personal life appeared to be in shambles. Sharing this information allowed the director to gain new insights into the reasons for some of

Maureen's difficulties. She now realized that Maureen was quite capable of being an excellent teacher, but the personal issues that were consuming Maureen were sapping her energy. The result was a lack of motivation.

Professional Orientation

Commitment to a center and overall motivation to perform certainly relate to commitment to the field of early childhood education. It stands to reason that those who are more committed to the field will have a stronger professional orientation. Professional orientation is characterized by an individual's emphasis on growth and change, skill based primarily on knowledge, autonomy in decision making, a reference-group orientation, the achievement of goals, and loyalty to clients and professional associations (Corwin, 1965; Jorde-Bloom, 1989b).

Most directors have an idea of where individual staff fit on a continuum relative to this concept. Some teachers are very active in NAEYC and ACEI affiliate groups, read professional books and journals on a regular basis, and see themselves as members of the early childhood profession. Many others, however, see their work with young children as a tolerable job and have little incentive to connect themselves to a professional organization. They perceive their work as a "job" as opposed to a "career."

The director may not be able to move all staff toward a career orientation. As in all professions, some people see teaching young children only as a vehicle for earning income and plan to get out of the field if something better comes along. This reality can be an area of frustration for directors; such an orientation does not promote organizational commitment or enthusiasm. For the purpose of individualized staff development, it is important for directors to know where individual staff members stand with respect to professional orientation.

As the profession of early childhood education gains credibility and career ladders become more established, the issue of professional orientation should receive more emphasis. Obviously, professionalism is interconnected with salary and incentive issues, as well as with the status of the field.

Beliefs and Values

In Ayers' *The Good Preschool Teacher* (1989), much of the focus is on the beliefs of the six teachers who are profiled. Anna thinks of herself as a substitute mother and "…struggles to achieve an intensity and investment in each child that will truly support and nurture and challenge" (p.127). Chana has come to some solid conclusions about the issue of separation in children's lives. She thinks of herself as a person "who understands what makes separations successful experiences from which to grow and build" (p. 127). Joanne's strongest belief is that children need to be empowered — that they need to be able to make decisions for themselves. For Darlene, patience is the key attribute of a good teacher. Michele emphasizes the importance of order and organization and productive work for children. "At the center of Michele's teaching is a strong valuing of education" (p. 128). And, finally, Maya infuses her teaching with a strong belief in warmth and respect. "She tells stories of her grandmother, who told her to respect herself and never to put herself in situations where she wasn't respected, and who insisted that she associate only with other children who were doing 'interesting things'" (p. 129).

The rich, descriptive profiles drawn by Ayers underscore the importance of looking at the beliefs and values of teachers in order to understand the meaning teachers give to their work. Again, it becomes the task of the director to listen closely to teachers to hear what values and beliefs support their teaching practices. Moreover, through an active, reflective listening process, the director can assist teachers in clearly identifying and articulating the beliefs and values that they bring to their present role which have been developed during their childhood, their educational training, or years of teaching experience.

The following comments illustrate some of the beliefs that undergird the classroom practices of teachers:

"This article on the Corporate Community School of America says that they have been able to teach children regardless of background to read and enjoy it. I'll bet they select-
ed only the smartest kids!" (Belief: Home background and inherited ability are more important than teaching as factors in learning.)

"I don't think teachers should dictate to children how they should spend their time, so I have long periods of free play for children; group time is just 10 minutes a day." (Belief: Autonomy is important; teachers should not intrude on children's learning.)

"Children, first of all, need structure. They feel safer with firm limits and rules. I can't buy into all of this talk about letting children make their own decisions." (Belief: Adults are the experts; they know what is best for children.)

"Parents need to be more connected to the classroom operation in day care. I'd like to see us encourage more visitation at lunch time and more discussion sessions with parents." (Belief: My role is only secondary to that of parents; I cannot effect change without parents' support.)

Such statements by teachers are based on beliefs and values. Often we can trace these beliefs back to the way we have been raised or educated. The values our parents and teachers inculcated have a deep and lasting impression on our belief system.

Regardless of their origin, it is important that beliefs be identified and articulated. Otherwise, teachers may try to implement new curriculum models or approaches and not understand that their beliefs may be in disagreement with the underlying assumptions of the curriculum models they are using.

Kim, a young first-grade teacher, accepted a job in a primary wing where they were experimenting with open classroom models and approaches. In the job interview, she was able to articulate quite well the theory and philosophy underlying open classroom practices; it had been part of her teacher training program. She had also done quite well in her student teaching experience in a traditional kindergarten program. However, once she got into a classroom with real children and real situations within a structure that promoted autonomy and flexibility, she became very frustrated with allowing children a lot of choice and decision making. She began using a loud, harsh voice to try to maintain a better sense of order. In a discussion with the principal following his observation of her teaching, she began recalling her own school experience. She was the product of a rigid parochial school. While she disliked aspects of this model, she also began to see, as she verbalized her feelings, that she believed children should "listen" to the authority figure. Overall, this teacher's belief system was in conflict with the model in which she was teaching. Identification of this dilemma helped the principal assess this teacher's needs for support and development opportunities.

Those teachers who move to a higher level of abstract thinking and altruistic motivation have reflected on their own values and beliefs in an attempt to clearly identify the linkages between their beliefs and their behavior. The director can be instrumental in assisting teachers to move in this direction.

Concomitant Roles

Also important for the director to consider is the number of roles teachers assume in their personal lives outside the center. This is a particularly important focus given the fact that the profession is dominated by women, many of whom wear many hats. One director expressed her feelings about this issue quite well:

"I'm amazed at how many different things my staff, all of whom are women, are involved in. Most of them are mothers; some of them are single parents. Two women, in particular, are very active in their husband's work as well as their own. Others are quite active in community activities — school, church, arts, social action programs. Three of my teachers are pursuing graduate degrees; two of them are finishing their bachelor's degree. In general, I believe

that all of this involvement makes them better teachers; but it does mean adjustment on my part at times. For example, when a teacher's child is sick, I try to make it possible for her to leave. I also provide a child care benefit for teachers with preschoolers. This practice promotes quality and retention, I think. And I've been trying to provide release time for some of the staff development activities like course attendance. Like I said, it's rough to respond to all of these things sometimes, but I think overall the program reaps the benefits."

Being aware of the concomitant roles of individual teachers further sensitizes the director to plan staff development and supervisory activities in a manner that allows for optimum flexibility, while still maintaining high standards for the overall program.

Tools for Assessing Individual Needs

In order to collect adequate data on individual staff members at a center, many different types of instruments can be used — some formal, some informal. Because of the inherent complexity of human beings, using multiple sources of evidence is important. In the appendix of this book are a number of tools for gathering data on individual staff members. You may not find all of them appropriate or relevant to the assessment of particular individuals. But hopefully, some of them will elicit information that will be helpful in designing individualized professional development plans.

The following provides a brief description of the areas assessed by these instruments. More detailed information about administering and scoring the assessments is included with each assessment tool in the appendix.

Teaching Practices

There are many different types of teaching practices that we want to evaluate in our centers and direct observation is typically the best way to collect this kind of data. NAEYC's guidelines for center accreditation (NAEYC, 1985a) provide a good overview of the many different types of teaching practices that can be observed. Assessment Tools #12, #13, #14, and #15 are modified versions of the four observation scales used in NAEYC's accreditation process. They are included here to provide a kind of overview of four critical areas of teaching practices: interactions among staff and children; the classroom curriculum; health, safety, and nutrition; and the physical environment.

Learning Style

Assessment Tool #16, "Appreciating Individual Differences," can be used to ascertain the learning style or preference of individual staff members. Part I elicits an individual's style of thinking. This section was adapted from the work of Wonder and Donovan (1984) and Torrance (1979). Part II looks at environmental, emotional, sociological, and physical elements related to learning style. This section was adapted from the work of Dunn and Dunn (1978). The results of this assessment can be used to plan staff development opportunities that match an individual's preferred learning style.

Temperament/Psychological Type

An understanding of different temperaments/ psychological types can elicit a deeper appreciation for those who function differently than we do. Assessment Tool #17 is based on the work of Jung (1923) and Myers (1980) and provides a brief assessment of psychological type along four dimensions: extraversion/introversion; sensing/intuition; thinking/ feeling; and judging/ perceiving. The information gleaned from this assessment will help you consider the implications of different typologies for your work situation.

Beliefs and Values

Assessment Tool #18 can assist a director in determining what particular values and beliefs seem to guide a teacher's attitudes and behaviors. A teacher's answers to the eight questions in Part I can serve as a springboard for a discussion about classroom environment, parent interactions, discipline, preferred instructional strategies, and other important issues related to teaching. Answers to Part II can serve to help teachers understand what traits they value in children and how they encourage the development of those traits through their practice.

Job Satisfaction

Job satisfaction may be defined as one's valuative reaction to a center. It is a kind of "psychological contract" between the worker and demands of the workplace that is influenced by personal needs, values, and expectations (Jones & James, 1979; Jorde-Bloom, 1989a; Mumford, 1972). Job satisfaction may be conceptualized as the discrepancy between real conditions and ideal conditions. When job satisfaction is high, the discrepancy between existing and ideal conditions will be small. Assessment Tool #19 is a modified version of the *Early Childhood Job Satisfaction Survey* (Jorde-Bloom, 1989a). It assesses five facets of job satisfaction: co-worker relations, supervisor relations, nature of the work itself, working conditions, and pay and promotion opportunities. Knowing in what facets of their work teachers are feeling content or discouraged can assist a director in designing organizational practices that facilitate higher levels of job satisfaction.

Professional Orientation

The "Professional Activities Questionnaire," Assessment Tool #20, can be used with staff to indicate their level of professional orientation. You may want to use this assessment in the initial hiring process to gather information about an individual's level of involvement in different types of professional activities.

Role Clarity

The clarification of roles for staff members at an early childhood center is of crucial importance, both for new staff and for veteran teachers. Program effectiveness is increased when role conflict and role ambiguity are low. Role conflict occurs when one's formal position has conflicting organizational expectations. For example, teachers are sometimes asked by parents not to have their childern take a nap in the afternoon because they will not be tired enough for bedtime at an early hour. For teachers, this presents a conflict in expectations between what the center requires (mandated naptime) and what the parent wants. There is an inherent tension in making decisions in the best interest of the child because different parties will interpret "best interest" quite differently. The role of teacher may be subject to a variety of different and incompatible expectations from divergent groups such as the center's board, the funding agency, the parents, and the director. Role ambiguity occurs when individuals do not have a clear understanding of the scope and nature of their jobs. Role ambiguity is often the result of vague job descriptions, center policies, and operating procedures.

Assessment Tool #21 assesses staff's perceptions about their roles. It is adapted from the work of Dyer (1984), Fox and Schmuck (1973), Rizzo, House, and Lirtzman (1970), and Seashore, Lawler, Mirvis, and Cammann (1983). The resultant information can assist directors in seeing where teachers' perceptions differ from their own. Assessment Tool #22 is specifically designed to be used with new staff. It should be given to staff approximately four weeks after they have begun the position. The results of this assessment should help alert the director to potential misunderstandings on the part of the new employee.

Organizational Commitment

Earlier in this chapter we defined organizational commitment as the relative strength of the staff's identification with and involvement in a particular center. Assessment Tool #23 provides information to a director about the level of commitment of a particular staff member. Since some items on this assessment tend to be of a sensitive nature, it is important that the director allow staff to use it as a self-survey. The results could then be brought by the teacher to a planning conference with her supervisor. This information may be useful in stimulating discussion between the director and teacher about ways to maximize commitment and motivation. Identifying a lack of commitment could lead to the identification of underlying problems and concerns.

Perceived Problems

Hall and Loucks (1978) believe staff develop-

ment can best be facilitated using a client-centered diagnostic/prescriptive model. Too often inservice training activities address the needs of trainers rather than those of the staff. Assessing teachers' perceived problems in the classroom is the first step to achieving this goal.

Teachers often feel overwhelmed by the myriad of problems they face on a daily basis. Helping them to zero in on the precise nature of their problems can serve as a first step in solving them. Johnston (1984) has prepared a "Prekindergarten Teacher Problems Checklist," which is provided in the appendix as Assessment Tool #24. This can be used as a vehicle for building staff development programs around teachers' perceived problems. The 60 items that comprise this instrument were generated by teachers themselves and represent the problems that were found to be significantly frequent, significantly bothersome, or both frequent and bothersome.

Flexibility/Openness to Change

Teachers vary greatly with respect to their willingness to accept new approaches and alternative ways of doing things. It is important for a director to be aware of potential resistance or receptiveness on the part of staff members. Assessment Tool #25 provides a means for an individual to develop a flexibility profile; the results indicate a person's approach to risk and change. Directors might have teachers use this tool as a self assessment and bring the results to a discussion meeting. It is important for the director to project that there are no right or wrong answers on the profile. The results may help explain why an individual has taken a particular stand on an issue at the center. Seeing behavior within such a framework can be useful in providing reasons and justifications.

A Final Word

The process of assessing teachers from an individualized, developmental perspective does not lend itself to quick and easy methods of analysis. Instead, the director must view this type of supervision as an ongoing, continuous collecting of relevant information that contributes in a meaningful way to individual growth. In many ways, it is more of a mindset on the part of the director. The process conveys respect for individuals in that they have a role in defining their own professional development. Any and all information concerning an individual teacher becomes data from which to build a comprehensive and personalized staff development action plan.

To be sure, the process itself is both time-consuming and complex. It grows out of the premise that the most important part of a director's job is staff supervision and development. Directors and other administrators give many excuses for not devoting time to such an in-depth process. Some of the excuses are valid; directors wear many hats and are indeed busy! But the energy and time devoted to individualized staff assessment will pay off in many ways, some of which will save the director time in other areas. For example, when staff are challenged in meaningful ways, when their personal goals are tied into the organi-zation's goals, and when they feel valued and respected, staff turnover will assuredly be less. Thus, the director will have to spend less time in hiring and interviewing processes.

Procedurally, recording developmental information on individual teachers in an ongoing manner is quite similar to anecdotal record keeping of children's behaviors and interests. Having a small notebook readily available at all times allows the director to jot down notes on individual staff members. These notes can include specific comments and examples of verbal interactions. From this notebook, more permanent entries can be made in each teacher's file.

One note of caution may be in order. We must be careful not to over diagnose people. If the director spends too much time on diagnosis, teachers may feel overwhelmed by the number of problems and be unable or unwilling to take action. Directors should be satisfied with a good overview of the situation and not get caught in a paralysis by spending too much time on analysis!

Chapter 6

Implementing an Individualized Model of Staff Development

The overall purpose of implementing a model of staff development in our programs is to improve the quality of the experiences of the children in our care. Beyond this overarching purpose, however, it is perhaps useful to keep in mind the multiple other purposes that provide a rationale for engaging in staff development activities. Stonehouse (1986) provides a useful summary of these reasons in Table 6.1.

As we can see from the variety of reasons detailed in this table, staff development goes far beyond the idea of training. Training programs are usually short-term, skill-oriented, and typically address only one aspect of teaching. For the most part, training deals with specific behavioral changes in people. The individualized model described in this chapter, on the other hand, addresses the overall education and professional development of a person. This model focuses on long-term growth and addresses change in individuals' thinking processes. It rests on the assumption that as thinking progresses to higher levels of complexity, an individual becomes more flexible and open to a wider range of stimuli (Dillon-Peterson, 1981). When viewed from this individualized perspective, the goal of staff development, then, is to move the individual to the next stage of professional competence.

Facilitating Change in Individuals

As we have stressed in previous chapters, staff development is most meaningful when viewed from an individual perspective. Adults, just as children, are at different levels of development and, therefore, have different needs and abilities. Thus their professional development plans should be differentiated based on a holistic view of the life span. What this means in practical terms is that planning staff development activities must be done in such a way as to accommodate individuals at different stages in their careers. Table 6.2 describes a model of staff development that embraces this principle. For each career development stage, a supervisory style, corresponding staff development goals, strategies, and content areas are suggested. In this chapter we will describe this model in detail. Before launching into a description of the specifics of the model, though, it is perhaps useful to review the assumptions upon which such an approach is premised.

Assumptions of Individualized Staff Development

The primary underlying assumption of an individualized model of staff development is that teachers are individual learners in various stages of adult growth and development. Research suggests that there are differences in adult learners on developmental variables such as cognition, ways of

> "Knowledge of how teachers can grow as competent adults is the guiding principle for supervisors in finding ways to return wisdom, power, and control to both the individuals and the collective staff in order for them to become true professionals."
>
> — Carl Glickman

Table 6.1

Why Have Staff Development?

To provide basic skills and an orientation to the profession for those staff who are untrained

To extend teachers' expertise and skills in specific areas

To provide opportunities for teachers to learn about new developments in a rapidly changing field

To remind staff about center expectations

To identify resources (people and materials) that staff can pursue themselves

To decrease professional isolation

To broaden teachers' perspective or professional "world view" of child care

To promote the establishment of informal support networks among teachers

To empower teachers to take a more active role in their own work, their own education, and their own professional development

To increase the enjoyment of work

To boost morale and self respect

Adapted from Stonehouse, A. (1986). *For us, for children: An analysis of the provision of in-service education for child care centre personnel in Australia.* Canberra: Australian Early Childhood Association, p. 13-16. Reprinted with permission.

thinking, and interpersonal orientation. These differences account for variation in the performance of teachers. According to Hunt (1971), teachers at higher stages of development function in a more complex way in the classroom. Thus, if we wish to improve the quality of education in the classroom, we need to consider the relationship between adult development and effective teaching.

A second assumption of the model is that teachers need to engage in identifying and helping to solve their own concerns and problems related to their development as individuals and as professionals. Such involvement empowers people by focusing on strengths and insights into their own developmental processes. Cookie-cutter approaches where inservice training and staff development programs are planned by the director for whole-group participation are bound to fail because there is no way they can meet the

different professional needs and interests of individual staff members.

Third, individualized staff development is based on an enabler model, not a deficit model. A deficit model implies that the teacher is unprepared or incompetent and that by using prescriptive techniques, we can "fix" the teacher just like we might fix a broken typewriter. An enabler or growth model focuses on the individual's strengths. It implies that teaching and learning are complex activities in which no one ever masters the totality of the profession (Hegland, 1984). An enabler model is developmental, not judgmental.

The philosophical premise of this staff development model is rooted in a Theory Y tradition of leadership rather than Theory X (McGregor, 1960). Theory X directors assume that their employees dislike work, and that they need coercion and tight supervision to get the job done. Theory Y direc-

Table 6.2

A Model of Staff Development

Career Development Stage	Supervisory Style	Goals of Staff Development	Staff Development Strategies	Content Areas of Staff Development
Survival	directive	Help develop specific competencies in the classroom and realistic expectations for measuring success and progress. Increase perceived level of competence and effectiveness.	– modeling/guidance – direct coaching – on-site workshops – college classes – support and encouragement – articles and books to read selected by director, mentor – hands-on activities	– instruction methods in art, music, science, math, language arts, drama, etc. – child development – nutritional practices – health and safety – arrangement of physical environment
Consolidation	directive, collaborative	Help individuals apply what they have learned about children to new situations. Help them begin to analyze belief system and effectiveness of different instructional strategies.	– released time to visit other centers – conferences and workshops – college classes – feedback from videotaped segments of instruction – self-selected books, articles – peer observation, coaching	– multiculturalism – parent relations – child observation and assessment techniques – children with special needs – children's learning styles – childhood stress
Renewal	directive, collaborative	Help individuals sustain enthusiasm about work. Help them explore their many interests and find ways to generate more challenging responsibilities.	– in-depth institutes – collegial support groups – sharing ideas with new staff – involvement in development of new curricular materials – visit other centers – expanded role in local professional organizations	– time management – stress management – child advocacy – cross cultural childrearing – adult learning styles – conflict management – curriculum innovations (e.g. computers)
Maturity	nondirective	Provide opportunities for them to expand their expertise in related areas. Help individuals broaden their sphere of responsibility for the training and supervision of others.	– classroom research – presentation at conferences – leadership role in professional organizations – in-depth institutes, seminars – involvement in development of new curriculum, policies – mentoring others	– program administration – budget/finance – grantsmanship – program evaluation – group dynamics – supervision techniques – public speaking and presentation skills – legal issues, social policy

tors, on the other hand, assume that people have integrity, will work hard toward objectives to which they are committed, and will respond to self-control and self-direction as they pursue their objectives. The Theory Y director's role thus becomes one of facilitating growth.

Supervisory Style

An individualized model of staff development necessitates a developmental approach to supervision. This approach focuses on the fact that individuals who function at different conceptual or developmental levels and who are at different stages of their careers should be supervised in qualitatively different ways. They require differentiated learning environments for optimal development. For example, teachers who are more concrete in their conceptualization or are in their first year of teaching will probably benefit more from a structured supervisory approach. At the other end of the spectrum, mature teachers who function at a high level of conceptualization or abstraction will appreciate more loosely structured approaches to staff development.

Glickman (1985), in delineating a model of developmental supervision, proposes that it is the job of supervisors to promote higher level thinking in teachers. He notes that teachers in general appear to be in a relatively low stage of ego and conceptual development — one characterized by dependence, simplicity, and concreteness. In order to move teachers forward in their thinking, the director needs to begin where each teacher functions by presenting ideas and opportunities that meet the identified developmental level. Sound familiar? This process parallels the developmental approach we advocate for young children.

At this point, you may want to assess your own supervisory beliefs and preferred style. Glickman (1981) has developed an instrument (Assessment Tool #26) to determine one's tendency toward directive, collaborative, or nondirective supervision. Assessing yourself from this perspective will allow you to see how much control you believe is necessary when supervising staff.

In ascertaining approaches to use with individual staff who may function at very different levels, we must remember that developmental levels of an individual are not static. Therefore, a director should take into account the current status of the individual and work to structure professional development opportunities which will stimulate growth to higher levels (Dillon-Peterson, 1981). Again, this emphasis directly parallels the cognitive-developmental philosophy being implemented in our early childhood programs with young children.

This perspective provides us with a framework for considering staff development from an individualized approach. While there are certainly exceptions to the rule, less developmentally mature individuals usually profit most from highly structured staff development environments. Conversely, individuals who are professionally mature are likely to profit more from low-structured staff development environments. If we translate this principle into practice, the director of a center, as the key person in the environment, would supervise staff different according to their assessed developmental levels.

Glickman (1985) puts a slightly different spin on this concept. He provides definitions of different supervisory styles which directly relate to the issue of control. Directive supervision is characterized by high supervisor control and low teacher control. When control is conceptualized more equally, the strategy is labeled collaborative supervision. Finally, low supervisor control and high teacher control is referred to as nondirective supervision.

All three approaches are valid as long as they are linked to the developmental needs of teachers and aim to increase teacher self-control, according to Glickman. When teachers are unskilled and unmotivated or are very new to the profession, a directive orientation may be the best approach. On the other hand, when teachers have had some experience, have shown some success and competency, and appear motivated, collaborative strategies will probably be a more successful approach. And for teachers who have had extensive background and experience, have demonstrated independence and autonomy, and have high problem-solving abilities, a nondirective orientation is most appropriate.

Glickman's Supervisory Behavior Continuum (Figure 6.1) provides a sequencing of supervisory behaviors matched to the three general approaches identified above. When the supervisor determines the actions for the teacher to follow, by directing what will be done, standardizing the time and criteria of expected results, and reinforcing the consequences, the approach falls into the directive category (far left on the continuum). A collaborative approach is evident when the supervisor participates in the discussion by presenting his or her own ideas, problem solving by having the teacher also propose alternatives, and then negotiating to find a common course of action. In this case, the control over the decision is shared by both teacher and director. On the far right of the continuum, the behaviors fall into the nondirective category of supervisory behavior. With this approach, the supervisor listens to the teacher, clarifies what the teacher says, encourages, and reflects. The supervisor is an active prober or sounding board for the teacher to make the decision.

Interactions between directors and teachers in early childhood programs are presented below to further clarify different supervisory styles and behaviors.

Directive Approach.

Director: "Have you looked through the new science materials that came in a few weeks ago? I haven't seen anything on your lesson plans that looks like you're using them."

Teacher: "I just haven't had any time to come in and review them. We need a lot more planning time to do things like that!"

Director: "I know you're busy, but science is an important part of our curriculum. I'd really like to see more science activities in your lesson plans. Perhaps you could take some of the things home this weekend and consider using them the following week."

Teacher: "Well, actually, I'm not sure what I'd want to do with them. The sand and water tables seem to be enough for my kids."

Director: "Why don't we get together next week to talk about this some more? I'll get your room covered and put a note in your box. Make sure you bring your lesson plans along, okay?"

Teacher: "All right. Any help would be appreciated."

A directive supervisory style can be useful when, as in this case, the teacher possesses little expertise in an area and doesn't seem motivated to find out about the subject on her own. Directive behaviors are also useful when the director cares about an issue, but the teacher doesn't see it as a priority.

Collaborative Approach.

Teacher: "I really think 4-year-olds still need naps!"

Director: "In general, I agree. But in the case of Josh, I'm not sure it's true. Having to lie on the cot for an hour and a half seems difficult for him."

Teacher: "But even resting is good for the kids. Otherwise they get real cranky later in the afternoon."

Director: "That might be true for a lot of children, but is it for Josh? Josh's mom is asking that we let him play quietly during naptime. She says he's very upset over having to lie there so long. Perhaps we should think about an adjustment of some kind for him."

Teacher: "But you know the problems that causes. Once one child is allowed the privilege, they'll all want it!"

Director: "On the surface, that's true. But maybe there's some other way to do it."

Teacher: "Maybe you're right. I was just thinking — maybe if we had him lie on his cot until everyone else was settled or asleep and then let him go to the books or manipulative area, it would work. I don't know. But it's probably worth a try."

Director: "Sounds so simple, but I think you might have something!"

The collaborative approach encourages a frank exchange of ideas. Differences of opinion are encouraged, not suppressed; equality in problem solving characterizes the nature of the exchange. Collaboration should be used when the teacher and supervisor have approximately the same degree of expertise on an issue (Glickman, 1985). In addition, for collaboration to work, both teacher and director must intensely care about the problem and be involved in carrying out the decision. In the case above, both teacher and director would deal with the parent to communicate the decision about naptime and explain the adjustment.

Nondirective Approach.

Teacher: "Boy, we sure had a mess in that room today!"

Director: "What happened? Sit down and relax a minute. You look exhausted!"

Teacher: "Well, one of the volunteers did the "footprint activity" today and didn't prepare for it well enough. Can you imagine how many places we got prints and drips when she forgot newspaper and towels? I thought I told the volunteers at the training session what they needed, but they came unprepared. I didn't notice until too late!"

Director: "I know how frustrating that is. You must have been ticked!"

Teacher: "Ticked is right! I'm going to have to think of how to inform these volunteers so they hear. I know they mean well, but they have to be better prepared."

Director: "Do you still give out the guideline sheets you developed last year? They seemed so clear."

Teacher: "Yes, I still do. But apparently I'm not placing enough emphasis on them."

Director: "You think they don't read them carefully?"

Teacher: "That's about it. They probably stick the papers in with everything else I give them about the center. I shouldn't be trusting that they read them without being prompted."

Director: "Well, you've always been good at setting expectations for our volunteers."

Teacher: "Yeah, I've thought so, too. I'll just have to get back to being more thorough again. Thanks for your ear!"

Nondirective supervision is based on the assumption that a teacher knows best what changes need to be made and has the ability to think and act on his or her own. The role of the director is one of assisting the teacher in the process of thinking through different possible courses of action. However, if the teacher lacks the expertise or capability, the nondirective approach is definitely an unwise choice. Only when teachers have expertise, take responsibility, and care about the issue will the nondirective supervisory approach prove viable.

A final consideration with respect to supervisory style is the recognition of the director's developmental level and continual growth. Caruso and Fawcett (1986) postulate that supervisors go through a series of phases as they move toward maturity (i.e., beginning, extending, and maturing). Like teachers, directors may move back and forth from one phase to another during their careers. Caruso and Fawcett note that even mature, educated, and talented directors may demonstrate some characteristics of beginners when they work in new roles, in unfamiliar settings, or with people they don't know.

An awareness of their own growth and development can assist directors in realizing that they cannot be all things to all people or know all the answers at all times. As directors gain experience, they are more comfortable in making decisions and soliciting group input into those decisions. There are times, though, when directors have to acknowledge that they may not have control over all the variables affecting their programs. Supervisors, just as teachers, are individuals with their own strengths and limitations.

Staff Development Strategies

Teachers who are in the survival or early consolidation stages, and who may function at a low level of abstraction, tend to focus on the practical. They are concerned with determining what to do in specific situations, rather than reflecting on philosophical principles and abstract ideas that can be generalized to multiple situations. Consequently, these teachers need more concrete, precise information on what to do, how to do it, and the circumstances under which it should be done (Dillon-Peterson, 1981). They benefit from lectures

Figure 6.1

Supervisory Behavior Continuum

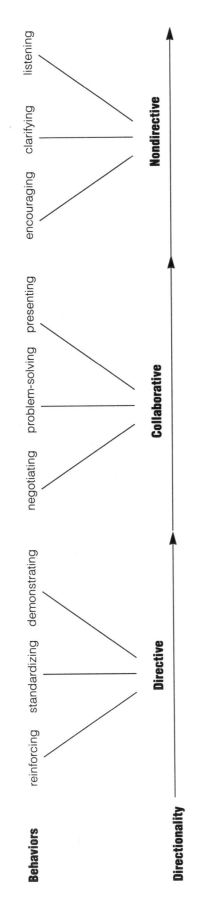

Behaviors

reinforcing   standardizing   demonstrating | negotiating   problem-solving   presenting | encouraging   clarifying   listening

Directive   **Collaborative**   **Nondirective**

Directionality

Control

teacher – low
supervisor – high

supervisor – low
teacher – high

Adapted from Glickman, C. (1985). *Supervision of instruction: A developmental approach.* Boston: Allyn Bacon, p. 49. Reprinted with permission.

on specific topics related to classroom situations and visits to other centers. Sample materials for their use should be clearly organized and sequenced.

Glickman (1985) identifies this group of teachers as low in abstract thinking and recommends an emphasis on demonstration of the new practice, skill, or program. Since these teachers are hesitant and inexperienced, workshops should focus on teachers' understanding of the personal advantages to be gained from the proposed changes. In early childhood centers, such inexperienced teachers benefit initially from a rather structured program of inservice activities and clearly organized goal plans. They need the support of the director in managing their classrooms and dealing with problem children.

Teachers who function at the career stage of consolidation or renewal and exhibit a moderate or high level of abstract thinking may resist mandatory staff development programs that appeal to teachers in the survival group. Although they may not have clarified their own point of view, these teachers express their criticisms of the way things are conducted and want to apply principles they have learned on their own (Dillon-Peterson, 1981). With this group, it is important that staff development activities allow opportunities for alternatives both with respect to content and presentation. Teachers at this level benefit from group discussions in which participants are given the chance to express and elaborate their own points of view.

Glickman (1985) sees this group of teachers as benefiting from applying newly learned principles to classroom activities. However, they are still in need of help from a supervisor in defining what they want to do and how to do it. Direct assistance from the director or peer supervision needs to be provided.

At the mature level of the career stage continuum, teachers frequently function at a very high level of abstraction. They require very different approaches with respect to staff development activities. Dillon-Peterson (1981) suggests that democratic decision-making procedures are particularly applicable at this level. By involving these teachers in the planning process, directors are allowing them to express their own uniqueness, knowledge, and experience. This group is expected to focus on the link between theory and practice, philosophical underpinnings, and more complex concerns. Glickman (1985) sees these teachers as contributing actively to brainstorming and group problem solving processes in a center.

Mature teachers function well in mentoring roles with new or inexperienced teachers, in conducting parent education programs, and in articulating the goals, curriculum, and philosophy of a center to the public. Presentations by these individuals at conferences provide opportunities for sharing their knowledge and experience and keeping them actively involved in the profession.

As Table 6.2 shows, there are many and varied staff development strategies that can be used with teachers at different developmental levels. While it is not our intent to go into an in-depth discussion of each of these strategies, an overview of some of them would seem appropriate.

Mentoring. The idea of using a knowledgeable and experienced person to guide another has gained credibility in education over the past 15 years. Gray and Gray (1985) believe that formalized mentoring, if implemented carefully, can meet the specific needs of beginning teachers and provide increased professional satisfaction to mature teachers acting as mentors.

Mentors, according to Gehreke (1988), are more than master teachers; they also serve as coach, positive role model, developer of talent, opener of doors, protector, sponsor, and successful leader. Driscoll, Peterson, and Kauchak (1985) studied teachers' perspectives of what actual functions performed by mentors were considered the most important. The top four items were: observes and comments on your classroom performance; gets involved in solving specific problems with curriculum, instruction, and people; assists you in knowing how well you are doing as a teacher; and helps you cope with the practical details of being a teacher. These researchers also present criteria for screening prospective mentors. These include the amount of time the individual has available to devote to mentoring, his/her concern for the needs of beginning teachers, the presence of a communicative-supportive personality, and overall level of professional competence.

Also of importance is the need for some type of structured support system for mentors themselves. Driscoll and her colleagues (1985) emphasize that if a mentor is to work closely with teachers in the classroom, he or she needs expertise in observation, conferencing, and clinical-teaching support. This assistance must be an integral part of the mentor system. If such a support system is in place, mentoring benefits the new teacher, the mentor teacher, and the students in the program.

Workshops. Workshops have long served as a vehicle for staff development in early childhood settings. The drawback of workshops, as Caruso and Fawcett (1986) point out, is that we tend to expect too much from them. "In one or a few sessions, participants are supposed to develop new skills or understandings, or to change attitudes toward children and parents. They are then presumed to be ready to demonstrate what they have learned on their return to the classroom. It is no wonder the results are often disappointing" (p. 204).

Workshops will be more successful as a staff development strategy if the following considerations are kept in mind. First, workshops need to be geared to the interests and developmental needs of participants. That means ensuring that there are multiple options for staff to select from. By having multiple options, teachers can self select those workshops that will be of most interest to them. A single topic workshop designed for all staff is bound to disappoint half or more of your teachers.

Second, the presenter should have an awareness of the specific context of the program and the real-life concerns of the teachers attending the session. There is nothing more disconcerting than a presenter who laces his/her presentation with examples that have no resemblance to the concerns or issues experienced by the participants.

Finally, sufficient follow-up needs to be planned to ensure that teachers have integrated the ideas and concepts into their day-to-day practice on the job. Workshops can be a viable means for increasing the knowledge and skills of teachers and even changing attitudes and their behaviors if

they are supported by supervisory processes that reinforce what has been learned. Stonehouse (1986) emphasizes that the most successful well-planned workshops embody both educative and supportive functions. In other words, they not only increase participants' knowledge and skills, they also enhance their self esteem and support systems in the field.

Professional reading. An important staff development strategy is to stimulate regular professional reading by staff members. Greenberg (1975) takes a very direct approach in this regard. She suggests that staff be given a regular reading assignment followed by problem solving sessions based on the readings. Finding time for professional reading is a worthwhile goal for staff at all levels of professional responsibility, but is particularly essential for teachers in the early stages of their careers.

Obviously, there are also less structured ways to encourage professional reading. Having a private staff area well-stocked with journals, books, and other resources will assist in the promotion of this strategy. Developing a resource file for parents will also cause staff to search for new and better articles and ideas.

Classroom research. The idea of teachers functioning as action researchers in their classrooms has been given renewed emphasis in the last decade (Loucks-Horsley, 1987; Rogers, Waller, & Perrin, 1987). This strategy is best utilized with mature teachers who are ready to systematically study and reflect upon some aspect of their classroom operation.

For teachers to undertake an action research project, they need support and guidance from the director. Release time will most likely be necessary for a teacher to stand back and observe her classroom at different points in the day or week. Assistance will also be necessary for designing the study (either from an outside resource person or from the director), as well as on-going discussion sessions to address data collection, procedural problems, data analysis, and implications. The time is well-spent, however, when a mature teacher is ready and interested in pursuing this staff development strategy. It allows the seasoned professional

Table 6.3

Content Areas for Staff Development

Child Care
- Legal issues
- Licensing
- Program evaluation
- Public policy
- Resource and referral
- School-age programs
- Summer camps

Child Development
- Child assessment
- Cognitive
- Emotional
- Language
- Moral
- Physical
- Sex roles
- Social

Exceptional Children
- Developmentally delayed
- Gifted
- Physically disabled

Families
- Parent education
- Parent involvement
- Single parent households
- Teen parents
- Blended families

Staff Needs
- Building team relationships
- CDA credential
- Communication skills
- Community resources and services
- Time management

Curriculum
- Art
- Children's literature
- Computers, child uses
- Curriculum development
- Environments/space
- Equipment/materials
- Health
- Infant stimulation
- Language arts
- Math readiness
- Movement/dance
- Multicultural/multilingual
- Music
- Nutrition
- Play
- Playgrounds
- Reading readiness
- Safety
- Science
- Social studies
- Staff-child interaction

Adapted from Abbott-Shim, M. S. (1990, January). In-service training: A means to quality care. *Young Children*, p. 16. Reprinted with permission.

to go beyond informal assessment of her classroom and learn new skills of systematic study. Such involvement usually serves to re-energize and challenge a teacher at this level.

In addition to the more formal strategies detailed above, there are numerous other informal strategies that we can utilize when identifying staff development strategies. Stonehouse (1986) suggests: visits to other centers to observe programs; opportunities to meet with staff from other centers for informal discussions; opportunities to meet with staff from other community services for children and families to discuss issues of mutual interest; individual on-site consultations with resource people possessing specialized expertise; participation in short courses, conferences, and seminars; and involvement in professional organizations.

Staff Development Content Areas

In the staff development model presented in Table 6.2, a number of different content areas are identified for staff development which match the developmental stages and goals. In general, these content areas move from concrete topics to those that are more abstract and complex. Thus, beginning teachers in the survival stage are usually not interested in or ready for a session on grantsmanship or child advocacy. Beginning teachers are focused on their classrooms and issues related to curriculum, health and safety, and the physical

Figure 6.2

Implementing an Individualized Model of Staff Development

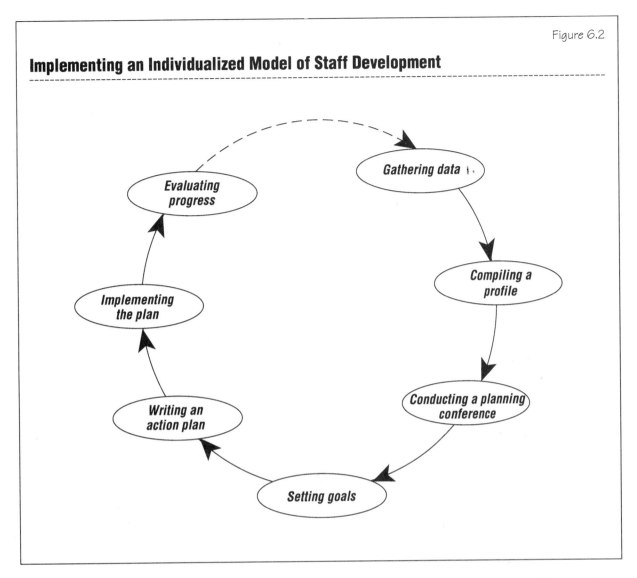

environment. Conversely, mature teachers will most likely be bored with topics which center on these issues; they are ready for discussions related to administration and supervision or mentoring approaches.

Another way to think about content areas is to group them into categories. Abbott-Shim (1990) provides a fairly comprehensive list of topic areas for staff development. Table 6.3 summarizes these areas. Abbott-Shim suggests using such a list as a training needs assessment survey that can be distributed to staff to assess their level of interest in different topics.

In considering actual content areas, directors must constantly be aware of the relationship between developmental stage and interest in a particular topic. These linkages are indeed no different from the ones we facilitate for young children. A 4-year-old will not be satisfied with putting objects in and out of a container like the 1-year-old. And just as children let us know the materials in which they are interested, so, too, will adults.

Implementing Individualized Staff Development

The primary goal of an individualized model of staff development is to have teachers understand their own professional growth needs and strengths as contributing members of the center in which they work. As directors allow teachers more choice and control over classroom practices, teachers will become more committed to improvement and to a cause beyond oneself (Glickman, 1985).

Individualized professional development plans cannot be done haphazardly; a systematic way to approach individuals is needed. Figure 6.2 details a seven-step process that can be used on an ongoing basis. While the seven steps here are visually displayed in a cycle, it is probably more useful to think of it as a "professional spiral," where new data are added, goals are refined, and new targets for professional growth are set each year. The seven steps in this process parallel the organizational problem solving process of change detailed in Chapter II. Where Figure 2.1 on page 29 focused on the center as the target of change, Figure 6.2 focuses on the individual as the target of change.

Gathering Data

 The initial interview with a new employee is a good place to begin collecting data on all aspects of the individual you have hired. The open, trusting relationship you establish at that time will provide a precedent for future interactions with that person. As director, it is important to acknowledge that you want to get to know this person better, that you want the person to come to you with concerns and problems, and that you wish to establish a good working relationship. Ask questions, look interested, and be concerned! In the final analysis, this interpersonal relationship is the key to meaningful dialogue.

With veteran staff, too, it is important to keep "checking back." How are things going? What's happening at the homefront? Have any problems surfaced since we last talked? As director, you set the tone of open communication. Your knowledge of individual staff increases daily through many and various informal and formal contacts. All of these contacts generate data for planning individualized professional development opportunities.

Relative to the job itself, there are many sources of data that directors can use. Teachers can be observed in action to assess the quality of their teaching practices using Assessment Tools #12, 13, 14, and 15. This data can be supplemented with informal daily observations that you record. Teachers frequently complain that their supervisors do not spend enough time observing in their classrooms. Brief, frequent visits by the director are less threatening to teachers than formal observations. Frequent visits convey a sense that the director is "in touch" with what is going on in the program. When the director is able, in a discussion session with a teacher, to present a number of specific instances of particular classroom practices, the director's credibility is greatly enhanced.

In using observational data for professional development purposes, we must try to suspend judgment on what is observed. In other words, there is a strong tendency when we observe teachers in action to judge whether the teacher is doing things "our way" or not. If the intention is to gather data to support someone's professional development, it is good to ask yourself "How can I account for what I am observing?" "Why is the teacher responding to the situation this way?"

Certainly the feedback we receive from parents and co-workers will also be helpful. Directors can gain valuable information about teachers through ongoing, informal exchange with parents and through conferencing with other staff who work with the teachers. But some of the most useful data will come from the individual teacher herself. Using the assessment tools in this book, or adaptations of them, will generate meaningful data in a number of areas — role clarity, job satisfaction, commitment, perceived problems, and temperament.

Anecdotal notes are another valuable source of data. Although it is time consuming to keep anecdotal records, they provide rich, descriptive examples of the way a teacher functions. These examples can be used in discussing a more abstract concept. For example, one director recorded the following exchange between a new teacher and a parent:

> Parent: "I thought you would be working on the alphabet with Jenny by now. She really seems ready for it."

Teacher: "Our program is more play-oriented. We don't believe in pre-reading activities."

The director was able to refer to this exchange when discussing parent communication with the teacher. Although this particular early childhood program was indeed play-oriented, the answer the teacher gave to this parent's question did not assist the parent in understanding why play and social interaction had been established as emphases of the program. Moreover, stating that there were no pre-reading activities was erroneous. Children were read to frequently, print was readily available in the classroom, and art work was often enhanced with children's dictations. This simple interaction identified several areas in which the director could work with the teacher. Having a specific example facilitated a meaningful discussion on important issues.

To simplify the recording of anecdotal entries, directors may wish to carry a small notebook or 3" x 5" cards around with them. Another method is to keep a notebook on the side of your desk so that items can be readily jotted down. The task here is quite similar to teachers' efforts to record anecdotal data on the children in their classrooms.

The overall goal of data gathering is to pinpoint staff's needs and confront rather than avoid problems. Without adequate information on an individual, it is impossible to devise a professional development plan that is worthwhile.

Compiling an Individual Profile

 After sufficient information has been gathered on an individual, it is time to create a profile on that person. The appendix includes blank sample forms that you can use in your program. This section includes examples of two sets of sample forms showing data compiled on two teachers from the Children's Corner — Pat, a mature, experienced teacher and Shelly, a new, inexperienced teacher. The areas noted on Sample Form #1 reflect the use of many of the different assessment instruments previously discussed. For example, there is a space for temperament type

and learning style. The accompanying observation sheets, Sample Form #2, show anecdotal entries on the two teachers which provide evidence for statements made on the profile. Obviously, these entries will be far more extensive after the individual has worked for the center for a period of time.

This first profile you prepare should be considered tentative until you have a planning conference with the teacher where you will elicit further information and clarification. Also, as you observe the classroom and receive ongoing feedback on the teacher, other modifications may need to be made.

Conducting a Planning Conference

It is important that a formal get-together, a planning conference, be conducted to begin the process of developing a professional development plan with the teacher. For new teachers, we suggest a planning conference six weeks into a new job and then every May or June. For veteran teachers it is usually sufficient to meet once a year. May or June provides a good time because it is a logical point to think about setting new organizational and individual goals for the following year.

Prior to the scheduled conference, it may be helpful to allow the teacher to prepare answers to some of the questions that will be presented. Sample Form #3 is provided for this purpose.

The goal of the planning session is to create the open, trusting atmosphere in which a teacher will openly share information and concerns. There are four types of information about teacher behavior that can be examined (Luft & Ingham, 1973).

The open self. Much of what we know is information which is known both to the teacher and others in the center. *Gina is a good piano player; she loves music activities.*

The secret self. Some information is known to the teacher but not to others. *Gina is terrified each time she has to conduct a parent conference.*

The blind self. There is information about the teacher's behavior which is known to others but not to the teacher. *Gina seems to reinforce sex role stereotypes in her classroom.*

The undiscovered self. Lastly, there is information which is unknown both to the teacher and to others. Through professional development opportunities these qualities may emerge. *Gina has the potential to be an outstanding mentor teacher to less experienced staff.*

The challenge to the director is to motivate the teacher to go beyond the open self and to delve into the secret and blind self when identifying improvement areas.

From the responses to Sample Form #3, we can begin to get an idea of what kind of activity or support the teacher needs. Pat, for example, is interested in gaining experience in the administrative side of child care. She has a desire to improve her supervisory skills. Perhaps a break from the long hours in the classroom might be appropriate for her. Obviously, we would need much more information on Pat before being able to put the pieces together. But the planning conference allows the teacher to articulate to the director her perceived needs and desires. All of us relish the opportunity to do this in relation to our work!

Be sure to allow the teacher the opportunity to initiate questions and raise concerns over and above your questions. The goal of the planning session is to establish an open, trusting atmosphere that helps teachers identify areas of strength and areas in need of improvement. At the conclusion of this session, you should be able to add more information to the profile you have begun to create on an individual teacher.

Developing a Goals Blueprint

 Toward the end of the planning conference, the focus should move to goal planning. Goal planning should be a joint process. When directors include staff in goal setting, they express confidence in their staff as reliable sources of information. The director's role is facilitative in the sense that she can help ensure that the individual is setting realistic and achievable goals that are congruent with the individual's developmental profile.

Begin the goal setting process by identifying and discussing the strengths of the teacher. By doing so, the process of goal planning begins on a positive note. Next, specific areas in need of improvement or growth can be noted. From this point, goals can be articulated. Sample Form #4 is provided for this purpose. Goals need not be grandiose, but they do need to be meaningful and moderately challenging.

The approach advocated here is a "needs analysis approach," one where teachers are helped to identify problem areas and then target specific objectives and activities that will reduce or eliminate those problems (Peters & Kostelnik, 1981). A needs analysis approach in working with individuals is essentially the same model that we used to assess center-wide needs. It is one that defines a problem as the discrepancy between what is and what is required or desired. In this case, it is the discrepancy between the knowledge, attitudes, or skills possessed by the teacher and those deemed desirable for the position.

It is important for directors to be mindful that there is often a difference between inferred and expressed needs. Many staff development programs in centers operate on an inferred needs basis. In other words, the director infers the training needs of staff based on her expert judgment alone. When teachers are permitted to express their own training needs, often different themes emerge (Peters & Kostelnik, 1981).

Writing a Staff Development Action Plan

A direct outgrowth of working together on goals is writing the staff development action plan. This plan breaks the goals down into activities, time, resources needed, and the how and when of evaluation. Sample Form #5 was designed for this purpose. The sample action plans on Pat and Shelly are quite different. Pat's activities reflect her maturity both in terms of her development and her career stage; they are directed beyond her classroom and emphasize her move into assuming a leadership role in the center. Shelly's plan, on the other hand, is focused on her classroom, as this is where she needs and wishes to concentrate her energies. Developmentally, this focus is appropriate because it addresses her survival orientation. Let's take a closer look and see how these action plans evolved.

At the conclusion of the goal setting conference, you might want to have the teacher complete Assessment Tool #27. This instrument was designed to assess the individual's level of motivation in tackling the goals and objectives that have been outlined on the action plan. If the results of this assessment reveal that the teacher has very little motivation for achieving the stated goals and objectives, then it will be important for the two of you to meet again to revise the action plan to more accurately reflect those goals that the teacher is sincerely interested in accomplishing. Otherwise, the entire goal setting endeavor will become merely a paper exercise.

Case Study: The Children's Corner

Martha and Shelly scheduled a time to meet to work on Shelly's action plan for the year. Martha thought a lot about how to handle this conference. Clearly, there were so many areas of Shelly's performance that needed attention — her lack of control of the children in the classroom, her overly structured instructional style, her inability to deal with parents effectively. The list seemed to go on and on. But Martha also realized that Shelly's self-esteem as a teacher was quite fragile. She was convinced that with the right kind of supervision and mentoring, Shelly could develop into a competent and capable teacher. That is why this first planning conference was so crucial. If Shelly left the conference overwhelmed by having to tackle too many improvements all at once, there was a good chance, Martha felt, that Shelly would simply burn out before she ever really made a commitment to the profession.

Martha decided to proceed cautiously. She let Shelly take the lead in the discussion regarding her perceived problems in the classroom. She was pleased at how Shelly opened up and how receptive she was to Martha's suggestions on ways they might work together to help solve some of Shelly's problems. Martha quickly realized that what Shelly needed most of all was to feel some sense of control over the management of her classroom. Trying to take on other goals right now such as improving her interactive style with parents would just be too much. First and foremost, Shelly needed to see herself as a competent teacher in control of her own classroom. Once that happened, Martha felt confident Shelly would be more ready to take on some of the other areas that needed improving such as parent relations.

In talking to Shelly, Martha began to see how instrumental her own role was in helping create a collegial and supportive atmosphere in the center. She talked to Shelly about doing some observations in Georgia's room. While Martha knew that Georgia wasn't ready to be a mentor, she did know that Georgia had a wonderful interactive style with the children and would serve as a good role model for Shelly in the area of classroom management. Martha also thought that this just might be the shot in the arm that Georgia needed to re-energize her own teaching. All kinds of possibilities were racing through Martha's mind. She thought, "Why couldn't Pat serve as Shelly's mentor, the person to meet with her each week to go over her progress in meeting her staff development objectives?" When she suggested this to Shelly, she liked the idea. Shelly stated that she always felt like she was "bothering" Martha every time she came to her with a problem because Martha was busy with so many other administrative responsibilities. Shelly liked the idea of having a "big sister" to go to with all her problems. Martha wasn't sure what she was getting herself into, but she said she would talk to Pat the next day at Pat's goal setting conference and see how Pat felt about the idea of mentoring Shelly.

When Pat and Martha met to work on Pat's action plan, the conference was, of course, far less directive from Martha's perspective. Martha listened intently as Pat talked about wanting to take on a more active role in the local AEYC group and how she wanted to "get up her nerve" to make a presentation at the state conference the following year. Martha proposed the idea of mentoring to Pat, thinking inside that Pat would graciously decline given how much additional work this would entail. She told Pat that she would revise Pat's schedule to give her two hours a week for mentoring, one hour to meet with Shelly and one hour to gather resources and plan for her session. Much to Martha's surprise, Pat was eager to take on the assignment. She told Martha how honored she was to be asked and that no supervisor had ever shown that much confidence in her before. Martha loaned Pat some books on supervision and mentoring and they scheduled a three-way meeting with Shelly to work out the details. Martha was elated.

Implementing the Action Plan

 Action plans often need revision as they become operational. It is important for the director and teacher to view them as being flexible, making changes as they seem warranted. The director is the key person in monitoring the staff development action plans that have been initiated. Without the exercise of leadership on her part, the entire process will crumble! Staff development does not happen just by talking about it. There must be active follow through to keep the process moving and relevant.

On Shelly's plan, for example, her third goal was to keep anecdotal records on the classroom operation. Through a review of these records as well as observations of the classroom, Martha and Pat (as Shelly's mentor) will try to determine if Shelly is more aware of interactions in the classroom and what might be influencing them. Once this awareness develops, the record keeping can be dropped and a new goal established.

Much of the director's time will be spent scheduling activities as appropriate and providing resources as needed for individuals to achieve goals. Often staff members need assistance in managing their time so they can attend to the action plan that has been agreed upon.

Sometimes the director can plan small group or even large group inservice workshops if there is high congruence among staff members in terms of needs and interests. This is a different approach than that of selecting a group topic that does not meet the goals of the individual teachers. The director is in a position to know in which direction to go on behalf of her staff.

"We are the architects

of our own future."

— Anonymous

Evaluating Progress

It is the director's responsibility through monitoring the action plans to evaluate progress on a continuous basis. Evaluation in this sense relates specifically to whether the goals have been attained, not to how well the teacher is doing her job from an overall perspective. Sometimes this responsibility can be partially delegated to a mentor, as in the case of Shelly. Martha is still responsible, however, for ensuring that the mentor/protege relationship is progressing smoothly. If not, she must intervene and make adjustments in supervising Shelly's progress in meeting her goals. Overall, it can be assumed that teachers in the survival or consolidation stages will require more time in assessing progress in meeting the goals stated on their individualized staff development plans. Teachers at more independent levels of functioning will require a supervisory style that is less directive.

Evaluation from this perspective, therefore, is linked directly to activities and their accomplishment. Most certainly the outcomes will be one piece of evidence in considering merit and pay increases or promotion to a new position of responsibility. Staff evaluation as it relates to overall performance appraisal from a more global framework will be presented in Chapter VII.

A Final Word

This chapter has focused on strategies and supervisory approaches for implementing individualized guided staff development. The emphasis has been on the "match" between the individual's developmental level and the selected supervisory behavior. Vygotsky (1978) uses the terms "scaffolding" and "zone of proximal development" to describe how teachers can facilitate the growth of children. We think the same terms apply to teachers' development. Your role as director in implementing an individualized model of staff development is to "stretch" teachers, helping them to move with competence and confidence to the next level of professional development. Clearly, the process is a time consuming one. We believe, however, that it focuses your time as director on the most important priority in your program — your staff. In the long-run, we are convinced it saves time by reducing, if not eliminating, many of the staff-related problems that impact the quality of program services.

Individual Profile

Name _Shelly_   Age _22_

Education/training _Associate's degree in early childhood._

Teaching experience _lab experience at the community college. No formal teaching experience. Worked at a summer camp for two years._

Professional orientation _Belongs to NAEYC and local affiliate. Reads Young Children and Pre-K Today regularly_

Special interests/skills/talents _runs in local marathons; has assisted in teaching an aerobics class at the community center; makes jewelry._

Relevant personal history _only child; father encouraged her in sports; parents divorced when she was 15; went to a parochial school as a child. Married her high school sweetheart._

Concomitant roles _wife (husband is in sales - away from home frequently) Belongs to a women's fitness group. Works in a local soup kitchen every weekend._

Stage of adult development/ego development _young adult stage; considering career options; wants to purchase home; reluctant to make certain decisions; frequently consults with others for the "right way" to do things._

Career stage _survival stage; frequently overwhelmed and frustrated; says it is difficult to keep track of all the things she is supposed to do as a teacher. Wants children to like her._

Personal traits and characteristics

Energy level *high energy level — very "peppy" and active; participates fully with the children on the playground.*

Level of abstract thinking *low; identifies problems but doesn't consider their relationship to her behavior; looks for quick solutions*

Temperament/psychological type *ESFJ; outgoing, cooperative; eager to please; likes routines clearly laid out; likes definitive answers*

Learning style *strong visual preference — likes handouts, lists, and visual configurations; terrific bulletin boards; neat, detailed lesson plans*

General dispositions *talkative, friendly, outgoing. Promotes good team spirit on staff; likes to give (and receive) praise.*

Self-confidence/self-efficacy *seems uncertain of herself in the classroom; confident in interpersonal relations with other staff.*

Degree of flexibility/openness to change *has right/wrong orientation to teaching; likes established routines; overwhelmed with changes*

Commitment/motivation *brings a lot of enthusiasm to her work; seems centered on having her own needs met instead of center goals; concerned with increasing financial incentives.*

Beliefs and values *Believes children learn best in a structured environment; has learned to espouse "developmentally appropriate practice"; values well-disciplined children who show respect for authority.*

Expectations/needs *appears to have a strong need for approval; important to be validated that she is doing a good job. Wants to be recognized as a "professional" and not a "babysitter."*

Observations

Name *Shelly*

Date: _10-15-90_

Shelly came in to ask my advice about the block corner. "These boys are out of control! They all want to be in the block area, but all they do is fight! I'm thinking of closing the block area for awhile."

Date: _11-3-90_

Shelly was talking to a parent outside the classroom. "Joe will _____ to learn to behave in here. He's been very disrespectful! I think you should talk to him about his behavior."

Date: _11-14-90_

At the staff meeting we discussed the problem of the lack of planned activities on the playground. Shelly chimed in, "I have an idea. Maybe a couple of days a week I could lead the children in doing some aerobic activities and exercises." The other teachers were very receptive to Shelly's suggestion.

Goals Blueprint

Teacher's name _Shelly_   Date _October 1990 – May 1991_

Strengths as a teacher

1. Enthusiastic; high energy level

2. Conscientious in preparing classroom and completing lesson plans

3. Promotes cooperation and team spirit among staff

Areas in need of improvement/growth

1. Needs to implement more effective classroom management strategies

2. Needs to improve physical arrangement of space to facilitate desired behavior

3. Needs to reflect on and clarify her role in the classroom

Goal   More positive interactions among children and better utilization of space, equipment, and materials

Objectives

1. To improve the physical arrangement of the learning environment

2. To improve classroom management strategies: redirection, prevention, and intervention

3. To monitor classroom interactions through anecdotal notes on children

Staff Development Action Plan

Name _Shelly_   Date _October 1990 - May 1991_

Objective #1 _To improve the physical arrangement of the classroom learning environment_

Activities	Time Needed	Resources Needed

1.-Read Greenman, J. _Caring Spaces_
  - View Dodge, D.T. _Room Arrangement as a Teaching Strategy_
  -View High/Scope video on space
2. Experiment: restructure space, observe behavior, assess and refine
	1. approx. 10 hours reading/viewing time
	
	2. weekly planning time with mentor 1 hr.
		1. Borrow book and video tapes from community college
		
		2. coverage for classroom 1 hr. per week

Evaluation (how/when) _weekly meetings with mentor. Use assessment Tool #15 as pre & posttest_

Objective #2 _To improve classroom management strategies_

Activities	Time Needed	Resources Needed
1. Observe Georgia's preschool class during freeplay period 2. Experiment with different strategies: prevention, redirection, and intervention. Keep journal to reflect on progress	1. 2 hrs/week for 3 weeks 2. ongoing - one entry per week	1. coverage for classroom 6 hrs x $8/hr = $48 2. Notebook

Evaluation (how/when) _Weekly meetings with mentor to discuss progress_

Objective #3 _To monitor classroom interactions through anecdotal notes_

Activities	Time Needed	Resources Needed
1. Keep notecard for each child Note examples of positive interactions 2. Read Day-Dopyera, M. _Becoming a Teacher of Young Children_ for observation guidelines	1. ongoing in classroom 2. approximately 8 hrs. total	1. notecards 2. borrow book from staff library

Evaluation (how/when) _weekly meeting with mentor to go over entries_

Individual Profile

Name ___Pat_____ Age ___38_____

Education/training ___B.A. in early childhood education; interested in getting master's___

Teaching experience ___Lead teacher - 3 yrs; assistant teacher - 7 yrs.___
___Volunteer in parent coop - 6 yrs.___

Professional orientation ___Reads widely - both professional journals and current news___
___events (subscribes to Education Week); attends conferences; active in local___
___NAEYC affiliate group; has made presentations at her church (parents' group)___

Special interests/skills/talents ___Active in support group for adoptive parents; plays___
___piano; sings in church choir; enjoys photography.___

Relevant personal history ___Has two children; stayed at home when they were___
___young and then active in parent coop nursery school; one child adopted;___
___experienced the death of her father last year.___

Concomitant roles ___Wife and mother; active in son's PTA; serves on two___
___local boards (women's shelter and community arts center).___

Stage of adult development/ego development ___Midlife stage; respects diverse___
___points of view and alternative life styles; shows autonomy___
___in thinking and decision-making.___

Career stage ___Maturity; still gets excited about her teaching; integrates___
___her knowledge and experience well; asks philosophical questions___
___about the meaning of educational experiences.___

Personal traits and characteristics

Energy level *moderate; puts a lot into her work but has to monitor hypoglycemia*

Level of abstract thinking *high; good problem solver; considers many sources of information before making a decision; able to evaluate actions*

Temperament/psychological type *ENFJ; outgoing with parents and colleagues warm and friendly; concerned about people's feelings; likes closure*

Learning style *strong auditory preference; enjoys group discussions; very self directed in learning; has impressive collective of books on tape.*

General dispositions *even-tempered; nurturing; curious about new ideas*

Self-confidence/self-efficacy *high; knows she is committed and is confident about abilities*

Degree of flexibility/openness to change *believes that change is healthy; quite open to new approaches and new ideas*

Commitment/motivation *self-motivated and committed to improving center; understands the concept of 'quality' from multiple perspectives and is committed to giving it her all.*

Beliefs and values *believes that children are intrinsically motivated to learn; values individuality and diversity; believes her role is one of facilitator.*

Expectations/needs *equity issues are important to her; wants to know that pay and benefits are distributed equitably. Often uses the word "fair" in explaining why she has made certain decisions.*

Observations

Name ___Pat___

NOTE: Pat's interactions with this family focus on solving problems, not judging their beliefs and actions

Date: ___10-15-90___

Pat discussed with me a conference she recently had with Michael's mother. She noted that Michael's mother advocates a "stronger" discipline program with Michael. Pat's comment: "This is a tricky situation. I need to respect her ideas, yet provide some guidance by offering alternative strategies for handling Michael."

Date: ___11-5-90___

In the classroom, Pat was sitting on the floor in the block area. The children had built a stage out of hollow blocks. Pat extended and enhanced their play by helping the children make signs, tickets, and programs for the audience. She was flexible in dropping her scheduled plans to capitalize on their interests.

Date: ___11-16-90___

I observed Pat supervising an aide in the classroom. She was pointing out some of the possible reasons for a child's negative behavior. Pat said, "Its frustrating, isn't it? It requires a lot of patience to be as understanding as we need to be."

Goals Blueprint

Teacher's name _Pat_ Date _Nov 1990 – May 1991_

Strengths as a teacher

1. _Excellent ability to integrate curriculum areas._

2. _Excellent communication skills with children and parents_

3. _Well-organized learning environment. Efficient use of time_

Areas in need of improvement/growth

1. _Needs opportunities to practice and refine supervisory skills_

2. _Needs opportunities to write (publish) and share her expertise with others_

3. _Needs opportunities to explore the theoretical foundations of early childhood in greater depth._

Goal _Achieve a greater sense of confidence and competence in communicating expertise to others_

Objectives

1. _to refine knowledge and skills in training/mentoring others_

2. _to publish an article_

3. _to increase confidence in making presentations_

Staff Development Action Plan

Name _Pat_   Date _Nov 1990 - May 1991_

Objective #1 _To refine knowledge and skills in training/mentoring others_

Activities	Time Needed	Resources Needed
1. Take course at university on clinical supervision (Fall semester) and adult learning theory (Spring semester)	1. 4 hrs/wk class time 4 hrs/wk study time	1. $50 books for each course
2. Serve as mentor to Shelly. Meet with her weekly	2. 1 hr./wk observation 1 hr/wk consultation	2. classroom coverage 2 hrs. per week

Evaluation (how/when) _meet with director in Dec. Feb and May to review progress_

Objective #2 _To publish an article_

Activities	Time Needed	Resources Needed
1. Write an article on the importance of block play in the classroom	1. Six months (approximately 80 hrs. total writing time.)	1. $25 for film and processing for photos of block play.
2. Submit to _Dimensions_, _Early Years_, _Pre-K Today_.	2. 2 hrs. each submission to write letter + follow up.	2. use center's computer

Evaluation (how/when) _copy of article_

Objective #3 _To increase confidence in making presentations_

Activities	Time Needed	Resources Needed
1. Present workshop to parents on the importance of block play in the classroom	1. Released time for preparation 6 hrs. total	1. classroom coverage 6 hrs x $8/hr = $48
2. Present workshop at state AEYC conference on block play	2. Released time (1 day)	2. $90 to cover conference registration and travel expenses

Evaluation (how/when) _copy of program from AEYC conference documenting presentation_

Chapter 7

Linking Staff Development to Performance Appraisal and a Career Ladder

One of the principles repeatedly emphasized in this book has been that in order to achieve effective and lasting change in one component of the system, it must be reinforced by change in other components of the system. The staff development process clearly reinforces the importance of this principle. The change in teachers' knowledge, skills, and attitudes we hope will occur as a result of implementing an individualized model of staff development will have a far better chance of succeeding if they are supported by changes in other organizational structures and processes. The individualized staff development processes a center has implemented will not become permanent fixtures of center functioning without supporting structures.

There are two center structures that are important in this regard — the center's performance appraisal system and a career ladder for professional advancement. Most centers already have in place some form of a performance appraisal system, but few tie that system to their staff development processes. This chapter will provide recommendations on how that might be done. Likewise, few centers have implemented a career ladder for professional advancement. As we will see later in this chapter, a career ladder for early childhood professionals makes eminently good sense. Career ladders have helped professionalize the field of education at the elementary and secondary level, and there is no reason why the same principles can't be applied to staff working with younger children.

Linking Staff Development to Performance Appraisal

Performance appraisal is a natural extension of the individualized staff development cycle we described in Chapter VI. It lays the foundation for ongoing planning and the charting of new goals and objectives for individual performance. So often we think of evaluation only as a way to judge performance, as a way to provide evidence on whether or not to renew a teacher's contract. But the performance evaluation process should serve as an effective tool for supporting change in individuals. Reviewing progress against previously set goals gives the evaluator and the teacher a yardstick by which to measure growth. This growth (or lack of growth) is the basis for change — change in knowledge, skills, and attitudes.

"People don't care what you know until they know that you care."

— Anonymous

Performance appraisal is a pivotal activity around which good directors manage their programs for staff development. When done right, it makes teachers aware of those areas of teaching performance in which they excel and those areas in need of improvement. In good programs, evaluation of staff is a continuous and ongoing process, one that focuses on change and improvement as well as reinforcing areas of strength. Figure 7.1 provides a visual display of the role of performance appraisal in the personnel management process. This process, of course, includes staff development.

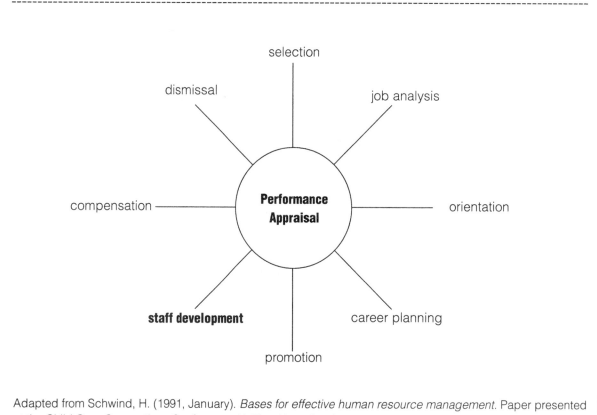

Figure 7.1

The Role of Performance Appraisal in the Personnel Management Process

selection

dismissal

job analysis

compensation — **Performance Appraisal** — orientation

staff development

career planning

promotion

Adapted from Schwind, H. (1991, January). *Bases for effective human resource management.* Paper presented at the Child Care Connections Conference, Halifax, Nova Scotia.

If performance appraisal plays such a vital role in organizational effectiveness, why is it that many directors dread the responsibility and see it as time-consuming and burdensome? Employees, as well, seem to share this ambivalence and often complain that the process is arbitrary and sometimes humiliating. This section will provide a rationale for viewing the performance appraisal processes of a center as a central vehicle for achieving center-wide change. It will look at the principles underlying effective performance appraisal and present some guidelines for implementing such a performance appraisal system in your center.

Principles Underlying Effective Performance Appraisal

Effective performance appraisal depends on the following variables: the teacher, the evaluator, and the context of the situation. For example, the background of the teacher with respect to educational level and degree of experience will dictate the kinds of information used in the performance appraisal process. As evaluator, your values and attitudes (your evaluation philosophy) will certainly affect how you interpret that information. And, the context of the situation in which you work will impact how that information is put to use. By understanding how these variables are defined differently in each situation, we can also understand why it is so important to individualize the performance appraisal process.

A number of excellent resources exist that identify effective performance appraisal processes (Albrecht, 1985; Bernardin & Beatty, 1984; Duke & Stiggins, 1986; Johnston, 1988; McGreal, 1983; Scallan & Kalinowski, 1990; Schwind, 1987). Using these resources as a guide, we can develop a comprehensive system to evaluate the staff in our early childhood programs. The following principles help us better understand how to make the evaluation process a productive one — one that is both individualized and individually guided.

Performance appraisal must be thorough. Time is such a scarce commodity in our administrative role as directors. Taking the time to do thorough evaluations of staff is perceived by many directors as a luxury. But when viewed through the lens of program effectiveness, the time we allocate to evaluating our staff pays tremendous dividends later on. Better teaching performance, higher morale, and lower turnover are but a few of the payoffs that come with reallocating our time and energy to providing feedback to staff through performance appraisal. Oddly enough, this is the one area that the teachers themselves feel so adamant about. The following scenario is not atypical of teachers' reactions to much of what passes for performance appraisal.

Mary, a Head Start teacher, was observed with her class at lunchtime on three different occasions during the year. Her yearly review stated that she showed poise, good manners, and self control. On the basis of this assessment, her teaching was regarded as excellent. To the director's surprise, Mary was unhappy with this evaluation of her performance. She felt the evaluation was very cursory, that the director's limited observation during lunch time could not possibly give her a representative sample of Mary's true performance. Even though the ratings were quite positive, Mary felt short-changed. She had worked hard preparing her lessons and providing an enriching classroom experience for the children. She really wanted to be validated for all her hard work.

Performance appraisal must be fair. One of the quirks of human nature is our tendency to let our personal biases cloud our judgments. In most situations, the consequences of this are fairly innocuous. In evaluating a staff's performance,

however, this tendency can be both damaging and counterproductive. The personal biases we bring to the evaluation task often serve to make the process unfair and viewed as arbitrary from the staff's perspective (Jensen, 1979). The following example serves to illustrate this point.

Before Ramona became a director, she had been a kindergarten teacher for 15 years. Ramona included poetry as an integral part of her teaching and felt that other teachers of young children should do the same. As a director, Ramona had provided her staff with many poetry collections in the professional library and often used poetry as a part of the staff bulletin board. Ramona clearly valued poetry. Bob, the experienced teacher in the four-year-old room, did not share this same enthusiasm for poetry. Ramona often would suggest appropriate poems for use in his classroom. The suggestions were ignored. Bob believed that the children's own writing should be the foundation of literacy. He felt strongly that he should exhibit books and songs the children had created. On Bob's performance appraisal form, he was rated "seldom" in promoting literacy. Bob felt the rating was unfair, that Ramona was using her high value of poetry as the basis for this judgment. He felt strongly that he provided a literacy-rich environment — just not the kind of literacy that Ramona preferred.

Staff should be actively involved in developing evaluation standards. Just as people and programs are fluid, so, too, should be performance appraisal. If evaluation methods accurately measure knowledge, skills, and attitudes of the staff, then teachers need to have an integral role in determining how their performance can best be evaluated.

The teachers of the public school prekindergarten program were amazed to find "dresses appropriately" on the performance appraisal form to be used to assess their teaching performance. After a team meeting, it was decided to ask for a conference with the school principal who would be serving as their evaluator. She met with the teachers and listened to them explain why an informal mode of dress was appropriate for teachers at the preschool level. They wanted more clarity in how "dresses appropriately" would be defined. The principal asked two of the prekindergarten teachers to serve on the district-wide committee to review the school's evaluation form. They eagerly agreed. The result was that a description was added to the criteria that acknowledged the special needs of prekindergarten teachers to wear comfortable, informal attire on the job.

Performance appraisal should build on the competencies of the individual. The perceptions of the performance appraisal process held by both the director and the staff member are important. It goes without saying that mutual trust between the evaluator and the staff member is necessary for effective performance appraisal. Evaluation must be viewed as a helping process, a time for building on old skills and acquiring new knowledge, rather than as a punitive measure. Besides, trying to remediate deficits is an uphill struggle; it is bound to fail. Feedback is most helpful if it focuses on strengths rather than weakness. Strengths change the focus of the interaction to one of talking about potential. In the end, this is what moves individuals to higher levels of performance and a stronger sense of self-efficacy and confidence. This principle of effective evaluation, of course, implies a sense of mutual trust and respect between the director and the teacher. If this quality is missing, the process is bound to be unproductive.

After observing Shawna struggle with the organization and management of her classroom block area, Stewart, the education coordinator of the center, shared the problems he had faced in his own classroom years before. "NAEYC has a great publication, the Block Book, that you may want to take a look at, Shawna," he said. "I found lots of good ideas and suggestions that helped me. Would you like me to find the center's copy for you?" When Shawna expressed an interest in the publication, Stewart was prompt in placing the book in her hands the next morning. The following week he observed again, and noticing new strategies in the block area, complimented Shawna specifically on the techniques he had observed. By using classroom observations as a vehicle to initiate change, Stewart was able to accent the positive and help Shawna become a better teacher. Shawna was empowered by seeing that her decisions and actions within the classroom made a difference.

Performance appraisal should focus on behavior and results rather than on personal traits. When we try to evaluate traits such as cooperativeness, loyalty, sociability, trustworthiness, initiative, creativity, or thoroughness, we find that it is next to impossible to pinpoint exactly what those qualities mean. What we are left with is a subjective judgment based on the evaluator's interpretation of just what these traits mean. Consequently, what typically happens is that the evaluator ends up making an overall judgment of the person and rates the specific trait items consistent with the judgment.

Jessica had worked as the infant caregiver for four years. She always smiled — the parents loved her. Often Bonnie, the program administrator, noticed that Jessica was less than careful about washing her hands when caring for the children. In fact, over the past six months, Bonnie had detected a trend of colds passing from one child to another in Jessica's classroom. Bonnie reminded Jessica of the importance of careful health habits, checked supplies to be sure soap and towels were always available, and modeled good health habits when she visited the room. But there seemed to be no change in Jessica's behavior and the illnesses continued to spread. On her annual performance appraisal form which only focused on personality traits such as "is pleasant," and "displays positive attitude," Bonnie rated Jessica as an excellent caregiver. This appraisal was unfortunate because Jessica's behavior in the area of providing an healthful environment clearly needed to be improved.

Traits are qualities that individuals bring to the job. They should not be the basis for performance appraisal because they are too abstract. Instead, our attention should focus on behaviors, those critical incidents that can be noted and assessed in terms of how frequently they occur. In defining behaviors, we have to be mindful that the specific criteria are sufficiently precise so as to provide a useful benchmark for performance. For example, "communicates with parents," as a criterion for judging performance is too vague to measure. Does this mean a "hello" and "goodbye" as parents drop off their child each day or does it mean weekly progress notes home, a monthly newsletter, and two parent conferences a year? Without more specific behavioral descriptors added to the criteria, the director and teacher may have conflicting expectations of just what "communicates with parents" really means.

Results relating to teaching effectiveness such as the degree to which children are actively involved, the gains children achieve on competence measures, or the degree to which parents are satisfied with the program, are important and useful ways to assess performance. But one must be cautious when interpreting certain outcome measures. Many programmatic outcomes in early childhood education are difficult to measure; others may be misleading. Take the case of Christine at the Children's Corner.

Case Study: The Children's Corner

Christine was a new teacher whom Martha had just hired. Martha had seen Christine in action at her previous preschool. She was a wonderful teacher, very much in touch with the needs of the young children. Her classroom was a child-centered learning environment rich in opportunities for free exploration and discovery learning. In a nutshell, Christine represented Martha's ray of hope for converting the other teachers to implementing more developmentally appropriate practices. Much to Martha's surprise, the parents were not happy with Christine's performance. They complained to Martha that Christine was not getting their children "ready for school." They wanted to know why Christine was not sending home school work like some of the other teachers.

Martha's experience shows us that results (in this case the parent's level of satisfaction with Christine's performance) can be misleading. The problem here is clearly not the teacher's performance, but rather the center's lack of communication to parents about how the philosophy and educational objectives of a developmentally appropriate program are translated into practice.

Multiple sources of evidence improve the reliability of performance appraisal. As professionals, we know the value of using multiple sources of information for assessing the progress of young children. When it comes to adults, however, we tend to rely on single instruments as the totality of our evaluation process. Particularly in child care centers where it is difficult to separate evaluation from supervision, it is imperative that a director use multiple sources of evidence to evaluate the performance of staff.

The kinds of evidence drawn into the performance appraisal process will be both formal and informal. Certainly, the director's and teacher's assessment of how well the goals on the Goals Blueprint have been met will serve as one source of evaluation information. But there are many other sources of evidence that can be gathered to provide a holistic view of a teacher's performance. McGreal (1983) and others provide a menu of suggestions:

▶ ***Standardized performance appraisal forms rating overall performance:*** Once a year it is wise to use at least one standardized evaluation instrument rating staff on their overall performance. This instrument should include some form of classroom observation as well as the evaluator's ratings on different preestablished criteria. Later on in this section we will describe how job descriptions can be used as the basis for constructing such an instrument.

▶ ***Feedback from parents:*** Feedback from the parents of students provides a rich source of evidence of the teacher's performance. You might want to send out a short questionnaire once a year (see Assessment Tool #11 for an example) or have the teacher gather together samples of parent notes and other correspondence that document parents' level of satisfaction.

▶ **Feedback from fellow teachers:** Feedback from colleagues is another important source of data about a teacher's performance. This feedback can be in the form of informal anecdotal notes that have been kept during the year or more formal peer observations that have been conducted. You may find Sample Form #6 useful for this purpose. Certainly, the master teacher serving in a mentoring role to teachers and assistant teachers should be provided an opportunity to give formal feedback on the individual's performance at least once a year.

▶ **Self assessment:** If we truly want to make the performance appraisal process meaningful, we must begin to help teachers realistically assess their own growth and performance. Journal reflections written on a regular basis may be one way for the teacher to gather this data during the year. At least once a year, teachers should do a self appraisal.

▶ **Videotaped segments of classroom instruction:** The wonders of technology can certainly help in our efforts to evaluate teaching performance. Why not have the teacher pull together a collection of highlights of different classroom activities conducted during the year? This videotape will not only serve as an excellent source of evidence regarding the teacher's performance, but it will also be treasured in years to come as the teacher looks back on her teaching career.

▶ **Examples of professional activities:** Teachers can keep copies of the programs from conferences they attend during the year as well as their notes from inservice workshops. They may also have certificates for specialized training they received outside the center. These and other artifacts provide evidence of teachers' professional growth during the year.

Effective performance appraisal depends on clear job descriptions. A clear and concise job description provides the foundation for fair and accurate evaluation. When job descriptions are clearly written and discussed at the initial hiring interview, the staff member has a better understanding of exactly what is expected in everyday performance. When job expectations are clearly understood right from the start, later evaluation is also easier and less biased; the whole process becomes a more effective tool for helping the employee be successful. A clear job description can provide baseline data for the level of expected performance because job descriptions, when done right, provide a concise picture of the competencies the employee needs.

The Child Development Associate (CDA) competency standards (CECPR, 1990) detailing six competency goals in early childhood settings can serve as a useful guide for constructing job descriptions for the teaching staff at your center. Table 7.1 illustrates how these categories have been used to construct a job description. This job description details the tasks for a teacher of preschool-aged children. The precise responsibilities indicated under each of these categories would need to be modified depending on the age level of children the teacher was working with. Thus job descriptions for teachers of infants, toddlers, or school-aged children would all be slightly different.

A good job description includes the following components: job title; a brief description highlighting key elements of the job; accountability — to whom the individual holding the position reports; minimum qualifications for the position; and key tasks and responsibilities required of the position. Writing job descriptions is tricky because you will want sufficient detail to give the individual guidance about what and how the job is to be carried out, but you also want it concise enough so as to be useful. Job descriptions that are too vague and brief or too detailed and wordy tend to get filed away and ignored. If a job description is to be useful, it must be able to fit the individual holding the position. That means your center will have some generic job descriptions for each category of jobs, in addition to specific detailed ones that reflect the scope of an individual position held by a specific person. There are several excellent resources that you may want to refer to when writing the job descriptions for your program (Sciarra & Dorsey, 1990; Storm, 1985; Travis & Perreault, 1981).

Concise, well-written job descriptions are essential because they can serve as a template for designing a performance appraisal form for each role. The appendix provides a blank performance appraisal form (Sample Form #7) for the position of Teacher. You can use this form as an example when constructing your own. This section includes sample peer observation and performance appraisal forms completed for Shelly at the Children's Corner.

Note how the performance appraisal form focuses on the frequency of behavior (from seldom to always) and on specific results the individual has achieved rather than providing a subjective evaluation (poor to excellent) of vague traits or behavior. This is purposeful. If you really believe that the primary goal of evaluation is to help your teachers improve, then your subjective judgments of their performance become less important. Your role should not be one of conferring judgment, but rather one of providing clear and honest feedback about behavior. The most useful part of this performance appraisal form will be the anecdotal notes you write in the comments section. It is here that you will provide a summary of the informal and formal observational data you have accumulated during the year as well as other data that has been collected which pertains to the specific criterion being evaluated.

Conducting the Performance Appraisal Conference

At least once a year you will want to schedule a formal performance appraisal conference. This session will include a discussion about the progress made on staff development action plans throughout the year. The scope of this conference is larger, however, than merely evaluating the progress of the teacher's action plan; it includes an appraisal of the teacher's overall performance during the previous year.

Teachers should be asked to complete a performance appraisal themselves and bring it to the conference with whatever documentation they wish. Particularly teachers at the consolidation, renewal, and maturity stages of their careers should be encouraged to develop portfolios as a means of compiling and tracking their activities and improvements during the previous year. This shift of responsibility is purposeful. It changes the nature of the teacher's role in the performance appraisal process from a passive one to an active one. The point is that the director should not be the only one held responsible for reviewing performance. Performance appraisal is a joint responsibility between the teacher and director and should be promoted as such.

If performance appraisal is perceived as an ongoing process throughout the year that culminates at the annual performance appraisal conference, then there should be no surprises for the employee. In other words, because the individual has had regular informal feedback through the year and has played an active role in documenting level of performance and areas in need of improvement, the director's role is dramatically altered from one of conferring judgment and assigning blame to one of nurturing reflection and problem solving. Certainly, the director and teacher will want to discuss those areas where there may be discrepant perceptions about the teacher's level of performance, but usually these are minor if a trusting, open relationship has existed throughout the year.

Albrecht (1989) underscores the importance of separating competency and compensation issues in a center's performance appraisal system. Performance appraisal that focuses on competency must be perceived by teachers as ongoing, involving informal feedback about the achievement of goals on the staff development action plan and more formal discussions such as the performance appraisal conference where overall performance is reviewed. Compensation, on the other hand, is discussed upon hiring and then again on a semi-annual or annual basis, with the outcome of the review being the determination of salary or wage change. Albrecht believes this allows the director to tie compensation to the larger context of the center. She states, "Whereas competency discussions

Table 7.1

Job Description - Preschool Teacher

Description:

The Teacher is responsible for the care and education of a group of children as part of a teaching team and functions as a team leader or co-leader. The Teacher plans and implements the curriculum and, with active participation of other members of the teaching team, works with parents and assesses the needs of individual children.

Accountability:

The Teacher reports to the Education Coordinator.

Minimum Qualifications:

Successful completion of an associate degree from a program conforming to NAEYC's *Guidelines for Early Childhood Education Programs in Associate Degree Granting Institutions* (1985b) or successful completion of an associate degree in a related field plus 30 semester hours of professional studies in child development or early childhood education including 300 hours of supervised teaching experience in an early childhood program.

Responsibilities:

To establish and maintain a safe and healthy environment

1. Designs appropriate room arrangement to support the goals of the classroom
2. Plans and implements a nutritious snack program
3. Promotes healthy eating practices
4. Maintains a safe environment
5. Posts necessary information to ensure the safety and well-being of the children
6. Maintains an orderly learning environment

To advance physical and intellectual competence

1. Provides a balance between child-initiated and teacher-initiated activities
2. Provides a balance between quiet and active learning activities
3. Uses equipment and materials for indoor and outdoor play that promote children's physical development
4. Involves children in planning and implementing learning activities
5. Provides an integrated curriculum that meets the needs of individual children
6. Plans and implements experiences that promote language and literacy development
7. Plans and implements activities that promote the acquisition of number concepts

----

To support social and emotional development and provide positive guidance

1. Plans and implements hands-on activities that develop positive self-esteem
2. Plans and implements hands-on activities that develop social skills
3. Plans and implements culturally diverse experiences
4. Uses and promotes positive guidance techniques
5. Provides a wide variety of creative and expressive activities
6. Establishes routines with smooth transition periods
7. Communicates with children at their developmental level
8. Encourages children to be independent

To establish positive and productive relationships with families

1. Relates assessment information to parents and offers support for dealing with children at different developmental stages
2. Plans and conducts home visits
3. Promotes communication with parents through weekly progress notes, a monthly newsletter, and semi-annual parent conferences
4. Provides a variety of ways that families can participate in the program
5. Encourages parents to participate in the program

To ensure a well-run, purposeful program responsive to participant needs

1. Assesses program supplies and materials needed prior to implementing activities
2. Coordinates and helps supervise aides, assistants, and volunteers working in the classroom
3. Maintains written plans on a weekly basis
4. Assesses children's needs and developmental progress on an ongoing basis
5. Uses the results of assessment to plan activities

To maintain a commitment to professionalism

1. Promotes the center's philosophy and educational objectives
2. Supports the center's code of ethical conduct
3. Engages in ongoing staff development to improve personal and professional skills
4. Supports the professional growth and development of colleagues by sharing materials and information and providing helpful feedback and encouragement
5. Attends staff meetings, workshops, and inservice training provided by the center

Peer Observation

Name of colleague observed **Shelly**   Date **4-23-91**

As you observe, please note comments about the following aspects of the classroom environment: interactions between the teacher and children; interactions between the teacher and other co-teachers or volunteers; interactions between the teacher and parents; the physical arrangement of space; the curriculum; and health, nutrition, and safety aspects of the program.

Aspects of this classroom I was impressed with include …

1. Wonderful gross motor activities! The obstacle course was a real hit with the children.

2. Great looking bulletin boards. Nicely organized science area, too. The butterfly display is impressive.

3. The dramatic play theme kits stimulated some wonderful creative play in the housekeeping corner this morning.

Aspects of this classroom that might be improved include . . .

1. You could include a few more books and pictures that promote cultural diversity.

2. Try not to schedule two art projects on the same day that require so much adult supervision.

3. You could use a few more challenging puzzles for your older 4s. Check with me — I have a few you can borrow.

Signed **Christine**

Performance Appraisal – Preschool Teacher

Name: _Shelly_   Date _5-20-91_

To establish and maintain a safe and healthy learning environment

	seldom	sometimes	frequently	always	Comments
1. Designs appropriate room arrangement			✓		Excellent progress in meeting target goal
2. Plans and implements a nutritious snack program				✓	Nice parent comments 11/90, 4/91
3. Promotes healthy eating practices		✓			Don't forget the handwashing!
4. Maintains a safe environment			✓		Peer comment 1/91 about cleaning supplies
5. Posts necessary health and safety information				✓	Contributed to resource bulletin board an article from young children. Has begun to label centers and
6. Maintains an orderly learning environment			✓		materials. Nice science area - peer comment 4/91

To advance physical and intellectual competence

	seldom	sometimes	frequently	always	Comments
1. Provides balance between child-/teacher-initiated activities		✓			Moving in this direction. Still somewhat inflexible in adapting plans. 1/91 obr
2. Provides a balance between quiet/active learning activities				✓	Excellent music/motor activities, peer comment 4/91
3. Uses equipment/materials to promote physical development				✓	Great aerobics activities, obstacle course per comment 4/91
4. Involves children in planning and implementing activities		✓			Moving toward this. Have observed increase in involvement of children at circle time.
5. Provides an integrated curriculum that meets the needs of individual children		✓			Still too much emphasis on whole group activities by separate content area
6. Plans and implements experiences that promote language and literacy development				✓	Excellent drama/story reenactment obr 1/91, 3/91
7. Plans and implements activities that promote the acquisition of number concepts			✓		Shared article w/ staff by C. Kamii. Improved use of concrete math materials in learning centers since Feb.

To support social and emotional development and provide positive guidance

	seldom	sometimes	frequently	always	Comments
1. Plans and implements hands-on activities that develop positive self-esteem		✓			activities still too craft oriented
2. Plans and implements hands-on activities that develop social skills			✓		From observations 3/91, 4/91 and from your journal reflections - good growth in this area
3. Plans and implements culturally diverse experiences	✓				Pass obs 4/91 We'll be having a workshop on this topic in the Fall.
4. Uses and promotes positive guidance techniques			✓		greatly improved *** good job!!
5. Provides a wide variety of creative/expressive activities				✓	wonderful dramatic play theme kits
6. Establishes routines with smooth transition periods			✓		journal reflections show improvement
7. Communicates with children at their developmental level			✓		interactive skills show improvement since 12/90
8. Encourages children to be independent		✓			let children serve snack

To establish positive and productive relationships with families

	seldom	sometimes	frequently	always	Comments
1. Relates assessment information to parents and offers support for dealing with children at different stages			✓		parent interactions sometimes abrupt and rushed at the end of the day on schedule, too! great
2. Plans and conducts home visits				✓	
3. Promotes communication with parents through progress notes, monthly newsletter, and parent conferences			✓		Be sure and let pat proofread your newsletters. Many typos ☺
4. Provides a variety of ways that families can participate in the program		✓			It is natural to feel uncomfortable in this area during your first year's teaching. It will be easier next year.
5. Encourages parents to participate in the program		✓			

To ensure a well-run, purposeful program responsive to participant needs

	seldom	sometimes	frequently	always	Comments
1. Assesses program supplies and materials needed prior to implementing activities				✓	well-organized system.
2. Coordinates and helps supervise aides, assistants, and volunteers working in the classroom			✓		This will become easier as routines established
3. Maintains written plans on a weekly basis				✓	always available and on time!
4. Assesses children's needs and developmental progress on an ongoing basis			✓		Increased observation time has aided this process. Anecdotal notes show progress
5. Uses the results of assessment to plan activities			✓		improving

To maintain a commitment to professionalism

	seldom	sometimes	frequently	always	Comments
1. Promotes the center's philosophy and objectives			✓		This will be easier in subsequent years
2. Supports the center's code of ethical conduct			✓		Watch the sharing of confidential information. One parent was very upset.
3. Engages in ongoing staff development to improve personal and professional skills				✓	Your enthusiasm and stamina in sticking to your action plan is commendable!
4. Supports the professional growth and development of colleagues by sharing materials and information				✓	Excellent! Very open and supportive. Shares ideas and resources freely.
5. Attends staff meetings, workshops, and inservice training provided by the center				✓	Didn't miss a single staff meeting!

Additional Comments: Shelly has experienced tremendous professional growth this past year. She established a good working relationship with her mentor, Pat. As a result, the organization and flow of her classroom saw a marked improvement. Her observation skills have aided in providing more individualized planning and a better managed learning environment.

Name of Supervisor _Martha Jackson_

focus on an individual's teaching skills, compensation discussions focus on the individual's connection with and contribution to the center as a whole" (p. 38). Albrecht goes on to say that compensation variables include regularity of attendance, initiative, progress toward completion of additional education and training, possession of special skills, special contributions to the management of the program, special training or certificates, and assignment of hours, in addition to overall teaching performance.

The performance appraisal conference should focus on the future. If a teacher needs improvement, it makes little sense to dwell on the past. Concentrating on the past seldom motivates people to improve their performance. Concentrating on the future, however, gives the teacher a blueprint for achieving change.

Perhaps most important to keep in mind is that your performance appraisal of each employee is a legal document. As such, it should chronicle performance and provide a time frame for needed improvements. This information may become critical should it become necessary to terminate an employee at some future date.

Common Errors in Conducting Performance Appraisal

Research conducted in business and industry about potential pitfalls of performance appraisal (Bernardin & Beatty, 1984; Schwind, 1987) is also relevant to the field of early childhood education. The following are several potential shortcomings of performance appraisal that the director must keep in mind if the process is to be a productive one.

Irrelevant or meaningless criterion. It seems so obvious that the criteria that form the basis for performance appraisal must be relevant and meaningful, yet many performance appraisal instruments fall short in this area. "Promotes an understanding of number concepts" may be a valid criterion for a preschool teacher, but is inappropriate as a criterion for an infant teacher. The best way to ensure that the performance appraisal criteria are relevant is to make sure they are derived from the job description — a job description that the employee has had input in refining.

Inappropriate scale anchors. The scale anchors used to assess performance (e.g. poor to outstanding or sometimes to always) must be appropriate for the specific criterion. Most behaviors are best assessed using a frequency scale (never, sometimes, frequently, always). Using a scale such as "poor to outstanding" is not wise because it implies a qualitative judgment that is more difficult to define. In other words, what constitutes "outstanding" when we're measuring a behavior like "promotes an understanding of number concepts"? Using such scale anchors can lead to misinterpretation about expectations for behavior.

Leniency. No one likes to play the role of the bad guy. Particularly in early childhood education, we pride ourselves on being empathetic and nurturing. But directors' desire to "be liked" by their employees can get in the way of effective performance appraisal. While candid, honest feedback is often difficult to give, successful directors understand it is necessary if staff are to improve.

Undersampling. Perhaps the most frequent complaint voiced by teachers is that their supervisors base their evaluations on too little evidence. "She observed me the morning that Michael decided to have a temper tantrum right in the middle of circle time!" "Wouldn't you know, it was raining, the gym was being painted and was off limits, so there I was trapped in the classroom with these hyper kids all day when my supervisor came to evaluate me." No doubt these frustrations surface when teachers feel their directors base their decisions about performance on an insufficient sampling of behavior. An annual performance appraisal that is based on just a couple of days of observation cannot possibly provide a full and accurate picture of a teacher's performance. As we have mentioned earlier, multiple sources of evidence gathered over an extended period of time are the best protection for ensuring that undersampling doesn't occur.

The halo effect. Another pitfall of performance appraisal is our tendency as evaluators to let one dominant or salient characteristic of a teacher cloud our judgment about behavior in other areas.

Bonnie's appraisal of Jessica's performance in the vignette shared earlier was in part due to the halo effect. Jessica's enthusiastic teaching style with the children led Bonnie to overlook her shortcomings in the area of maintaining a healthful environment. Just being conscious of this tendency can help you diminish the possibility of having the halo effect impact your judgment. Precise criteria also help.

The 'recent event' effect. Given the complexity of the director's job and the countless number of interactions every day, it is quite understandable that we can forget events that transpired a week, a month, or a year ago. Consequently, there is a tendency on our part to remember more recent critical events in staff's performance. This could be a problem if the recent events are not representative of overall performance for the year. If a parent has just complained to you about a teacher, for example, you are more likely to weight that piece of evidence more heavily than earlier assessments of this teacher's performance. Anecdotal notes and frequent recorded observations can serve to provide a more accurate profile of a teacher's overall performance throughout the year. Such records also help us see patterns in behavior rather than focusing on single recent incidents.

Refining Your Present Performance Appraisal System

McGreal (1983) reminds us that teachers change their behavior in the classroom only when they want to do so. They must perceive themselves as partners in the system. The best way to establish and/or change your methods of performance appraisal is to ask for help from your teachers. If the staff is large, recruit a representative group. Try to get a variety of teachers at different career stages. A good place to begin is to ask what components of the present performance appraisal system they like, what parts they don't, and why not?

A necessary part of this review should be the critical examination of current job descriptions and performance appraisal forms. The examples provided in the appendix will provide a template for you and your staff to refine those that you already have in place. By starting with an analysis of each job, the teacher is intimately involved in structuring the support system to guarantee higher levels of performance in the future. In addition, the cooperative endeavor will set a precedent for future collaborative improvement projects that you will consider.

Linking Staff Development to a Professional Career Ladder

Staff development and performance appraisal practices cannot exist in a vacuum. There needs to be an organizational framework to support them. A career ladder is such a framework. Establishing a career ladder for personnel in the early childhood setting is a logical step for a program wishing to implement a comprehensive model of professional development. A professional career ladder provides the organizational framework to support good staff development and performance appraisal practices. The differentiated staffing patterns that comprise a career ladder occur when job roles are clearly defined and delineated. Each level in the ladder has certain expectations and specific responsibilities, indicating a minimum level of education. The experience necessary for the position is also indicated. Job title, salary, benefits, and rewards are defined by the level of job within the career ladder.

Career ladders, by definition, place the employee with the lowest amount of education and experience at the base of the vertical scale. Job responsibilities, salary, rewards, and benefits would also be at the lowest level. As the education, experience, and responsibilities of the employee increase, the worker progresses up the career ladder. Salary, benefits, and duties increase accordingly.

A career ladder clearly establishes the guidelines for advancement within the profession and, in this way, supports the personal and professional development of the individual. The value of a career ladder model for a child care center is that each individual, in consultation with the director or supervisor, is allowed to move at his/her own pace, setting personal priorities and goals that are consistent with the overall goals of the center. The model supports equity and fairness in pay and opportunities for promotion. Further, by tracking the upward career movement of staff, the director can better anticipate staffing needs. This allows the director to better plan staffing patterns and anticipate hiring of needed staff.

While the model proposed in this chapter appears hierarchical on paper, it still embodies what Dresden and Myers (1989) call a "career path." From a career path perspective, an individual may move not necessarily from a position of lesser authority to one of greater authority, but from a position that emphasizes one set of skills to a position that offers different kinds of challenges for additional learning and growth. This perspective underscores the number of options available in the field, not just "the next step on the ladder."

Assumptions about Career Ladders

Although career ladders are relatively new in the field of early childhood (Morgan, 1991; NAEYC, 1990b), a substantial amount of research has been conducted regarding career ladders in public school programs at the elementary and secondary level (ATE, 1985; Burden, 1987; Christensen, 1989; Cornett, 1985). From this research, several reasons emerge as a rationale for implementing a professional career ladder in the field of early childhood education.

▶ A career ladder strengthens and unifies the structure and organization of a school and improves the teaching/learning process by providing clear job responsibilities. When workers know what is expected of them, they are able to do a better job. This, in turn, empowers teachers and helps them be more effective.

▶ A career ladder results in a more effective use of teachers' talents and abilities. A hierarchy of roles and responsibilities rewards teachers who are good and provides incentive for those who need improvement. Identifying the most capable teachers on a staff allows administrators to use these teachers as models for others. For example, a teacher who encourages children to develop gross motor skills by using equipment in a variety of

innovative ways should be encouraged (and rewarded) for sharing this ability with others.

▶ A career ladder provides incentives for staff at different career stages. Currently, the teaching profession is "front-loaded" — that is, most rewards are given to teachers within the first five years of service. This practice discourages longevity in the field. Promotion within the ranks of teaching results in a stronger commitment to the profession and a greater retention of competent teachers.

▶ A career ladder encourages a better pattern of initial teacher preparation, improves induction into teaching, and gives focus to on-the-job development. By firmly establishing a system of master teachers who serve as mentors to younger, less experienced staff, the beginning teacher is automatically provided with a support system to aid and encourage development.

Mertens and Yarger (1988) view the differentiation of staffing as a way to make teaching more professional and a more attractive career. They concur with other educational leaders that "career ladders provide ways staff members can rise to positions of importance with more responsibility, leadership, and status within a setting" (p. 33). In sum, a considerable amount of evidence points to the conclusion that career ladders provide a way to empower teachers and encourage them to stay in the field of early childhood education.

Developing a Career Ladder for Your Center

Because each child care center is unique in its philosophy, goals, and needs, each center must develop its own distinctive version of a career ladder. By reviewing the roles and responsibilities of staff, budget limitations, and the professional goals of the center, a director can design a career ladder that is responsive to the center's unique character.

A good career ladder provides a hierarchy based on differing roles for personnel within the center. Education and experience needed for each role must be clearly defined as are the corresponding salaries and benefits. The five-step progression of professional categories presented in Table 7.2 provides a useful model from which to develop a career ladder for your center. The structure of this model is consistent with the professional categories proposed by the National Association for the Education of Young Children (1990b).

Table 7.2 begins with a preprofessional level. This level represents a precredential teacher's aide position within the center. While the NAEYC model notes that this position is essentially one filled by an untrained individual enrolled in a program of study, individual state standards may require this entry-level worker to have higher requisite qualifications.

While a few individuals will be hired with the minimal qualifications required of this position, most employees will enter the organization with higher qualifications. At the time of initial hiring, an assessment of overall qualifications can be made and a decision regarding the appropriate level of entry. For example, a teacher having just completed a baccalaureate degree in early childhood education with no formal experience would probably qualify to begin work at Level III, Step I. Then as the teacher increased her qualifications with added experience and education, an advancement to the next step or level would be appropriate.

While this model is broad and intended to encompass a wide range of positions in the field, it can be tailored to meet the specific demands of your early childhood program. Each step requires the professional to achieve the needed education and experience before applying for the next level within the organization. A variety of roles are available at each of the five professional levels, leaving options for those career professionals at the higher levels who choose to stay in the classroom yet want to diversify their service within the early childhood field.

Step 1. Identify roles. Earlier in this chapter when discussing the performance appraisal process, we defined the responsibilities for a typical preschool teacher in a center-based program. Table 7.3 provides a brief description of the other roles that may exist in a program along with requisite qualifications. The different roles any particular center has will vary, of course,

depending on the size of the program and the needs of the center. A small program may not necessitate a Social Service Coordinator or a Parent Education Coordinator. Likewise, in a small program, the director may serve as both Education Coordinator and Program Administrator.

One of the strongest benefits resulting from an established set of professional categories such as those proposed by NAEYC is a consistency in the nomenclature used in child care programs around the country. As Hostetler and Klugman (1982) pointed out almost a decade ago, the lack of consistency in job titles in the field of early childhood education is one of the principal roadblocks to achieving professional status. Currently, there still exists much confusion from program to program about job titles and requisite qualifications. When fully implemented, a comprehensive career ladder for the field that uses agreed-upon professional categories with corresponding roles and job titles should help eliminate this confusion. In fact, when fully implemented, the very job title that we have used consistently throughout this book, "director," may well become obsolete.

Step 2. Set salaries. Using an index scale, salaries can be included as part of your center's career ladder. With 1.00 as the baseline for the professional employee at Level I, Step I, the index allows the center administrator to set a prorated system that increases salaries as the staff member moves up the ladder during his/her career. For example, if the salary index of 1.00 is equal to $10,000 per year, the index of 1.25 would be equal to $12,500. A salary of 1.50 would be equal to $15,000; 2.00 is equal to $20,000 per year. By using an index as a basis for salary increases, fair and equitable advancements can be incorporated into the center's organizational structure. Budget planning becomes easier as the present and projected salary needs become clear.

Because advancement to the next professional category largely depends on the attainment of additional education and training, a center may also want to include a parallel system of small increments within each step that are based on years of

Table 7.2

Professional Categories

Level	Step	Index	Education	Experience	Roles*
V	1	3.75	Ph.D or Ed.D. in early childhood education or related discipline	3 or more years	Program administrator Education coordinator
IV	3	3.50	Step 2 plus an additional 15 s.h.	2 or more years	Program administrator Education coordinator Master teacher
	2	3.25	Step 1 plus 15 s.h.	1 or more years	Program administrator Education coordinator Teacher, Master teacher
	1	3.00	MA in early childhood education or related discipline**		Program administrator Education coordinator Teacher, Master teacher
III	3	2.75	Step 2 plus an additional 15 s.h.	2 or more years	Program administrator Education coordinator Teacher, Master teacher
	2	2.50	Step 1 plus 15 s.h.	1 or more years	Program administrator Education coordinator Teacher, Master teacher
	1	2.25	BA in ece or BA in related field with 45 s.h. in cd/ece**		Teacher
II	3	2.00	Step 2 plus an additional 15 s.h.	2 or more years	Teacher*** Assistant teacher
	2	1.75	Step 1 plus 15 s.h.	1 or more years	Teacher*** Assistant teacher
	1	1.50	AA in ece or general AA and 30 s.h. in cd/ece		Teacher*** Assistant teacher
I	2	1.25	CDA plus 30 s.h. in child dev or early childhood educ	1 or more years	Teacher*** Assistant teacher
	1	1.00	CDA		Assistant teacher
Preprofessional		.75	High school diploma or GED		Teacher aide

* The specialty roles of Early Childhood Special Educator, Early Childhood Subject Area Teacher, Parent Education Coordinator, and Social Service Coordinator are not included on this table. The roles of Education Coordinator and Program Administrator require three years of successful teaching experience and specialized course work (see Table 7.3).

** Including supervised field experience (150 hours at primary level and 150 hours at preschool or infant/toddler level).

*** Teacher at this level is under the supervision of a Master Teacher.

Table 7.3

Differentiated Staffing Roles for a Center-Based Program

PREPROFESSIONAL ROLE

Teacher Aide

Description: The Teacher Aide assists in the implementation of program activities under the direct supervision of members of the early childhood teaching team. The Aide performs the daily, routine tasks that establish the basic foundation for a healthy and safe environment. The Aide works under the direct supervision of a Teacher or Master Teacher.

Minimum Qualifications: The Teacher Aide position is a precredential position that requires no formal training in early childhood education or child development. The Teacher Aide must be 18 years of age and enrolled in a course of study leading to acquisition of requisite knowledge and abilities for professional entry into the early childhood career ladder.

PROFESSIONAL ROLES

Assistant Teacher

Description: The Assistant Teacher is responsible for implementing program activities as part of a teaching team, providing help to the Teacher in all areas of the classroom program. This includes, but is not limited to, implementing curriculum, supervising children, communicating with parents, and providing a healthy and safe environment for children. The Assistant Teacher works under the direct supervision of a Teacher or Master Teacher.

Minimum Qualifications: Successful completion of a program conforming to the Model CDA Curriculum of the Council for Early Childhood Professional Recognition (CECPR, 1990) or successful completion of a systematic, comprehensive training program that prepares an individual to successfully acquire the CDA Credential through direct assessment.

Teacher

Description: The Teacher is responsible for the care and education of a group of children as part of a teaching team and functions as a team leader or co-leader. The Teacher plans and implements the curriculum and with active participation of other members of the teaching team, works with parents, and assesses the needs of individual children.

Minimum Qualifications: Successful completion of an associate degree from a program conforming to NAEYC's *Guidelines for Early Childhood Programs in Associate Degree Granting Institutions* (1985b) or successful completion of an associate degree in a related field plus 30 semester hours of professional studies in child development/early childhood education including 300 hours of supervised teaching experience in an early childhood program.

PROFESSIONAL ROLES (cont'd)

Master Teacher

Description: The Master Teacher provides a model classroom environment, articulates good early childhood practices, mentors and helps supervise other Aides, Assistant Teachers, and Teachers, develops and initiates new curriculum, and provides leadership to the teaching staff.

Minimum Qualifications:

► Successful completion of a baccalaureate degree from a program conforming to NAEYC's *Early Childhood Teacher Education Guidelines: Basic and Advanced* (1990a) or successful completion of a baccalaureate degree in a related field with 45 semester hours in child development and early childhood education including a minimum of 150 hours of supervised teaching experience at the primary grades and a minimum of 150 hours with either infants and toddlers or 3- to 5-year olds.

► 15 semester hours of post baccalaureate course work in any of the following areas: group dynamics; child, family, and community; adult development theory; curriculum development; child assessment; supervision and staff development.

► One year of successful teaching experience.

SPECIALTY ROLES

Early Childhood Special Educator

Description: The Special Educator is responsible for the care and education of a group of children which may include children with special needs or working with other Teachers to support the mainstreaming of children with special needs into their classrooms.

Minimum Qualifications: Successful completion of a baccalaureate degree in early childhood education or special education which includes a minimum of 30 semester hours of specialized course work in early childhood special education.

Early Childhood Subject Area Teacher

Description: Responsible for planning and implementing a curriculum in a specialty area such as art, music, physical education, or foreign language. May work directly with children or as part of a teaching team.

Minimum Qualifications: Successful completion of a baccalaureate degree in child development/ early childhood education with a subject area specialization or a comparable degree in a specialty field with at least 30 semester hours of course work in child development/early childhood education.

SPECIALTY ROLES (cont'd)

Parent Education Coordinator

Description: The Parent Education Coordinator is responsible for the planning and implementation of a parent involvement/parent education program.

Minimum Qualifications:

▶ Successful completion of a baccalaureate degree from a program conforming to NAEYC's *Early Childhood Teacher Education Guidelines: Basic and Advanced* (1990a) or successful completion of a baccalaureate degree in a related field with 45 semester hours in child development and early childhood education and 300 hours supervised field work with families.

▶ 15 semester hours of post baccalaureate course work in any of the following areas: family systems theory; family support; or parent education.

▶ One year of successful experience working with families.

Social Service Coordinator

Description: The Social Service Coordinator is responsible for the coordination of child and family services for a program or agency offering early childhood services, including nutrition, health, counseling, and special needs.

Minimum Qualifications:

▶ Successful completion of a baccalaureate degree from a program conforming to NAEYC's *Early Childhood Teacher Education Guidelines: Basic and Advanced* (1990a) or completion of a baccalaureate degree in a related field with 45 semester hours in child development or early childhood education and 300 hours supervised social service field work.

▶ 15 semester hours of post baccalaureate course work in any of the following areas: family systems theory; family support; social work; or human services.

▶ One year of successful experience working in the provision of social services.

Education Coordinator

Description: Responsible for implementing the educational goals and objectives of the center. The Education Coordinator supervises, trains, and evaluates staff; designs and monitors curriculum planning; and oversees the implementation of the curriculum by the teaching teams.

Minimum Qualifications:

▶ Successful completion of a baccalaureate degree from a program conforming to NAEYC's *Early Childhood Teacher Education Guidelines: Basic and Advanced* (1990a) or successful completion of a baccalaureate degree in a related field with 45 semester hours in child development or early childhood education including a minimum of 150 hours of supervised teaching experience at the primary grades and a minimum of 150 hours with either infants and toddlers or 3- to 5-year olds.

▶ 15 semester hours of post baccalaureate course work in any of the following areas: group dynamics; child, family, and community; curriculum development; curriculum evaluation; supervision and staff development; or program evaluation.

▶ Three years of successful teaching experience.

Program Administrator

Description: The Program Administrator monitors the administrative systems of the center including: the fiscal management of the program; recruiting and hiring personnel; facility management; board relations; and marketing and public relations. The Program Administrator also serves as a liaison with professional associations and regulatory agencies.

Minimum Qualifications:

▶ Successful completion of a baccalaureate degree from a program conforming to NAEYC's *Early Childhood Teacher Education Guidelines: Basic and Advanced* (1990a) or successful completion of a baccalaureate degree in a related field with 45 semester hours in child development or early childhood education including a minimum of 150 hours of supervised teaching experience at the primary grades and a minimum of 150 hours with either infants and toddlers or 3- to 5-year olds.

▶ 15 semester hours of post baccalaureate course work in any of the following areas: human resource management; legal issues, licensing, and regulations; program evaluation; financial management; proposal writing; public policy and child advocacy; or organization and administration of early childhood programs.

▶ Three years of successful teaching experience.

working experience at the center. It is important that such a system not undermine the intent of the career ladder — to encourage individuals to increase their level of education and training.

Unfortunately, implementing a career ladder doesn't automatically solve the perennial issue facing directors of how to increase the total pool of money allocated for salaries; it only allows one, as Jensen (1979) noted, to "distribute dissatisfaction more equitably." The issue of increasing funding is beyond the scope of this book, but there are a number of excellent resources that will help you find creative ways to raise salaries (Boyer, Gerst, & Eastwood, 1990; CCEP, 1990; Whitebook, Pemberton, Lombardi, & Galinsky, 1990).

Step 3. Establish a menu of benefits. Providing ample employee benefits is problematic for most small businesses in this country (Perreault, 1990). Centers that are part of a large agency network or those sponsored by a parent corporation are fortunate in that they may already have in place a comprehensive benefits plan for their employees. But even small centers can work to increase the amount and variety of benefits offered to staff. Some benefits like paid preparation time or free lunches can be provided to all employees. Other benefits, however, can be tied to longevity at the center and the individual's position on the center's career ladder. One way to accomplish this is to establish an indexed menu of benefits.

An index of benefits operates in much the same way as a salary index. Two categories of benefits, professional and personal, can be offered to employees. Professional benefits could include such things as membership in professional organizations, paid days to visit other programs, reimbursement for college classes, subscriptions to professional journals, and paid conference registrations. Personal benefits could include such things as health insurance, dental insurance, retirement/pension, child care tuition, paid vacation days, and sick days. Table 7.4 provides a list of the possible personal and professional benefits and an example of how the distribution of benefits would be awarded according to the employee's index level.

How such a benefit system is actually put into practice would out of necessity vary from center to center. For example, it might be decided that an employee at the 1.00 index level could choose one benefit from each of the personal and professional categories. At the 1.25 index level, another benefit choice could be added; and still another at 1.50. Under such a system, each employee would have the opportunity to choose from the menu of professional and personal benefits. From year to year, choices may change as the needs of the employee change. For example, an employee with a young child may be more interested in health insurance and partial payment of child care tuition. An older employee may choose dental insurance and reimbursement for conference fees. The attractiveness of such a plan is that it is not only equitable, but it also accommodates the changing needs of the individuals working at the center.

While the record keeping involved may be viewed as cumbersome, offering a menu of benefits is clearly advantageous to the employer. Increasing the type and variety of benefits offered to employees can have a direct impact on their level of commitment to the center. By assessing the kinds of benefits employees select from year to year, the center administrator can plan a budget for benefits that meets the changing needs of the staff. A center with a staff of young teachers who are using child care tuition as a major benefit each year would be able to plan for the lost revenue on child care slots within the center. A center with a staff of older employees who are interested in extended vacations or release time to visit other facilities would be able to budget for the hiring of substitutes. Accommodating staffs' changing needs in this fashion can't help but increase employee satisfaction and result in less staff turnover.

Step 4. Determine how individuals advance within the center. The final step in developing a career ladder for your center is to decide on the configuration and progression of steps for advancement. Table 7.5 provides an example of a career ladder configuration for a center. (This ladder does not include the preprofessional role of Teacher Aide or

Table 7.4

Personal and Professional Benefits

Each of these items constitutes one UNIT of benefit.

Personal	**Professional**
25% health insurance	membership to a professional association
25% dental insurance	1 day released time to visit another center
25% life insurance	1/4 tuition reimbursement for a college class
25% retirement/pension plan	subscription to a professional journal
25% child care tuition	conference/workshop registration
5 vacation/personal days	
5 sick days	

Benefit Index

An employee may choose according to his/her individual needs using the following guidelines.

Index Level

0.75 – 1 personal unit
1.00 – 1 personal unit and 1 professional unit
1.25 – 1 personal unit and 2 professional units
1.50 – 2 personal units and 2 professional units
1.75 – 2 personal units and 3 professional units
2.00 – 3 personal units and 3 professional units
2.25 – 3 personal units and 4 professional units
2.50 – 4 personal units and 4 professional units
2.75 – 4 personal units and 5 professional units
3.00 – 5 personal units and 5 professional units
3.25 – 5 personal units and 6 professional units
3.50 – 6 personal units and 6 professional units
3.75 – 6 personal units and 7 professional units

For example, an employee at the 2.50 index level may choose to use 4 personal units for health insurance (50% paid) plus 10 sick days and 4 professional units for 2 paid days to observe another school plus 1/2 tuition reimbursement for a college class.

Career Ladder Configuration for a Center-Based Program

Table 7.5

Level / Role	Assistant Teacher	Teacher	Master Teacher	Education Coordinator	Program Administrator
V				Step 1	Step 1
IV		Step 2 Step 1	Step 3 Step 2 Step 1	Step 3 Step 2 Step 1	Step 3 Step 2 Step 1
III		Step 3 Step 2 Step 1	Step 3 Step 2	Step 3 Step 2	Step 3 Step 2
II	Step 3 Step 2 Step 1	Step 3* Step 2* Step 1*			
I	Step 2 Step 1	Step 2*			

* denotes that teacher at this level is under the supervision of a Master Teacher

several of the specialty roles.) By plotting where each teacher is on the career ladder, you can plan staffing configurations and budget salaries and benefits. For example, Table 7.6 shows the staffing pattern of a full-day program with 140 preschool children divided into 7 classrooms of 20 children each. In this center, the Education Coordinator also assumes the role of Parent Education Coordinator. In a smaller center, individuals may have additional overlapping roles. For example, the Education Coordinator and the Program Administrator could be the same person.

The professional categories listed earlier in Table 7.2 designate a natural progression to be followed as an employee advances within the center. By obtaining education and/or job experience, the employee becomes eligible to assume new roles and responsibilities. Because salaries and benefits are indexed according to each of the steps within the career levels, the incentive to advance is clearly seen by the employee and can be used in charting new staff development goals.

At the time when progress toward achieving staff development goals is assessed, short-term and long-term professional opportunities for the staff member should be discussed. Helping an employee reach new professional goals is the responsibility of both the employer and the employee. Together a plan can be implemented to aid the professional advancement of each staff member. In this way, a center shows a commitment to staff and a willingness to retain and improve the quality of work life for its employees.

A Final Word

In this chapter we have seen how performance appraisal procedures and a career ladder for professional growth can serve as the organizational framework to support staff development. These two aspects of center functioning will play an integral role in ensuring that goals for individual change become a reality.

The performance appraisal processes detailed in this chapter rest on the premise that all employees, regardless of how outstanding their current teaching performance, can stretch and grow. The constructive feedback gleaned from the performance appraisal conference process provides the rationale for different areas that need to be addressed in a teacher's staff development action plan. The entire nature of the experience is thus changed from an adversarial one to a helpful and supportive one. The performance appraisal process thus serves a dual purpose; it acknowledges and rewards teachers' strengths while helping to expand their field of vision of what they could become.

If individualized staff development and performance appraisal processes are tied into a career ladder for professional advancement, then true lasting individual change has a chance to take hold. By clearly setting the standards and rewards for advancement, a career ladder helps individuals make decisions based on personal needs and goals. In essence, staff are helped to take control over their own career development. When implemented, these organizational structures and processes will serve as the supporting framework to energize employees to higher levels of performance and fulfillment.

Table 7.6

Sample Staffing Pattern for Center with 140 Students

TEACHING STAFF

Classroom	Staff	Career Ladder Level	
1	Teacher	Level III,	Step 2
	Assn't Teacher	Level II,	Step 3
	Teacher Aide		
2	Master Teacher	Level IV,	Step 2
	Assn't Teacher	Level I,	Step 1
	Teacher Aide		
3	Teacher	Level III,	Step 1
	Assn't Teacher	Level II,	Step 2
	Assn't Teacher	Level I,	Step 1
4	Master Teacher	Level III,	Step 3
	Teacher	Level II,	Step 2
	Teacher Aide		
5	Teacher	Level III,	Step 2
	Assn't Teacher	Level I,	Step 2
	Assn't Teacher	Level I,	Step 1
6	Teacher	Level IV,	Step 1
	Assn't Teacher	Level I,	Step 1
	Assn't Teacher	Level I,	Step 1
7	Master Teacher	Level IV,	Step 1
	Teacher	Level I,	Step 2
	Assn't Teacher	Level II,	Step 1

SPECIALTY ROLES

Education Coordinator/Parent Education Coordinator	Level IV,	Step 2
Program Administrator	Level IV,	Step 1
Music Teacher (1/2 time)	Level III,	Step 1
Early Childhood Special Educator (1/2 time)	Level III,	Step 3

SUPPORT STAFF

Secretary/receptionist
Cook

Chapter 8

Meshing Organizational and Individual Needs

As we have seen in preceding chapters, the development of individuals within a center and the development of the center itself are interrelated. Understanding the center as an integrated whole composed of many interconnected parts helps a director see the "big picture" of how the center's problems relate to individual problems experienced by staff. The director, as change agent, creates a collaborative work environment based on individualized staff development. This kind of staff development is ongoing, and focuses on enabling teachers to understand their own professional growth needs. The result is change, both individual and organizational. Figure 8.1 visually captures this dynamic relationship.

Meaningful growth and change, then, is accomplished through an understanding that the people who work at a center must be empowered and supported in their efforts to grow professionally. The role of the director is to act as a catalyst in identifying problem areas and helping teachers analyze the situation to find workable solutions. Strategies for achieving change flow out of the shared responsibility experienced by the director and staff.

How does this meshing of organizational and individual needs happen? This chapter will explore

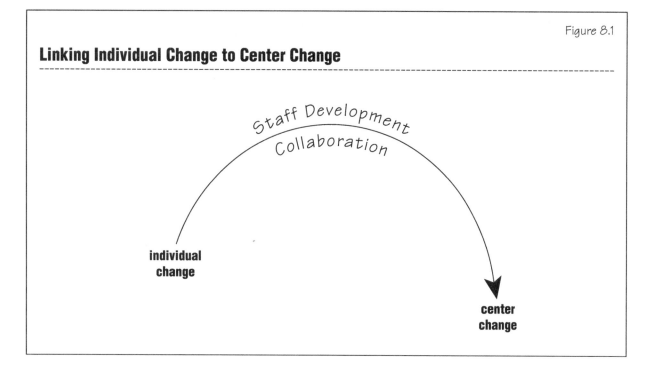

Figure 8.1

Linking Individual Change to Center Change

Staff Development
Collaboration

individual change

center change

the issue from two directions. First it will look at how directors can reduce resistance to change; then it will explore how they can establish a collaborative environment. To set the stage for this discussion, let us return to our case study, the Children's Corner, as an example of the change process in action.

Case Study: The Children's Corner

Martha was pleased. Her decision to keep anecdotal notes and develop an individual profile on each teacher helped her to get to know each of them better and understand why they were resisting change. She felt her interest in finding out about her teachers' personal lives, their previous teaching experience, career patterns, and special interests was beginning to break down the norms of isolation and competition that had permeated her center. It was also beginning to dissipate the dominant coalitions that had existed previously. Martha was particularly pleased with her decision to have Shelly observe in Georgia's classroom. This really bolstered Georgia's confidence and seemed to reduce some of her resistance to new ideas.

At her goal setting conference with each teacher in the fall, Martha asked the teachers to assess their own strengths and weaknesses. Together they talked about teaching goals that emphasized the teacher's strengths and ways to improve weaknesses. Martha felt that there were still problems to solve and she understood that change would not come swiftly. But she also knew she couldn't rush the process. She was hopeful that if she could win her teachers' trust on a one-to-one basis, she could then get them to begin to work more cooperatively as a group.

Overcoming Resistance to Change

Just as child care centers are dynamic systems which move toward organizational change in complex ways, so too do individual relationships within a center reflect complexity. The way individuals get along together, trust one another, feel loyalty toward the center, respond to authority, and take initiative are measures of how organizational processes support their personal and professional needs. As we have seen, understanding the individual within the child care setting is an essential ingredient affecting organizational change. This is particularly true when individuals resist change.

Resistance to change occurs for a variety of reasons, but most often resistant behaviors are rooted in fears of loss of autonomy and self-esteem or fear that one might fail in the midst of the change process. Dealing with resistance involves not only an understanding of the change process, but also an awareness of what the change represents to individuals on a personal level. Administrators who work objectively to depersonalize resistance try to build rapport with teachers and support staff with an empathic point of view (Saxl, 1989).

The Psychological Element

It is not uncommon to think of change in schools as an impersonal event rather than a highly personal process. However, it is people who change. Each individual in a center is different and responds to change in unique ways. How a director is attuned to the psychological states of teachers involved in the change process determines one of the conditions for successful change. Directors set the stage for change when they cue into teachers' levels of concern, the problems they perceive as inherent in the change process, and the resistances teachers exhibit.

Hopkins (1990) studied school climate and the psychological state of individual teachers. He assessed how teachers with different psychological states who worked in different school climates utilized educational ideas. Hopkins describes teachers' psychological states in terms of teachers' level of confidence, their overall interest in growth, the intensity of their interest in seeking out new experiences, and their sense of collegiality and belonging to the group. He found that those teachers who performed at a higher level of self-fulfillment and who were situated in schools which valued collaboration and collegiality were more likely to make use of new educational ideas. Hopkins concluded that when a school is committed to a more democratic work climate in which collegiality, collaboration, and communication are prevalent forms of school management, individual teachers adapt more readily to school changes.

What is perhaps most relevant from Hopkins' research to our present discussion of change in child care centers is his analysis of how teachers change in their psychological states. Hopkins analyzed four categories of teachers with respect to their psychological states. Teachers at the lowest self-actualizing level expressed a lack of self-confidence. Their main concern was focused on protecting themselves from losing control of their class. Hopkins found that these teachers were far less able to implement new ideas in practice than more confident teachers who had a strong self-concept and whose energy was focused on growth. Hopkins stresses that for teachers demonstrating a low-level of self-actualization, it is important to introduce change slowly and in small doses.

The connection between center climate and the teacher's psychological state cannot be overemphasized. The role of the director is crucial in establishing a positive, open atmosphere which actively supports teachers' growth. Dogmatic directors, as well as those who give only passive support, inhibit teachers from embracing change and achieving their goals. Unquestionably, teachers' degree of receptiveness to change is significantly affected by their perception of their administrator's support. It follows, then, that expanding opportunities for staff to formally discuss, help plan, and implement new curriculum and educational ideas provides the climate of administrative support for change to take hold.

Risk of Failure

One of the most common reasons that center staff find change difficult is that they view a specific change as representing a personal risk of failure. For many individuals, center change becomes a leap into the unknown. New beginnings, no matter how simple, are experienced by teachers as both fearful and hopeful (Wallenberg, 1980). It is this unknown, fearful aspect of change, attached to feelings of failure, which can become overwhelming for the teacher. "I just can't do this." "I'm too old to learn something new." "I have always done it this way. Why should I do it a different way?" These phrases indicate that teachers are opposed to changes because change raises the specter of failure in a highly

personal way. Teachers themselves, however, may not necessarily be aware of why they feel intimidated, angry, or opposed to specific changes.

Carol, a talented veteran teacher, was given a new age group of children to teach. She had difficulty adjusting since she had to adapt most of her tried and true activities for younger children. Patricia, her supervisor, visited Carol's class for the purpose of evaluating the curriculum. She expected to see the competent, experienced teacher she knew. Instead, she saw a chaotic room and a teacher suffering from low self-esteem. Patricia resolved to visit more often. Carol saw these visits as intrusive and not supportive. She began to dread her supervisor's observations and just couldn't seem to do anything right when Patricia was there. She became more angry, uncooperative, and resistant. Patricia felt rejected by Carol and annoyed at what appeared to be Carol's negative reaction to her new class. She began to think that Carol wasn't such a good teacher after all.

What can be done to remedy this situation? The supervisor is caught up in her own subjective point of view and thus is unable to help Carol view her situation objectively. The new class represents personal failure for Carol. Even experienced teachers like Carol begin to doubt themselves when faced with new situations in which they are not immediately successful. New situations can psychologically remove teachers from areas in which they feel very successful to areas of unfamiliarity and in which they feel unsuccessful, even out of control. Consequently, oppositional behavior such as passive and active withdrawal of support for proposed changes, limiting resources of time and energy, blocking, stalling, and procrastinating may be exhibited. These behaviors serve the function of preventing teachers from viewing themselves as failures (Saxl, 1989). Let's return now to our vignette about Carol and her supervisor

"Habits can't be thrown out the upstairs window. They have to be coaxed down the stairs one step at a time."

— Mark Twain

to see how their situation might be handled in a proactive, positive way.

Patricia was worried about the difficult relationship she had with Carol and she was determined to turn this potentially explosive situation around and make it a positive growth experience. She knew Carol was a teacher with extensive background and a great deal of experience. Ordinarily she demonstrated independence and autonomy. Because of Carol's need to adjust to a new age group of children, Patricia decided, for the time being, that Carol needed additional supervisory support. She initiated another conversation with Carol in which she acknowledged how difficult it must be for Carol to make the transition to a new age group. Patricia asked Carol what strategies might be implemented to assist her in building her confidence level. Carol stated that she had felt so physically exhausted lately that she had not had time to track down some of the books and curriculum aids she wanted to used with the children. Patricia felt she could offer direct help in this area. She then asked Carol if she would like to exchange visits to observe another teacher at the center. When Carol enthusiastically agreed, Patricia said she thought she could arrange for subs to take both classes once in a while so the two teachers could share information and plan together.

Change as Loss

Change often represents a personal loss for individuals. It may be as simple as a change in secretarial support or a change in the way a classroom is staffed. These seemingly uneventful changes may be experienced as a temporary loss of security until familiarity in the new situation is established. Change requires adjustment — adjustment in new relationships or adjustment in unlearning or modifying old behaviors. When change is introduced, individuals often feel that their former work was not worthwhile in the eyes of administrators or that it was not appreciated. The loss of what was formerly done becomes personally intimidating. "I have never done group time like that!" "Your idea for a math curriculum will never work here." "We've tried a substitute system like that before, and it didn't work at all."

Change can be perceived as a loyalty conflict where individuals feel that by embracing new approaches, they must reject the old. Unlearning old behaviors is a difficult process, one which involves the feelings and personal concerns of individuals. It is a wise director who understands the link between center change and personal change and views resistance as a means for the individual to preserve autonomy and a feeling that one's work is worthwhile and successful. Resistance is another way for teachers to say, "Your changes threaten my sense of security." Resistance, then, is a form of protection for teachers who worry that not only their work but their ideas, philosophy, and personal beliefs, are threatened by the proposed changes.

Not Everyone Sees Things the Same Way

We've shared several vignettes in this book that provide colorful examples of how individuals view the same situation in vastly different ways. Differing perceptions of reality occur because individuals come to any situation with varied experiences, diverse values and beliefs, and different expectations. Individuals holding different positions in the center are also privy to different types of information. This in itself can contribute to different perceptions of events. Because not everyone sees things the same way, the likelihood for resistance to change is increased.

McGreal (1983) asserts that a major hindrance to change in teacher performance is related to the incongruence between organizational expectations and what teachers are in fact required to do. For example, supervisors may expect teachers to improve classroom performance by conducting complicated screening procedures for children and keeping detailed records. Teachers may also be expected to perform these record-keeping procedures during class time when children are present, thus effectively hindering change in classroom performance. Resistance to change may simply be the teachers' only means of protesting unrealistic center expectations.

Establishing a Collaborative Environment

Collaboration is the vehicle for linking individual change to organizational change. Saxl (1989) defines collaboration as creating relationships in which influence is mutually shared. Establishing a collaborative work environment involves structuring specific workplace conditions that support cooperative relationships. The process is achieved by developing goal consensus and supporting opportunities for shared decision making. These elements enable teachers to reduce resistance and see the change process as their own.

Working Toward a Common Vision — Achieving Goal Consensus

Achieving lasting organizational change occurs only when individuals in a center feel a sense of commitment and connection to the center. In other words, they share a common vision of what the center should be. But before a staff can achieve a common vision, they need to achieve some degree of consensus as to just how a center's philosophy is put into practice through its goals and educational objectives. Having a clear, agreed-upon set of purposes directly affects the center's ability to carry out its mission. If a center's goals are ambiguous, then teachers will feel uncertain about their own teaching practices (Arbuckle & Murray, 1989; Smith & Scott, 1990).

Educational goals and objectives really center on priorities — those things we want children to do, to be, or to have as a result of their early childhood experience. But because staff have different values, their educational priorities may be different. Goal consensus, in many ways, reflects both a consensus of value orientations and the ability of individuals to compromise and tolerate differences of opinion. When teachers share goals in work settings, it is an indication that a harmony of purpose exists among the individuals in the center.

A good place to begin in establishing goal consensus among staff is with the center's stated philosophy. This statement can serve as a starting point to help discern differences in interpretation. This is more difficult than it may appear on the surface. Most philosophical statements are written in vague, abstract language. They are filled with cliches like "child-centered," "developmentally appropriate," and "individualized instruction." These are important concepts, but if true goal consensus is to be achieved, staff need to be able to articulate in behavioral terms just what they mean.

Involving Staff in Decision Making

Directors who are intent on building a collaborative work environment need to see shared decision making as a priority by setting aside time for teachers to meet concerning different aspects of the program. It is the interaction itself, more than the invitation, which leads to collaboration. Involvement in decision making can take a variety of forms. Joint planning, problem solving, and evaluating are but a few of the ways that staff can work together.

Rosenholtz (1989) notes some of the ways teachers benefit from shared decision making. She states that when teachers have the opportunity to debate issues, they clarify and broaden their own point of view when confronted with their colleagues' varied perspectives. When staff can reason through problems together, it reinforces the notion that a mutual exchange of ideas is the best way to improve everyone's teaching practice. The most valuable benefit derived from shared decision making, however, is that teachers find out that their colleagues have competencies and special skills which complement their own. The process can help teachers identify with and take pleasure in the work of their colleagues. This cannot help but strengthen their own connection to others in the center.

Setting Conditions for Collaboration

Collaborative work environments don't just happen. Learning to work cooperatively takes skill — skill that may not be in a teacher's repertoire of behaviors. Some teachers may be products of previous work environments that fostered competition rather than cooperation, where alienation and

Case Study: The Children's Corner

Martha planned several in-depth staff meetings for the sole purpose of "dissecting our philosophy...to arrive at a shared understanding of why we do what we do with children in our classrooms." She felt the first meeting was an unmitigated disaster. Every teacher seemed to be on the defensive. This was particularly true of some of the old-timers who seemed to assume this was a forum for espousing their point of view. Martha felt no one was really listening to one another. At the second meeting, however, things improved. Martha asked Bea to facilitate the discussion. All of a sudden, what had been a defensive, self-righteous posture on her behalf now became one of support and encouragement. Martha was heartened. She really felt some progress was being made in the group dynamics of the teachers.

At the third meeting, the teachers really began to open up. The discussion now focused on how they as individual teachers translated the center's philosophy into specific curricular practices. As the discussion unfolded, some concerns began to surface. Margaret, one of the younger teachers, admitted that she felt intimidated by the parents — most of whom, she felt, had unrealistic expectations for their children. "They equate learning with worksheets! I just don't know how to respond when they expect that I should be giving their four-year-olds direct instruction in reading," she confessed. Margaret's comment opened a floodgate of similar concerns. Several other teachers stated that they felt "developmentally appropriate" was a fuzzy term and weren't really sure what it meant precisely.

Martha suggested that since the staff had identified a problem, maybe it was time to collect some data to find out some possible solutions. Teachers agreed to fill out questionnaires on their values and beliefs as well as their perceptions about the center's degree of goal consensus. They also suggested that Martha do a formal observation of teaching practices in each classroom to see how the staff differed in their approaches. Without exception, the teachers expressed an interest in learning more about developmentally appropriate teaching practices.

In a subsequent meeting when some of the data were shared, Martha couldn't believe the growth in self analysis that was taking place. Teachers began to connect general philosophical terms such as "child-initiated" and "individualized instruction" to specific teaching practices. They analyzed their behavior in how they scheduled children's time, how they arranged their classroom space and materials, and how they interacted with children.

Previously, the teachers had stated that their problem was "parents who had unrealistic expectations for their kids." Now the problem was being recast. Instead of assigning blame to the parents, the teachers were beginning to see that the problem was their own inability to articulate and defend "developmentally appropriate" practices. Collectively they decided that the best place to start figuring out appropriate teaching practices might be to involve themselves in NAEYC's center accreditation process. Martha agreed that the self-study phase of accreditation was an excellent place to start. She was confident that as the teachers increased their own awareness of developmentally appropriate practices, their level of confidence would also increase. This in turn would change the adversarial relationship they were experiencing with parents into one where they could perceive themselves as helping to educate parents as partners in the education of their children.

isolation, the "everyone for himself," attitude prevailed. Without experience in collaborative decision making, teachers may not know how to adjust their own point of view in order to support group planning. Learning to work cooperatively also takes time. It is not uncommon for teachers first introduced to cooperative group experiences to become frustrated with the slowness of the process. It takes time to nurture reciprocity, trust, and supportive relationships. This means that directors must structure multiple opportunities for staff to make decisions together, to solve staff problems together, and to work together in the mutual exchange of instructional ideas and materials that will help improve program practices.

Rosenholtz (1989) explains why some teachers do not readily collaborate with their colleagues. Most individuals avoid situations which threaten to give away or highlight their instructional uncertainty. She says, "Indeed, under conditions of high uncertainty, colleagues are most apt to interpret requests for help as clear evidence of performance inadequacy" (p. 43). Teachers may or may not be willing to seek help from one another or from the director if the result is embarrassing or threatening to the individual. This is probably why in the previous vignette, Carol resisted the initial attempts of her supervisor to help her.

One way to help teachers work collaboratively is to acquaint them with current research on cooperative learning (Johnson & Johnson, 1987; Johnson, Johnson, & Holubec, 1986; Slavin, 1990). Staff development programs on cooperative learning encourage staff to learn and model cooperative behaviors as they develop strategies to use with their children. As they learn about different cooperative learning strategies for children, a conscious parallel is drawn between their actions and children's behavior. Collaboration emphasizes highlighting staff's common goals and arranging tasks so that goals can only be achieved by pooling the collective talent of individuals.

Another way that cooperation and collaboration can be enhanced is to acquaint teachers with the research on learning styles. In Chapter V, we provided some background information on learning styles and temperaments. Sharing this information with staff and allowing them opportunities to assess their own learning styles and temperaments can increase their appreciation for differences among people. Without this broader perspective of human behavior, we are apt to think of ourselves as the "norm" and anyone not like us as the aberration. Appreciating individual differences is the first step to building the sense of cohesion that binds people together in a cooperative spirit. It was for this reason that Martha included a staff inservice on the topic of learning styles as one of her objectives on the action plan that you read at the end of Chapter IV.

Team teaching and mentoring are also powerful tools for increasing helping behaviors among teachers. Individuals who team teach, equally sharing classroom responsibilities, have built-in, ongoing opportunities to talk about what they do in the classroom. In contrast to teachers in isolated settings, team teachers communicate more, are more experienced in decision making, and work more closely with their supervisors regarding decisions. Rosenholtz (1989) also believes that team teaching results in a substantial increase in the teachers' ability to give and take advice.

Mentoring has also been shown to be particularly effective in reducing teacher isolation and increasing staff cohesiveness (Loucks-Horsley, 1987). The supportive role that the mentor plays in guiding the professional development of a less-experienced teacher has the ancillary effect of reducing some of the supervisory responsibility of directors. Driscoll, Peterson, and Kauchak (1985) state, "What separates new teachers from experienced professionals is not only years of experience, but also the knowledge and skills that have developed over those years. Mentoring systems provide a process for passing on this knowledge to beginning teachers in a systematic rather than haphazard way" (p. 108).

In their research, Driscoll and her colleagues found that mentoring programs not only increase teachers' productivity, but also their commitment to the profession, thus preventing teacher attrition. This is important because the foundation for collegial, cooperative relationships rests in large part on the sense of staff stability at a center. Centers that experience high turnover will have more difficulty in both initiating and sustaining collaboration.

What Have We Learned From the Children's Corner?

Let's review the case study we've shared in this book and see what lessons we can learn from Martha's experience. We've followed her progress over her first year as director of the Children's Corner. Clearly, the most important lesson Martha learned was that change takes time. In September, Martha was confronted with the challenge of changing the discrepancy between the stated philosophy of the center's structure and the every day teaching practices that were in place. She was also confronted with some staff members that were uncooperative and sometimes hostile. But Martha was patient and determined.

Martha began with a top-down model of change in order to modify the center norms of isolation and resistance. She hoped her efforts would create a more collaborative climate for teachers. Her goal was to build a unified team out

Martha did not want to lose the momentum generated at the last few staff meetings. She feared that if summer vacation came without a well-thought-out plan of action committed to paper, the enthusiasm and cooperation she had seen during the previous month might be lost. She sent a memo to the staff suggesting a half-day retreat on a Saturday in mid-May. Initially, Bea and Mary indicated that they had conflicting plans, but when Georgia and the rest of the staff enthusiastically supported the idea, even Bea and Mary rearranged their schedules to be free.

At the retreat, Martha and the teachers spent some time deciding how much it would cost and how to arrange the time that would be needed to conduct the accreditation self study. They looked at the possibility of purchasing new equipment and how to allocate dollars in the following year's budget for this purpose. They also decided to begin a peer mentoring program based on Shelly's and Pat's experience. Finally, several younger staff members made a case for getting substitute teachers so that staff could visit other centers. They felt these visits would give a basis of comparison with their own program. They agreed that the whole accreditation process would take about eighteen months. The teachers met on two more occasions to develop a center action plan so that work could be divided equitably. Individual goal-setting conferences were planned. The individual and organizational change process was underway.

of her staff. She began by making some changes in her own administrative behavior that would model the cooperative, trusting behavior she hoped to nurture in her staff.

As the year progressed, Martha and her staff implemented individual action plans that furthered the goal of achieving a collaborative environment for the center as a whole. Teachers began sharing resources, observing each other's rooms, and working together to try out new ideas. Staff meetings evolved from a top-down directed approach to one where teachers took a more active role in determining the agenda and facilitating the discussion.

It was not until spring that teachers internalized a collective sense of responsibility for center change and improvement. When it happened, though, the effect was powerful. Martha was amazed at how the teachers zeroed in on a very fundamental problem in the center — the lack of a shared vision of what "developmentally appropriate" practice really meant in action. Martha facilitated the problem clarification discussion, helped the teachers articulate a goal, and assisted them in deciding where they wanted to put their energies the following year. Martha felt their action plan was a bit too ambitious, but she also knew good action plans are not engraved in stone. This one could be modified as activities were initiated the following September. In the meantime, Martha was busy meeting with individual teachers to develop their goals blueprints and staff development action plans for the following year. At their orientation meeting in late August, she would then be prepared to show them how their individual goals meshed with the center's goals (Sample Form #8). We've included copies of Martha's working papers to show you how she did this.

All in all, Martha's experience was a positive one. She had grown professionally in learning how to practice the collaborative skills she embraced philosophically. She looked forward to her second year on the job with a sense of pride and anticipation. She knew there was still a lot to do, but she felt ready and eager to handle the challenges ahead.

A Final Word

In collaborative child care work environments, organizational change is a shared goal between director and teachers. Teachers view one another as mutual facilitators in achieving individual professional goals and those goals of the center. Collaboration offers many benefits to a center-based program. Positive interpersonal relationships increase teachers' self esteem and encourage them to support the work of colleagues. Acceptance and instructional sharing, in turn, lead to a shared vision, greater productivity, and cohesion as a staff. Center-based change is achieved when individuals develop a commitment to make the goals of the center their own.

In this book we have seen that an important part in creating the climate for change depends on how events are planned and how effectively time is

Action Plan

Goal: Staff will have a shared vision of "developmentally appropriate" practice and be able to communicate that vision to parents

Objectives	Action Steps	Who Responsible	Time	Resources Needed (people, materials, $$$)	Evaluation Checkpoints
To clarify the center's philosophy and educational objectives	1. Complete Assessment Tools #5, #2 2. Committee write draft of philosophy. Bring to whole staff 3. Staff read Developmentally Appropriate Practice. Discuss at 6 staff meetings	1. all staff, martha tabulate results 2. Pat, Christine, Georgia, Scott 3. Two staff lead each meeting	1. ½ hr staff 1 hr. martha 2. 20 hrs during fall 3. 3 hrs to read book. 1 hr to prepare group discussion	1. Xeroxing $5 2. Each committee member to get 4 hrs released time 3. Read on own time. Discussion leaders get 2 hrs. prep time = $84. Books $6 each × 15	1. August 2. Draft philosophy in Nov. final in Dec. 3. Do Assessment Tool #10 after 14th meeting. Do Assessment Tool #5 in December
To initiate the self-study phase of NAEYC center accreditation	1. get materials from NAEYC 2. get approval from board. 3. conduct classroom observations. Tools #12, 13,14,15. to assess areas in need of improvement	1. Martha 2. Martha 3. Bea and Shelly to coordinate observations. all staff notate observations 2 in Fall, 2 Spring	1. 1 hr. 2. 2 hrs. write proposal 3. 3 hrs to observe ea. classroom × 2 times × 7 classes	1. initial fee + misc. expenses $150 2. Xeroxing for board + copies of NAEYC accreditation criteria guidelines $60 3. Released time for observations substitutes = $192	1. By Sept 15 2. Presentation in October 3. ½ observations done by 12/31 rest done by 5/31
To increase parents' understanding of developmentally appropriate practices	1. Xerox handouts for monthly newsletter 2. conduct 6 parent education meetings 3. Distribute Tool #11 to parents	1. Scott 2. Pat to coordinate parent meetings 3. Martha	1. during planning time 2. Pat - 1 hr 1a. month. 6 items to 2 staff ca. 5 hrs. each team 3. 2 hrs to tally.	1. Approx $35/month (4 pages, 165 parents) 2. Paid planning time 30 hrs @ $8/hr =$240 food = $150 misc supplies = $50 3. Xeroxing $15 postage $25	1. one article per month 2. workshops in Nov to April 3. Distribute Tool #11 again in May.

Working Together Toward a Common Vision

Date: *June, 1991*

Center Goal

Staff will have a shared vision of "developmentally appropriate" practice and communicate that vision to parents.

Objectives

To clarify the center's philosophy and educational objectives

To initiate the self-study phase of NAEYC center accreditation

To increase parents' understanding of developmentally appropriate practices

Name: *Pat*
- *coordinate committee for parent workshops*
- *conduct one workshop on math/science*
- *serve on committee to rewrite philosophy*

Name: *Shelly*
- *with Bea coordinate classroom observations*
- *conduct 4 observations*
- *conduct staff meeting w/ Margaret on DAP*

Name: *Georgia*
- *coordinate committee to rewrite philosophy*
- *conduct parent workshop on guidance*
- *coordinate refreshments for staff meetings*

Name: *Bea*
- *with Shelly coordinate classroom observations*
- *conduct 4 observations*
- *make posters announcing parent workshops*

Name: *Scott*
- *select articles for parent newsletter*
- *conduct staff meeting w/Christine on DAP*
- *conduct 4 observations*

Name: *Christine*
- *serve on committee to rewrite philosophy*
- *conduct staff meeting w/ Scott on DAP*
- *coordinate refreshments for parent workshops*

used during the change process. Teachers and directors need enough time to identify the problem, gather data, develop an action plan, implement it, and evaluate progress. Not allocating sufficient time for any one of these steps in the change process can jeopardize the entire process.

Individuals also need time to get to know one another, share ideas and information, and to learn how to work together. If teachers are eager to work on implementing a new curriculum but meetings are sporadic and twenty minutes long, then it will be difficult for them to feel they can successfully complete their work. Time is all too often a neglected resource. Ensuring a realistic time line for the change process is a necessary condition for successful change.

Before embarking on a course of change, it is important to consider whether the center can provide the resources needed to accomplish its intended goals. Financial resources are necessary for materials and equipment, for hiring substitutes, for evaluation materials, and a host of other related expenses. Providing necessary resources also includes resources of energy and expertise. And we can't neglect the human element. It is a tremendously important energy resource to give teachers undivided attention to listen to their concerns. Allowing time to develop relationships with staff and support their needs is a precondition for successful change. Information and expertise may also be seen as resources. Building a network of consultants and links to the community through parents, professionals, and professional associations who can provide expertise is a necessary element in the change process.

Successful change, as we have seen, is dependent on concrete, individual and center action plans. The action plans must begin with a clear statement of the proposed goal so that staff members will have a common vision of what the changes will be. Explicitly delineating objectives, the activities, and who will carry out the activities is essential to the smooth implementation of the change process. In addition, carefully planning evaluation procedures helps participants see that progress is being made. Disorganized and haphazard action plans make it difficult to avoid ambiguity, role confusion, and conflict.

Finally, in order to improve our centers, we must make changes in the structures and processes of the center that will support change in individuals. This book has shown that the professional development of staff is the vehicle for achieving center-based change. A holistic view of change that meshes individual needs and goals with center needs and goals is tied to an understanding that a program is an integrated whole made up of different, though interrelated parts. Such a systems view can help directors better understand why people resist change and the conditions necessary for successfully accomplishing the change process. Lasting center change will only occur when the participants build a shared vision linking organizational needs to the needs of individual people. Collaboration, shared decision making, and building a cohesive sense of purpose are all elements that will help ensure this happens.

References

Abbott-Shim, M. (1990, January). In-service training: A means to quality care. *Young Children*, 14-18.

Albrecht, K. (1989, December). Helping teachers grow: Separating competency from compensation. *Child Care Information Exchange*, 37-38.

Albrecht, K. (1985, March). Monitoring, measuring, and evaluating teacher performance. *Child Care Information Exchange*, 8-10.

Anderson, K., & Durant, O. (1989, Winter). Orchestrating staff development for all school personnel. *Journal of Staff Development*, *10*(1), 14-17.

Anderson, E. & Shannon, A. (1988, January/February). Toward a conceptualization of mentoring. *Journal of Teacher Education*, 38-42.

Arbuckle, M., & Murray, L. (1989). *Building systems for professional growth: An action guide*. Andover, MA: The Regional Laboratory for Educational Improvement of the Northeast and Islands.

Arends, R., & Arends, J. (1977). *Systems change strategies in educational settings*. New York: Human Sciences Press.

Association of Teacher Educators. (1985). *Developing career ladders in teaching*. Reston, VA: Author.

Ayers, W. (1989). *The good preschool teacher*. New York: Teachers College Press.

Bandura, A. (1982). Self-efficacy mechanism in human agency. *American Psychologist, 37*, 122-147.

Baratta-Lorton, M. (1976). *Mathematics their way*. Menlo Park, CA: Addison Wesley

Barker, L., Wahlers, K., Watson, K., & Kibler, R. (1987). *Groups in process*. Englewood Cliffs, NJ: Prentice Hall.

Bean, R., & Clemes, H. (1978). *Elementary principal's handbook: New approaches to administrative action*. West Nyack, NY: Parker Publishing Co.

Beer, M. (1980). *Organization change and development: A systems view*. Glenview, IL: Scott, Foresman and Company.

Berman, P., & McLaughlin, M. W. (1976). Implementation of educational innovations. *Educational Forum, 40*, 345-370.

Bernardin, H. J., & Beatty, R. W. (1984). *Performance appraisal: Assessing human behavior at work.* Boston: Kent Publishing.

Berrueta-Clement, J., Schweinhart, L., Barnett, W., Epstein, A., & Weikart, D. (1984). Changed lives: *The effects of the Perry Preschool Program on youth through age 19.* Ypsilanti, MI: High/Scope.

Blake, R., & Mouton, J. (1969). *Building a dynamic corporation through grid organization development.* Reading, MA: Addison-Wesley.

Bowditch, J., & Buono, A. (1982). *Quality of work life assessment.* Boston: Auburn House.

Boyer, M., Gerst, C., & Eastwood, S. (1990). *Between a rock and a hard place: Raising rates to raise wages.* Minneapolis, MN: Child Care Workers Alliance.

Bronfenbrenner, U. (1979). *The ecology of human development.* Cambridge, MA: Harvard University Press.

Burden, P. R. (1987). *Establishing career ladders in teaching.* Charles Thomas.

Burke, P., Christensen, J., & Fessler, R. (1984). *Teacher career stages: Implications for staff development.* Bloomington, IN: Phi Delta Kappa Educational Foundation.

Caruso, J.J., & Fawcett, M. T. (1986). *Supervision in early childhood education: A developmental perspective.* New York: Teachers College.

Child Care Employee Project. (1990). *How and why of salary schedules.* Oakland, CA: Author.

Christensen, J. (1989). Master teacher: A way to restructure the profession. In J. A. Braun, Jr. (Ed.), *Reforming teacher education: Issues and new directions* (pp. 49-65). New York: Garland Publishing.

Christensen, J., McDonnell, J., & Price, J. (1988). *Personalizing staff development: The career lattice model.* Bloomington, IN: Phi Delta Kappa Educational Foundation.

Cogan, M. (1973). *Clinical supervision.* Boston: Houghton Mifflin.

Colette, C., & Russell, J. (1988, Spring). Facilitating educational change through data-based staff development. *Journal of Staff Development, 9*(2), 16-21.

Cornett, L. (1985, November). Trends and emerging issues in career ladder plans. *Educational Leadership, 43*(3), 6-10.

Corwin, R. G. (1965). Professional persons in public organizations. *Educational Administration Quarterly, 1,* 19-28.

Council for Early Childhood Professional Recognition. (1990). *Child Development Associate assessment system and competency standards for preschool caregivers.* Washington, DC: Author.

Dillon-Peterson, B. (1981). *Staff development/organizational development.* Reston, VA: ASCD.

Dodge, D. T. (1988). *The creative curriculum.* Washington, DC: Teaching Strategies.

Dresden, J., & Myers, B. K. (1989, January). Early childhood professionals: Toward self-definition. *Young Children,* 62-66.

Driscoll, A., Peterson, K., & Kauchak, D. (1985). Designing a mentor system for beginning teachers. *Journal of Staff Development, 6*(2), 108-117.

Duke, D., & Stiggins, R. (1986). *Teacher evaluation.* Washington, DC: National Teachers Association.

Dunn, R., & Dunn, K. (1978). *Teaching students through their individual learning styles*. Reston, VA: Reston Publishing.

Dyer, W. (1984). *Strategies for managing change*. Reading, MA: Addison-Wesley Publishing.

Erikson, E. H. (1968). *Identity: Youth and crisis*. New York: W. W. Norton.

Feeney, S., & Kipnis, K. (1989, November). Code of ethical conduct and statement of commitment. *Young Children*. 24-29.

Firestone, W. A., & Corbett, W. (1988). Planned organizational change. In N. Boyan (Ed.) *Handbook of research on educational administration* (pp. 321-340). White Plaines, NY: Longman.

Fliegel, F., & Kivlin, J. (1966). Attributes of an innovation as factors in diffusion. *American Journal of Sociology, 72*, 235-248.

Fox, R., & Schmuck, R. (1973). *Diagnosing professional climate of schools*. Fairfax, VA: Learning Resources Corp.

Fullan, M. (1991). *The meaning of educational change* (2nd edition). New York: Teachers College Press.

Fuller, F. (1969). Concerns of teachers: A developmental conceptualization. *American Educational Research Journal, 6*, 207-226.

Gehreke, N. J. (1988, January-February). On preserving the essence of mentoring as one form of teacher leadership. *Journal of Teacher Education*, 43-45.

Getzels, J., & Guba, E. G. (1957, Winter). Social behavior as an administrative process. *The School Review, 65*, 423-441.

Giammatteo, M. C. (1975). *Training package for a model city staff. Field paper no 15*. Portland, OR: Northwest Regional Educational Laboratory, 30.

Glickman, C. D. (1981). *Developmental supervision: Alternative practices for helping teachers*. Alexandria, VA: Association for Supervision and Curriculum Development.

Glickman, C. D. (1985). *Supervision of instruction: A developmental approach*. Boston: Allyn & Bacon.

Gray, W., & Gray, M. (1985, November). Synthesis of research on mentoring beginning teachers. *Educational Leadership, 43*(3), 37-47.

Greenberg, P. (1975). *Day care do-it-yourself staff growth program*. Winston-Salem, NC: Kaplan Press.

Greenman, J. (1988). *Caring spaces, learning places*. Redmond, WA: Exchange Press.

Guskey, T. (1986, May). Staff development and the process of teacher change. *Educational Research*, 5-12.

Hackett, G., & Betz, H. (1981). A self-efficacy approach to the career development of women. *Journal of Vocational Behavior, 18*, 326-339.

Hall, G., & Loucks, S. (1978, September). Teacher concerns as a basis for facilitating and personalizing staff development. *Teachers College Record, 80*(1), 36-55.

Hall, J. (1988). *The competence connection*. The Woodlands, TX: Woodstead Press.

Havelock, R. G., & Havelock, M. C. (1973). *Training change agents*. Ann Arbor, MI: Institute for Social Research.

Hegland, S. M. (1984, May). Teacher supervision: A model for advancing professional growth. *Young Children*, 3-10.

Hersey, P. & Blanchard, K. (1982). *Management of organizational behavior*. Englewood Cliffs, NJ: Prentice-Hall.

Herzberg, F. (1966). *Work and the nature of man*. New York: World Publishing.

Hohmann, M., Banet, B., & Weikart, D., (1979). *Young children in action*. Ypsilanti, MI: High/Scope.

Hopkins, D. (1990). Integrating staff development and school improvement: A study of teacher personality and school climate. In B. Joyce (Ed.), *Changing school culture through staff development* (pp. 41-67). Reston, VA: ASCD.

Hord, S.M., Rutherford, W., Huling-Austin, L., & Hall, G. (1987). *Taking charge of change*. Alexandria, VA: ASCD.

Horn, J. L., & Cattell, R. B. (1967). Age differences in fluid and crystallized intelligence. *Acta Psychologica*, *26*, 107-129.

Hostetler, L., & Klugman, E. (1982, September). Early childhood job titles: One step toward professional status. *Young Children*, *37*, 13-22.

Hoy, W., & Miskel, C. (1987). *Educational administration*. New York: Random House.

Hunsaker P., & Alessandra, A. (1980). *The art of managing people*. New York: Simon & Schuster.

Hunt, D. (1971). *Matching models in education*. Toronto: Ontario Institute for Studies in Education.

Jensen, J. (1979). *Basic guide to salary management*. Los Angeles: The Grantsmanship Center.

Johnson, D., & Johnson, R. (1987, November). Research shows the benefits of adult cooperation. *Educational Leadership*, 27-30.

Johnson, D., Johnson, R., & Holubec, E. (1986). *Circles of Learning: Cooperation in the classroom*. Edina, MN: Interaction Book Company.

Johnston, J. (1984, March). Assessing staff problems: Key to effective staff development. *Child Care Information Exchange*, 1-4.

Johnston, J. (1988, September). A performance based approach to staff evaluation. *Child Care Information Exchange*, 10-13.

Jones, A. P., & James, L. R. (1979). Psychological climate: Dimensions and relationships of individual and aggregated work environment perceptions. *Organizational Behavior and Human Performance*, *23*, 201-250.

Jorde-Bloom, P. (1982). *Avoiding burnout: Strategies for managing time, space, and people in early childhood education*. Lake Forest, IL: New Horizons.

Jorde-Bloom, P. (1986a, July). Organizational norms — our blueprint for behavior. *Child Care Information Exchange*, 5-9.

Jorde-Bloom, P. (1986b, Fall). The administrator's role in the innovation decision process. *Child Care Quarterly*, *15*(2), 182-197.

Jorde-Bloom, P. (1988a). *A great place to work*. Washington, DC: National Association for the Education of Young Children.

Jorde-Bloom, P. (1988b). Closing the gap: An analysis of teacher and administrator perceptions of organizational climate in the early childhood setting. *Teaching & Teacher Education: An International Journal of Research and Studies*, *15*(4), 9-11.

Jorde-Bloom, P. (1988c). Factors influencing overall job satisfaction and organizational commitment in early childhood work environments. *Journal of Research in Early Childhood Education, 3*(2), 107-122.

Jorde-Bloom, P. (1989a). *Measuring work attitudes: Technical manual for the Early Childhood Job Satisfaction Survey and the Early Childhood Work Environment Survey.* Brandon, VT: Psychology Press.

Jorde-Bloom, P. (1989b, Winter). Professional orientation: Individual and organizational perspectives. *Child and Youth Care Quarterly, 18*(4), 227-240.

Jorde-Bloom, P., & Ford, M. (1988). Factors influencing administrators' decisions regarding the adoption of computer technology. *Journal of Educational Computing Research, 4*(1), 31-47.

Joyce, B. (Ed.). (1990). *Changing school culture through staff development.* Alexandria, VA: ASCD.

Joyce, B., & McKibbin, M. (1982, November). Teacher growth states and school environments. *Educational Leadership*, 36-41.

Joyce, B., & Showers, B. (1988). *Student achievement through staff development.* New York: Longman.

Jung, C. (1923). *Psychological types.* New York: Harcourt Brace.

Kagan, S. L. (1990). *Policy perspectives: Excellence in early childhood education — Defining next-decade strategies.* Washington, DC: U. S. Department of Education, Office of Research and Improvement, Information Services.

Kast, F. S., & Rosenzweig, J. E. (1970). *Organization and management: A systems approach.* New York: McGraw-Hill.

Katz, D., & Kahn, R. (1978). *The social psychology of organizations.* New York: Wiley.

Katz, L. (1972). Developmental stages of preschool teachers. *Elementary School Journal, 73,* 50-55.

Katz, L., & Ward, E. (1978). *Ethical behavior.* Washington, DC: National Association for the Education of Young Children.

Katz, L., & Raths, J. (1986). Dispositions as goals for teacher education. *Teaching and Teacher Education,* 1(4), 301-307.

Keirsey, D., & Bates, M. (1978). *Please understand me.* Del Mar, CA: Prometheus Nemesis.

Kilman, R. H. (1984). *Beyond the quick fix.* San Francisco: Jossey Bass.

Kirton, M. J. (1976). Adaptors and innovators: A description and measure. *Journal of Applied Psychology, 61,* 622-629.

Kroeger, O., & Thuesen, J. (1988). *Typetalk.* New York: Dell Publishing.

Kurtz, R. (1991, Jan/Feb). Stabilizer, catalyst, troubleshooter, or visionary — Which are you? *Child Care Information Exchange,* 27-31.

Lawrence, G. (1982). *People type and tiger stripes.* Gainsville, FL: Center for Applications of Pscyhological Type, Inc.

Lay-Dopyera, M., & Dopyera, J. (1990). *Becoming a teacher of young children.* New York: McGraw Hill.

Levine S. (1989). *Promoting adult growth in schools.* Boston: Allyn & Bacon.

Lewin, K. (1951). *Field theory in social science.* New York: Harper & Row.

Lightfoot, S. (1983). *Good high schools: Portraits of character and culture.* New York: Basic Books.

Little, J. W. (1982). Norms of collegiality and experimentation: Workplace conditions of school success. *American Educational Research Journal, 19,* 325-340.

Loevinger, J. (1976). *Ego development.* San Francisco: Jossey-Bass.

Loucks-Horsley, S. (1987). *Continuing to learn: A guidebook for teacher development.* Andover, MA: Regional Laboratory for Educational Improvement of the Northeast and Islands.

Luft, J., & Ingham, H. (1973). The Johari Window. *Annual handbook for group facilitators.* San Diego, CA: University Associates.

McCarthy, B. (1980). *The 4 MAT system.* Oak Brook, IL: EXCEL, Inc.

McDonnell, J., Christensen, J., & Price, J. (1989, March). *Teachers' career stages and availability and appropriateness of incentives in teaching.* Paper presented at the annual meeting of the American Educational Research Association, San Francisco.

McGreal, T. (1983). *Successful teacher evaluation.* Reston, VA: ASCD.

McGregor, D. (1960). *The human side of enterprise.* New York: McGraw-Hill.

McLaughlin, M. W., & Pfeifer, R. S. (1988). *Teacher evaluation: Improvement, accountability, and effective learning.* New York: Teachers College Press.

Maslow, A. A. (1954). *Motivation and personality.* New York: Harper and Row.

Mertens, S. & Yarger, S. (1988, January-February). Teaching as a profession: Leadership, empowerment and involvement. *Journal of Teacher Education,* 32-37.

Miles, M. B. (1965). Planned change and organizational health: Figure and ground. In M. Miles (Ed.), *Change processes in the public schools* (pp. 11-34). Eugene, OR: University of Oregon, Center for Advanced Study of Educational Administration.

Moos, R. H. (1976). *The human context.* New York: Wiley.

Morgan, G. (1991). *Career development systems in early care and education: A concept paper.* Boston: Wheelock College Center for Career Development in Early Care and Education.

Mowday, R., Steers, R., & Porter, L. (1979). The measurement of organizational commitment. *Journal of Vocational Behavior, 14,* 224-247.

Mumford, F. (1972). *Job satisfaction.* London: Longman.

Myers, I.B. (1980). *Gifts differing.* Palto Alto, CA: Consulting Psychologist Press.

Myers, I. B. (1980). *Introduction to type.* Palo Alto, CA: Consulting Psychologists Press.

Nadler, D., & Tushman, M. (1983). A general diagnostic model for organizational behavior: Applying a congruence perspective. In J. R. Hackman, E. Lawler, & L. Porter (Eds.), *Perspectives on behavior in organizations* (pp. 112-124). New York: McGraw Hill.

National Association for the Education of Young Children. (1984). *Accreditation criteria and procedures.* Washington, DC: Author.

National Association for the Education of Young Children. (1985a). *Guide to accreditation*. Washington, DC: Author.

National Association for the Education of Young Children. (1985b). *Guidelines for early childhood education programs in associate degree granting institutions*. Washington, DC: Author.

National Association for the Education of Young Children. (1990a). *Early childhood teacher education guidelines: Basic and advanced*. Washington, DC: Author.

National Association for the Education of Young Children. (1990b). *NAEYC model of early childhood professional development* (Draft). Washington, DC: Author.

Neugebauer, B. (1990, August). Evaluation of director by staff. *Child Care Information Exchange*, 20-21.

Neugebauer, B. (1990, September/October). Are you listening? *Child Care Information Exchange*, 62.

Owens, R. G. (1981). *Organizational behavior in education*. Englewood Cliffs, NJ: Prentice-Hall.

Parkay, F., & Damico, S. (1989, Spring). Empowering teachers for change through faculty-driven school improvement. *Journal of Staff Development*, *10*(2), 8-14.

Perreault, J. (1990, September/October). Improving employee benefits. Doing the right thing. *Child Care Information Exchange*, 35-38.

Peters, D. L., & Kostelnik, M. (1981). Current research in day care personnel preparation. In S. Kilmer (Ed.), *Advances in Early Education and Day Care* (vol. 2, pp. 29-60). Greenwich, CT: JAI Press.

Peters, T. J., & Waterman, R. H. (1982). *In search of excellence: Lessons learned from America's best-run companies*. New York: Random House.

Pofahl, D., & Potaracke, R. (1983, July). Staff development: A cooperative approach. *Young Children*, *38*(5), 14-20.

Porter, L. W., & Lawler, E. E. (1968). *Managerial attitudes and performance*. Homewood, IL: Dorsey.

Public Management Institute. (1980). *Non-profit management skills for women managers*. San Francisco: PMI.

Reddin, W. J. (1970). *Managerial effectiveness*. New York: McGraw-Hill.

Rizzo, J., House, R., & Lirtzman, S. (1970). Role conflict and role ambiguity in complex organizations. *Administrative Science Quarterly*, *15*, 150-163.

Rogers, E. (1983). *Diffusion of innovations* (3rd ed.). New York: The Free Press.

Rogers, D., Waller, C., & Perrin, M. (1987, May). Learning more about what makes a good teacher good through collaborative research in the classroom, *Young Children*, 34-39.

Rosenholtz, S. (1989). *Teachers' workplace*. New York: Longman.

Saxl, E. (1989). *Assisting change in education: Trainer's manual*. Alexandria, VA: Association for Supervision and Curriculum Development.

Scallan, P. (1988, Oct.). In search of excellent training: Tuning in to right brain/left brain thinking. *Child Care Information Exchange*, 7-11.

Scallan, P., & Kalinowski, M. (1990, June). Improving staff performance. *Child Care Information Exchange*, 15-18.

Schwind, H. (1987). Performance appraisal: The state of the art. In S. Dolan and R. Schuler (Eds.), *Personnel and human resources management in Canada* (pp. 197-210). Toronto: West Publishing.

Schwind, H. (1991, January). *Bases for effective human resource management.* Paper presented at the Child Care Connections Conference, Halifax, Nova Scotia.

Sciarra, D., & Dorsey, A. (1990). *Developing and administering a child care center.* Albany, NY: Delmar Publishers.

Schein, E. (1985). *Organizational culture and leadership.* San Francisco: Jossey-Bass.

Schmuck, R. A., & Runkel, P. J. (1985). *The handbook of organization development in schools.* Prospect Heights, IL: Waveland.

Seashore, S. E., Lawler, E., Mirvis, P., & Cammann, C. (1983). *Assessing organizational change.* New York: John Wiley & Sons.

Sergiovanni, T., & Elliott, D. (1975). *Educational and organizational leadership in elementary schools.* Englewood Cliffs, NJ: Prentice Hall.

Slavin, R. E. (1990). *Cooperative learning: Theory, research, and practice.* Englewood Cliffs, NJ: Prentice-Hall.

Smith, S., & Scott, J. (1990). *The collaborative school.* Reston, VA: National Association of Secondary School Principals.

Stonehouse, A., (1986). *For us, for children: An analysis of the provision of in-service education for child care centre personnel in Australia.* Canberra: Australian Early Childhood Association.

Storm, S. (1985). *The human side of child care administration.* Washington, DC: National Association for the Education of Young Children.

Torrance, E. P. (1979). *Your style of learning and thinking,* Athens, GA: University of Georgia.

Travis, N., & Perreault, J. (1981). *Day care personnel management.* Atlanta, GA: Save the Children.

VanderVen, K. D. (1988). Pathways to professional effectiveness for early childhood educators. In B. Spodek, O. Saracho, and D. Peters (Eds.), *Professionalism and the early childhood practitioner* (pp. 137-160). New York: Teachers College Press.

Vygotsky, L. S. (1978). *Mind in society.* Cambridge, MA: Harvard University Press.

Wallenberg, I. (1980). *The emotional experience of learning and teaching.* London: Routledge and Kegan Paul.

Wedgwood, H.C. (1967, July/August). Where committees go wrong. *Personnel,* 64-65

Weiner, B. (1980). *Human motivation.* New York: Holt, Rinehart & Winston.

Whitebook, M., Pemberton, C., Lombardi, J., & Galinsky, E. (1990). *From the floor: Raising child care salaries.* Oakland, CA: Child Care Employee Project.

Wonder, J., & Donovan, P. (1984). *Whole-brain thinking.* New York: William Morrow.

Wu, P. C. (1988, Spring). Why is change difficult? Lessons for staff development. *Journal of Staff Development, 9*(2), 10-14.

Zaltman, G., & Lin, I. (1971). On the nature of innovations. *American Behavioral Scientist, 14,* 651-673.

Assessment Tools

The assessment tools included in this appendix are available for purchase from the publisher as a separate packet. The masters included in the packet may be freely reproduced for professional development activities at your center. Permission for systematic large-scale reproduction for other training and research purposes or for the inclusion in other publications must be obtained from the copyright holder. The authors would appreciate any feedback from individuals using the assessment tools included in this book. This appendix includes the following assessment tools:

1. Reacting to Change

2. Concerns About an Innovation

3. Organizational Climate

4. Leadership Style

5. Goal Consensus and Communication

6. Collegiality and Collaboration

7. Decision-making Processes

8. Supervision and Evaluation Processes

9. Organizational Norms

10. Group Meeting Processes

11. Parent Satisfaction

12. Teaching Practices: Interactions Among Staff and Children

13. Teaching Practices: Curriculum

14. Teaching Practices: Health, Safety, and Nutrition

15. Teaching Practices: Physical Environment

16. Learning Style

17. Temperament/Psychological Type

18. Beliefs and Values

19. Job Satisfaction

20. Professional Orientation

21. Role Clarity

22. Role Clarity (new staff)

23. Organizational Commitment

24. Perceived Problems

25. Flexibility/Openness to Change

26. Supervisory Beliefs

27. Goal-Setting Motivation

Reacting to Change

Rationale:

Assessing employee reactions to a proposed organizational change is the first step in identifying those initial concerns staff might have about the change. This is important because organizational change implies altering established ways of thinking about one's job. The information gleaned from such an assessment can help directors tap into staff's feelings, assumptions, fears, and concerns about a proposed change. Assessment Tool #1 is an informal measure of how individuals anticipate a proposed change will impact their work, their self perception, and their relationship with others. This instrument was adapted from the work of W. J. Reddin (1970).

Directions:

Distribute the "Change-Reaction Checklist" and a blank envelope to all staff who will be affected by a proposed change. Place a box labeled "Questionnaire Return Box" in your center's office or staff room and ask respondents to deposit their completed surveys in this box. Ensure staff of the confidentiality of their responses.

Scoring:

This instrument can be scored in two ways.

1. To generate an average positive impact (+), negative impact (–), and no impact (n/i) score for the center, combine individual staff scores at the bottom of the page for each of these three categories and divide by the total number of respondents who completed surveys.

2. To do an item analysis, tally the number of times staff indicated a positive (+), negative (–), and no impact (n/i) for each item. Those items with the highest negative impact scores are those areas where staff express the deepest concern about the proposed change. The results of this informal assessment can be used as a springboard for discussion at a staff meeting about the proposed organizational change.

Change-Reaction Checklist

Proposed change: _____

In the space provided after each statement, indicate if you anticipate the proposed change will have a positive (+) impact, a negative (–) impact, or no impact (n/i) with respect to your work, yourself, and your relationship with others.

Work

1. How will the amount of work I do change?   _____
2. How will my interest in my work change?   _____
3. How will the importance of my work change?   _____
4. How will the challenge of my work change?   _____
5. How will the work pressures change?   _____
6. How will the skill demands on me change?   _____
7. How will my physical surroundings change?   _____
8. How will my hours of work change?   _____

Self

9. How will my advancement possibilities change?   _____
10. How will my salary change?   _____
11. How will my future with this center change?   _____
12. How will my view of myself change?   _____
13. How will my formal authority change?   _____
14. How will my informal influence change?   _____
15. How will my view of my prior values change?   _____
16. How will my ability to predict the future change?   _____
17. How will my status change?   _____

Others

18. How will my relationship with my co-workers change?   _____
19. How will my relationship with my supervisor change?   _____
20. How will what my family thinks of me change?   _____

total   +   _____
total   –   _____
total   n/i _____

Adapted from Reddin, W. J. (1970). *Managerial effectiveness*, New York: McGraw-Hill, p. 163. Reprinted with permission from McGraw-Hill, Inc.

Concerns About an Innovation

Rationale:

Because change is experienced differently by every individual, the concerns associated with implementing any proposed organizational change will also vary from one individual to another. Hall and Loucks (1978) have identified seven stages of concern about implementing educational innovations. These concerns move from self, to task, to the innovation's impact (see Table 3.1).

Assessment Tool #2 is an abbreviated version of the concerns questionnaire developed by Hall and Loucks (as cited in Hord, Rutherford, Huling-Austin, & Hall, 1987). This shortened version uses the High/Scope curriculum as an example of an early childhood innovation. This instrument will provide a quick assessment of an individual's most intense concerns about a proposed innovation. To generate a more extensive profile of teachers' stages of concern, it is recommended that directors use the questionnaire described in *Taking Charge of Change* by Hord, Rutherford, Huling-Austin, and Hall (1987).

Directions:

The "Concerns Questionnaire" will need to be adapted for the specific innovation you are planning to implement. In each instance where "High/Scope curriculum" is noted, the name or type of innovation being considered can be substituted. Distribute the "Concerns Questionnaire" and a blank envelope to all staff who will be involved in implementing the proposed change or innovation. Place a box labeled "Questionnaire Return Box" in your center's office or staff room and request that respondents place their completed questionnaires in this box.

Scoring:

On the scoring sheet provided, put the total number of points the individual assigned next to the corresponding number of the questionnaire item. Then total the points for each column. This score will represent the individual's total score for that type (stage) of concern. Scores for each type of concern will vary from 0 to 15. Note the two or three areas where the individual scored highest. Below the scoring section are some suggestions for facilitating change for individuals who have strong concerns in each of these seven areas. Since facilitating change should be handled on an individual basis, it is not recommended that scores be collapsed to generate a combined staff profile. A center-wide average on this instrument can mask the enormous variation that can exist in the type of concerns that individuals will experience.

Concerns Questionnaire

Name _____

    The purpose of this questionnaire is to determine how you feel about using the High/Scope curriculum. Please respond to the items in terms of your present concerns, or how you feel about your involvement or potential involvement with High/Scope. Some of the items on this questionnaire may have little relevance to you at this time. For the completely irrelevant items, please circle "0" on the scale. Other items will represent those concerns you do have, in varying degrees of intensity, and should be marked higher on the scale.

irrelevant	not true of me now		somewhat true of me now		very true of of me now
0	1	2	3	4	5

1. I am concerned about how the students will react to the High/Scope curriculum.   0 1 2 3 4 5

2. I know of some other curriculum approaches that might work better than High/Scope.   0 1 2 3 4 5

3. I don't even know what the High/Scope curriculum is.   0 1 2 3 4 5

4. I am concerned about not having enough time to organize myself to implement this curriculum.   0 1 2 3 4 5

5. I would like to help the other teachers in their use of the High/Scope curriculum.   0 1 2 3 4 5

6. I am concerned about how I can carry out all my responsibilities with respect to the High/Scope curriculum.   0 1 2 3 4 5

7. I would like to know who will make decisions regarding the High/Scope curriculum.   0 1 2 3 4 5

8. I would like to explore the possibility of using the High/Scope curricular approach.   0 1 2 3 4 5

9. I would like to know what resources are available to implement the High/Scope curriculum.   0 1 2 3 4 5

10. I am concerned about my inability to manage all that the High/Scope curriculum requires.   0 1 2 3 4 5

11. I am concerned about evaluating my impact on students' learning with respect to High/Scope.   0   1   2   3   4   5

12. am too occupied with other things right now to consider implementing High/Scope.   0   1   2   3   4   5

13. I would like to modify and revise the High/Scope curriculum.   0   1   2   3   4   5

14. I would like to coordinate my efforts with other staff to maximize High/Scope's effect.   0   1   2   3   4   5

15. I would like to have more information on the time and energy commitment required to implement the High/Scope curriculum.   0   1   2   3   4   5

16. I would like to know what other staff are doing with respect to implementing High/Scope.   0   1   2   3   4   5

17. At this time, I am not really interested in learning about the High/Scope curriculum.   0   1   2   3   4   5

18. I would like to determine how to supplement and enhance the High/Scope curriculum in this center.   0   1   2   3   4   5

19. I am interested in getting feedback from the students to improve the way I implement the High/Scope curriculum.   0   1   2   3   4   5

20. I would like to know how my role will change if I implement the High/Scope curriculum.   0   1   2   3   4   5

21. I would like to know how the High/Scope curriculum is better than what we have now.   0   1   2   3   4   5

When I think of the High/Scope curriculum, my primary concern is…

Adapted from Hord, S., Rutherford, W., Huling-Austin, L., & Hall, G. (1987). *Taking charge of change.* Alexandria, VA: ASCD, pp. 47-49. Reprinted with permission.

Concerns Questionnaire Scoring Sheet

Stage 0 Awareness Concerns	Stage 1 Informational Concerns	Stage 2 Personal Concerns	Stage 3 Management Concerns	Stage 4 Consequence Concerns	Stage 5 Collaboration Concerns	Stage 6 Refocusing Concerns
3 _____	8 _____	7 _____	4 _____	1 _____	5 _____	2 _____
12 _____	9 _____	15 _____	6 _____	11 _____	14 _____	13 _____
17 _____	21 _____	20 _____	10 _____	19 _____	16 _____	18 _____
_____ total	_____ total	_____ total	_____ total	_____ total	_____ total	_____ total

Facilitating Change for Individuals at Different Stages of Concern*

Stage 0 — Awareness Concerns

▶ Involve teachers in discussions and decisions about the innovation and its implementation.

▶ Share enough information to arouse interest, but not so much that it overwhelms.

▶ Acknowledge that a lack of awareness is expected and reasonable, and that no questions about the innovation are foolish.

▶ Encourage unaware persons to talk with colleagues who know about the innovation.

▶ Take steps to minimize gossip and inaccurate sharing of information about the innovation.

Stage 1 — Informational Concerns

▶ Provide clear and accurate information about the innovation.

▶ Use a variety of ways to share information — verbally, in writing, and through any available media. Communicate with individuals and with small and large groups.

▶ Have individuals who have used the innovation in other settings visit with your teachers. Visits to other centers could also be arranged.

▶ Help teachers see how the innovation relates to their current practices, both in regard to similarities and differences.

▶ Be enthusiastic and enhance the visibility of others who are excited.

Stage 2 — Personal Concerns

▶ Legitimize the existence and expression of personal concerns. Knowing these concerns are common and that others have them can be comforting.

▶ Use personal notes and conversations to provide encouragement and reinforce personal adequacy.

▶ Connect these teachers with others whose personal concerns have diminished and who will be supportive.

▶ Show how the innovation can be implemented sequentially rather than in one big leap. It is important to establish expectations that are attainable.

▶ Do not push innovation use, but encourage and support it while maintaining expectations.

Stage 3 — Management Concerns

▶ Clarify the steps and components of the innovation. Information from innovation configurations will be helpful here.

▶ Provide answers that address the small specific "how-to" issues that are so often the cause of management concerns.

▶ Demonstrate exact and practical solutions to the logistical problems that contribute to these concerns.

▶ Help teachers sequence specific activities and set timelines for their accomplishment.

▶ Attend to immediate demands of the innovation, not what will be or could be in the future.

Stage 4 — Consequence Concerns

▶ Provide these individuals with opportunities to visit other settings where the innovation is in use and to attend conferences on the topic.

▶ Don't overlook these individuals. Give them positive feedback and needed support.

▶ Find opportunities for these individuals to share their skills with others.

▶ Share with these persons information pertaining to the innovation.

Stage 5 — Collaboration Concerns

▶ Provide these individuals with opportunities to develop those skills necessary for working collaboratively.

▶ Bring together those persons, both within and outside the center, who are interested in collaboration.

▶ Help the collaborators establish reasonable expectations and guidelines for the collaborative effort.

▶ Use these people to provide technical assistance to others who need assistance.

▶ Encourage the collaborators, but don't attempt to force collaboration on those who are not interested.

Stage 6 — Refocusing Concerns

▶ Respect and encourage the interest these individuals have for finding a better way.

▶ Help these individuals channel their ideas and energies in ways that will be productive rather than counterproductive.

▶ Encourage these individuals to act on their concerns for program improvement.

▶ Help these persons access the resources they may need to refine their ideas and put them into practice.

▶ Accept the fact that these persons may replace or significantly modify the innovation.

---

* Adapted from Hord, S., Rutherford, W., Huling-Austin, L., & Hall, G. (1987). *Taking charge of change*, Alexandria, VA: ASCD, pp 44-46. Reprinted with permission.

Organizational Climate

Rationale:

Organizational climate describes the collective perceptions of staff regarding the overall quality of work life at the center. Assessment Tool #3 is the short form of the *Early Childhood Work Environment Survey* (Jorde-Bloom, 1988a, 1989a). It was designed to measure staff's perceptions about ten different dimensions of organizational climate: co-worker relations; opportunities for professional growth; supervisor support; clarity; reward system; decision-making structure; goal consensus; task orientation; physical environment; and innovativeness. The attached table provides a fuller description of these ten dimensions. The instrument is short and can be administered to staff annually to take a quick pulse of organizational functioning. Centers wishing to have a fuller profile of staff's perceptions regarding the dimensions of organizational life tapped by this assessment may want to administer the longer version of this instrument. It may be obtained from the Early Childhood Professional Development Project at National-Louis University.

Directions:

Distribute the short form of the *Early Childhood Work Environment Survey* to all staff who work a minimum of ten hours per week at the center. In addition to your teaching staff, this will probably include some support staff (for example, secretary, nutritionist, or social worker). Each individual should also be given a blank envelope. Designate one person on your staff to be responsible for collecting all the completed surveys. Before distributing the survey to your staff, decide who will be tabulating the results and summarizing the data. The staff should be informed who this person will be.

Scoring:

The organizational climate scores on this survey will range from 0 – 100. Tabulate individual scores by simply adding up the numerals next to each statement. To determine the average organizational climate score, total all the individual organizational climate scores and divide by the total number of individuals completing the survey.

This instrument is most useful when used as a pre and post assessment of staff's perceptions of the quality of work life. If the center is engaged in any kind of center improvement effort, the information gleaned from comparing pre and post scores on this assessment will provide helpful information as to the success of the center improvement efforts.

The Ten Dimensions of Organizational Climate

Dimension	Definition
Collegiality	Extent to which staff are friendly, supportive, and trust one another. The peer cohesion and esprit de corps of the group.
Professional Growth	The degree of emphasis placed on personal and professional growth.
Supervisor Support	The degree of facilitative leadership that provides encouragement, support, and clear expectations.
Clarity	The extent to which policies, procedures, and responsibilities are clearly defined and communicated.
Reward System	The degree of fairness and equity in the distribution of pay, fringe benefits, and opportunities for advancement.
Decision Making	The degree of autonomy given to the staff and the extent to which they are involved in center-wide decisions.
Goal Consensus	The degree to which staff agree on the goals and objectives of the center.
Task Orientation	The emphasis placed on good planning, efficiency, and getting the job done.
Physical Setting	The extent to which the spatial arrangement of the center helps or hinders staff in carrying out their responsibilities.
Innovativeness	The extent to which the organization adapts to change and encourages staff to find creative ways to solve problems.

From Jorde-Bloom, P. (1989). *Measuring work attitudes in the early childhood setting*. Brandon, VT: Psychology Press.

Early Childhood Work Environment Survey

(Short Form)

This survey is designed to find out how you feel about this early childhood center as a place to work. The success of this survey depends on your candid and honest responses. Please know that your answers are completely confidential. When you have completed the questionnaire, put it in the attached plain envelope, seal it, and give it to your staff representative. Indicate in the space provided the numeral (0 - 5) which most accurately describes how you feel about each statement.

never	seldom	sometimes	somewhat regularly	frequently	always
0	1	2	3	4	5

_____ Staff are friendly and trust one another.

_____ Morale is high. There is a good team spirit.

_____ Staff are encouraged to learn new skills and competencies.

_____ The center provides guidance for professional advancement.

_____ Supervisor(s) are knowledgeable and competent.

_____ Supervisor(s) provide helpful feedback.

_____ Communication regarding policies and procedures is clear.

_____ Job responsibilities are well-defined.

_____ Salaries and fringe benefits are distributed equitably.

_____ Promotions are handled fairly.

_____ Teachers help make decisions about things that directly affect them.

_____ People feel free to express their opinions.

_____ Staff agree on school philosophy and educational objectives.

_____ Staff share a common vision of what the center should be like.

_____ The program is well planned and efficiently run.

_____ Meetings are productive. Time is not wasted.

_____ The work environment is attractive and well-organized.

_____ There are sufficient supplies and equipment for staff to do their jobs.

_____ Staff are encouraged to be creative and innovative in their work.

_____ The center implements changes as needed.

What three words describe the climate of this center as a place to work?

What do you perceive to be the greatest strengths of this center?

What areas do you feel could use some improvement?

Leadership Style

Rationale:

The leadership style of the director of a child care center is perhaps the most potent factor influencing organizational effectiveness. The director must create an environment based on mutual respect in which individuals work together to accomplish collective goals. The success of this endeavor rests in large part on the director's ability to balance organizational needs with individual needs. The research in this area suggests that leaders who head the most effective organizations tend to be those that apply a transactional leadership style — an ability to adjust their style to the demands of each situation so that both organizational needs and individual needs are met.

Part I of this assessment tool was adapted from the work of Blake and Mouton (1969), Getzels and Guba (1957), Giammatteo (1975), Hersey and Blanchard (1982), and Reddin (1970). It assesses three different leadership styles: the task-oriented style emphasizing organizational needs; the people-oriented style focusing on people and their individual needs; and the transactional style stressing an appropriate emphasis on both the center's needs and the individual worker's needs depending on the situation. Part II of Assessment Tool #4 was developed by Exchange Press (Neugebauer, 1990). It provides staff with an opportunity to evaluate the director's overall administrative/management style.

Directions:

Distribute the five-page "My Director..." questionnaire and a blank envelope to each individual who works at the center more than ten hours per week. (If the director is a male, some of the questions will need to be changed first to reflect masculine pronouns.) For more accurate results, it is advisable to distribute questionnaires to both teaching staff and support staff. Place a box labeled "Questionnaire Return Box" in your center's office or staff room and ask respondents to deposit their completed surveys in this box. Ensure staff of the confidentiality of their responses. It is suggested that the director also complete a survey of his/her perceived style. The results of this self-assessment may then be compared to the collective perceptions of the staff.

Scoring:

The composite results of Part I summarize the staff's perceptions of the director's dominant leadership style. The following scoring sheet includes a brief description of the three leadership styles assessed by this questionnaire.

To score Part I, tally the responses by noting with a mark each time staff checked a particular response:

1. _____   9. _____   17. _____

2. _____   10. _____   18. _____

3. _____   11. _____   19. _____

4. _____   12. _____   20. _____

5. _____   13. _____   21. _____

6. _____   14. _____   22. _____

7. _____   15. _____   23. _____

8. _____   16. _____   24. _____

Now total the marks for the following responses:

Task-oriented: 1, 6, 8, 10, 14, 17, 19, 22   Total _____

Achieving center goals is most important in this leadership style. Strong concern for high performance and accomplishing tasks. Emphasis is on planning, directing, following procedures, and applying uniform standards and expectations for all. This director may be viewed as too structured, bureaucratic, and inflexible.

People-oriented: 2, 4, 7, 11, 15, 18, 20, 24   Total _____

Achieving harmonious group relations is foremost in this leadership style. Strong emphasis on maintaining comfortable, friendly, and satisfying working conditions. Allows staff to exercise control and be self-directed with minimal intrusion of center-wide policies and procedures. Staff working in centers with this style of leadership may complain about the lack of order and coordination.

Transactional: 3, 5, 9, 12, 13, 16, 21, 23   Total _____

Achieving both center goals and maintaining high morale is important in this leadership style. This director is flexible and fair, recognizing that different situations may require a different emphasis on center-wide needs or individual needs.

For a fuller description of each style, refer to Chapter III.

For Part II, add up the total score for each respondent. (Scores will range from 25 to 125.) Add together all respondents' scores and divide by the number of individuals returning questionnaires. This will yield an average score regarding the staff's evaluation of the director's performance in a wide range of administrative and supervisory behaviors.

On any assessment such as this where perceptions may vary considerably, it is important to note the range of scores (the lowest score and the highest score). Also, it is helpful to do an item analysis to discern those two or three items that staff rated the director lowest and those two or three items where the director consistently scored highest. This will provide the director specific feedback about those perceived areas where staff may feel he or she has the greatest skill and those areas in need of improvement.

"My Director..."

Dear Staff:

One of the hallmarks of an early childhood professional is the ability to reflect on one's performance. Your feedback about my leadership style is important in helping me improve and grow professionally. Please take a few minutes to complete this questionnaire. When you are finished, insert it in the attached plain envelope and put it in the "Questionnaire Return Box" in the office. There is no need for you to put your name on the questionnaire.

Thank you

PART I. Place a check (✔) in front of the statement that most nearly reflects your director's leadership style in different situations. (Check only one response in each group).

With respect to planning, my director...

1. _____ does most of the planning herself by setting goals, objectives, and work schedules for staff to follow. She then works out procedures and responsibilities for staff to follow.

2. _____ does very little planning, either by herself or with the staff. She tells the staff she has confidence in them to carry out their jobs in a responsible way.

3. _____ gets staff members together to assess center-wide problems and discuss ideas and strategies for improvement. Together they set up goals and objectives and establish individual responsibilities.

With respect to work assignments and the day-to-day operation of the center, my director...

4. _____ checks with staff regularly to see if they are content and if they have the things they need. She does not see the necessity of precise job descriptions, preferring instead to let the staff determine the scope and nature of their jobs.

5. _____ is flexible in adapting job descriptions and changing work assignments as needed. Updates center polices and procedures depending on the needs of the staff, parents, children, and board.

6. _____ tends to go by the book. Expects staff to adhere to written job descriptions. Follows policies and procedures precisely.

With respect to leadership philosophy, my director...

7. _____ tends to emphasize people's well-being, believing that happy workers will be productive workers.

8. _____ tends to emphasize hard work and a job well done. We are a results-oriented program.

9. _____ tends to emphasize both what we do and what we need as people.

During meetings, my director...

10. _____ keeps focused on the agenda and the topics that need to be covered.

11. _____ focuses on each individual's feelings and helps people express their emotional reactions to an issue.

12. _____ focuses on differing positions people take and how they deal with each other.

The primary goal of my director is...

13. _____ to meet the needs of parents and children while providing a healthy work climate for staff.

14. _____ to keep the center running efficiently.

15. _____ to help staff find fulfillment.

In evaluating the staff's performance, my director...

16. _____ attempts to assess how each individual's performance has contributed to center-wide achievement of goals.

17. _____ makes an assessment of each person's performance and effectiveness according to predetermined established criteria that are applied equally to all staff.

18. _____ allows people to set their own goals and determine performance standards.

My director believes the best way to motivate someone who is not performing up to his/her ability is to...

19. _____ point out to the individual the importance of the job to be done.

20. _____ try to get to know the individual better in an attempt to understand why the person is not realizing his/her potential.

21. _____ work with the individual to redefine job responsibilities to more effectively contribute to centerwide goals.

My director believes it is her role to...

22. _____ make sure that staff members have a solid foundation of knowledge and skill that will help them accomplish center goals.

23. _____ help people learn to work effectively in groups to accomplish group goals.

24. _____ help individuals become responsible for their own education and effectiveness, and take the first step toward realizing their potential.

What three words or phrases most accurately describe the leadership style of your director:

_____   _____   _____

PART II. Circle the numeral that most nearly represents your assessment of your director in each of the areas described.

My director is...

	strongly disagree				strongly agree
...knowledgeable. She knows what is going on in the program for staff, children, parents, board, and administrators.	1	2	3	4	5
...in control. She has a handle on things and is actively and effectively in charge of the center's programs and operations.	1	2	3	4	5
... dedicated. She demonstrates interest in learning more about her job from peers, professional groups, and reading material.	1	2	3	4	5
...confident. She has a sense of mission and a clear vision for the center.	1	2	3	4	5
... enthusiastic. She has the energy to cope with the daily demands of her job.	1	2	3	4	5
...an effective communicator. She keeps us well informed about policies, procedures, activities, and schedules.	1	2	3	4	5
...responsive. When adults or children need her attention, she is able to focus on their needs.	1	2	3	4	5
...available to parents. She knows the families and encourages them to participate in the program.	1	2	3	4	5
...open. She encourages employees to participate in decision-making and welcomes their suggestions.	1	2	3	4	5
...fair. She investigates all sides of an issue and distributes criticism and praise with grace and equity.	1	2	3	4	5
...predictable. Expectations are clearly defined, and policies are routinely followed.	1	2	3	4	5
...a trainer. She encourages my professional growth by providing opportunities for on-going training and development.	1	2	3	4	5
...a delegator. She uses authority with fairness and according to the staff's talents and time.	1	2	3	4	5

	strongly disagree				strongly agree
...prepared. She has a sense of priority about the center and the requirements of her role.	1	2	3	4	5
...respectful. She understands people as individuals and shapes her expectations of them accordingly.	1	2	3	4	5
...understanding. She realizes that each of us has different interests, abilities, attitudes, and personalities.	1	2	3	4	5
...available. I am comfortable bringing my concerns, criticisms, problems, and successes to her.	1	2	3	4	5
...efficient. She handles the day-to-day routines of the center promptly and skillfully.	1	2	3	4	5
...supportive. She looks for opportunities to give feedback and offer praise.	1	2	3	4	5
...a motivator. She encourages each of us to give our best effort.	1	2	3	4	5
...realistic. She has a sense of humor and is able to keep things in perspective.	1	2	3	4	5
...an influence in the community. She is an advocate for children and quality care.	1	2	3	4	5
...genuine. She greets me warmly and demonstrates interest and concern. I know where I stand with her.	1	2	3	4	5
...flexible. She encourages creative problem solving, facilitates personal growth, and keeps things interesting.	1	2	3	4	5
...resourceful. She knows where to go and what to do to get things done. She makes good use of community resources.	1	2	3	4	5

Part II from Neugebauer, B. (1990, August). Evaluation of director by staff. *Child Care Information Exchange*, pp. 20-21. Reprinted with permission.

Goal Consensus and Communication

Rationale:

The hallmark of any successful organization is a shared sense among its members about what they are trying to accomplish. Agreed-upon goals and ways to attain them provide the foundation for rational planning and action. One cannot assume, however, that just because a center's goals and objectives are committed to paper that there will be uniform agreement among staff about their importance. Assessment Tool #5 assesses staff's rankings of various educational goals and objectives. From this information, you will be able to determine the degree of goal consensus that exists among your staff. The six educational objectives included on this questionnaire are common educational objectives for most early childhood programs. Feel free to reword them to make them more appropriate for your program.

Goal consensus rests in large measure on the effectiveness of communication in the center. Communication of information takes many forms in child care centers; it can be written or oral, formal or informal, and personal or impersonal. Communication networks also vary in centers. They may be vertical (from supervisor to teacher) or horizontal (between teachers). Assessment Tool #5 also assesses staff's perceptions of the effectiveness of communication at the center. The questions on this assessment tool were adapted from the work of Bean and Clemes (1978), Jorde-Bloom (1989a), and Rosenholtz (1989).

Directions:

Distribute the "Goal Consensus and Communications Questionnaire" and a blank envelope to all teaching staff who work at the center more than ten hours per week. Place a box labeled "Questionnaire Return Box" in your center's office or staff room and ask staff to put their completed questionnaires in this box.

Scoring:

Tally the results of Part I by noting the number of individuals who ranked each educational objective as 1, 2, 3, 4, 5, 6. When you have completed, you will have a profile of the distribution of staff's perceptions of the importance of different educational objectives. If there is strong goal consensus among your staff, the responses should cluster. In other words, you should see a strong agreement among staff about which one or two educational objectives are most important and which objective is least important. Even in centers where there is strong goal consensus, it is rare to see strong agreement among the third, fourth and fifth rankings. Remember, the larger your staff, the more difficult it is to achieve goal consensus. Thus large programs (with more than 20 staff completing the questionnaire) should expect to see a wider distribution of responses.

For Part II of the questionnaire, merely tally the number of individuals who checked the statement as being an accurate reflection of center practices. Divide this number by the total number of respondents to get a percentage of staff who agreed with the statement.

For Part III of the questionnaire, total the individual scores of respondents. They will range from 10 – 50. Then sum all respondents' scores and divide by the number of staff completing the questionnaire. This will yield an average score. Scores between 40 – 50 indicate that staff perceive the communication processes of the center to be quite positive. Scores between 10 – 20 indicate staff feel this is an area that may need some improvement.

Goal Consensus and Communication Questionnaire

This questionnaire has three parts. Part I assesses your perceptions of the priority of different goals and educational objectives in our center. Part II asks you to indicate all those statements that accurately reflect how you feel about goal consensus at our center. Finally, Part III assesses your attitudes about the effectiveness of different communication processes in our center. Your honest and candid responses to these questions are appreciated. When you have completed your questionnaire, please put it in the envelope you have received and place it in the "Questionnaire Return Box" in the office. There is no need to include your name.

PART I. Rank order the following program objectives according to how important you feel they are at this center. Put a "1" by the most important, a "2" by the next most important and so on until you get to "6" for the least important. *Each objective must only have one number next to it.*

_____ to help children develop language and problem solving skills

_____ to help children build strong friendships and learn to share

_____ to help children master concepts needed for reading and arithmetic

_____ to help children develop skill and independence in caring for themselves

_____ to help children develop physical coordination

_____ to help children develop a healthy self-esteem and positive self-concept

PART II. Please check all those statements that accurately describe how you feel.

_____ At this center, we agree on the objectives we're trying to achieve with students.

_____ The director's values and philosophy of education are similar to my own.

_____ Most teachers at this center have values and philosophies of education similar to my own.

_____ There are explicit guidelines at this center about the things teachers are to emphasize in their teaching.

_____ Discussion about school goals and means of achieving them is a regular part of our staff meetings.

_____ Before teachers are hired at this center, they are asked about their philosophy of teaching.

PART III. Circle from 1 (strongly disagree) to 5 (strongly agree) how you feel about the following statements:

	strongly disagree				strongly agree
Written communication at this center is clear	1	2	3	4	5
Staff seem well-informed most of the time	1	2	3	4	5
The information I receive is usually accurate	1	2	3	4	5
Parents seem well-informed about issues and events	1	2	3	4	5
Communication between teachers is open and direct	1	2	3	4	5
Communication between the director and staff is open	1	2	3	4	5
Expressing my feelings is valued and easy to do here	1	2	3	4	5
People feel comfortable to disagree with one another	1	2	3	4	5
The director makes an effort to solicit feedback	1	2	3	4	5
Policy manuals and written procedures are clear	1	2	3	4	5

What suggestions do you have for improving communication processes at this center?

Collegiality and Collaboration

Rationale:

Collegiality is the glue that holds a center together. It is that esprit de corps, that feeling of sharing and caring for one another that is so essential to a team effort in improving center functioning. Assessment Tool #6 assesses the staff's perceptions regarding their overall co-worker relations, specifically, the extent to which they feel teaching at the center is a team effort directed toward the collaborative goal of improving center effectiveness. Rosenholtz (1989) states that "collaborative norms undergird achievement-oriented groups, they bring new ideas, fresh ways of looking at things, and a stock of collective knowledge that is more fruitful than any one person's work alone" (p. 41). Whether or not teachers work mutually depends in large part on the harmony of their interests within the center — the degree to which they share similar goals and objectives. It should not be surprising, then, if the results of this assessment are similar to those of the goal consensus (Assessment Tool #5). The questions on this assessment tool were adapted from the work of Rosenholtz (1989).

Directions:

Distribute the "Collaboration Index" and a blank envelope to all teaching and support staff who work at the center more than ten hours per week. Place a box labeled "Questionnaire Return Box" in your center's office or staff room and ask staff to put their completed questionnaires in this box.

Scoring:

Since many of the questions on this instrument deal with sensitive social relationship issues, it is wise to have an outside person tabulate the results and summarize the responses to the open-ended question. The scores for this instrument will range from 0 to 10. To determine your center's collaboration index:

a. Tally the number of checks next to items #1, 3, 5, 6, 9,   Total _____ (a)

b. Tally the number of checks next to items #2, 4, 7, 8, 10   Total _____ (b)

c. Individual total score equals (a) – (b) + 5 = _____ (c)

d. Sum all the individual scores and divide by the total number of staff completing the questionnaire to determine your center's collaboration index. A score of 7 to 10 indicates that your staff has quite positive feelings about teamwork at your center. A score lower than 4 would indicate that there is room for improving the climate of collaboration.

Collaboration Index

This questionnaire assesses your perceptions of the degree to which this staff functions as a team. Your honest and candid responses to these questions are appreciated. When you have completed your questionnaire, please put it in the envelope provided and place it in the "Questionnaire Return Box" in the office. It is not necessary for you to include your name on this questionnaire.

Put a check (✓) next to those items which accurately reflect how you feel.

_____ 1. Other teachers at this center regularly seek my advice about professional issues and problems.

_____ 2. I don't offer advice to other teachers about their teaching unless they ask me for it.

_____ 3. I regularly share teaching ideas, materials, and resources with other teachers at this center.

_____ 4. I believe that good teaching is a gift; it isn't something you can really learn from anyone else.

_____ 5. If teachers at this center feel that another teacher is not doing a good job, they will exert some pressure on him/her to improve.

_____ 6. The director encourages teachers to plan together and collaborate on instructional units, field trips, and classroom activities.

_____ 7. Substitutes at this center often do not know what is expected of them.

_____ 8. Most of the time the other teachers at this center don't know what I do in my classroom with my group of children.

_____ 9. I see myself as part of a team and share responsibility for our center's successes and short comings.

_____ 10. I can go for days at this center without talking to anyone about my teaching.

Select the three words that most accurately describe other staff at this center.

cooperative	friendly	isolated	cautious
competitive	trusting	guarded	helpful
caring	cliquish	open	mistrustful

What suggestions do you have that might increase opportunities for collaboration and teamwork at our center (for example, modifying work schedules, changing the layout of space, etc.)?

Decision-Making Processes

Rationale:

The opportunity to participate in center-wide decision making is an important factor in the morale of teachers. It is also an essential ingredient in achieving a collaborative model of center improvement. Since every center is unique, however, the nature of decision making processes will also be unique. Thus, the roles that teachers and director play in decision making will vary according to the nature of the issue being considered and the background and interests of the parties affected. Not all teaching staff want the same degree of decision-making influence in all areas of program functioning.

Assessment Tool #7 was designed to assess staff's perceptions of their current and desired levels of decision-making influence in five areas. The purpose of this assessment is to measure the discrepancy between perceived levels of current and desired decision-making influence. Assessment Tool #7 also includes questions about how staff perceive the decision-making processes of the center. The information gleaned from this instrument will give you a clearer picture of the areas in which staff desire a greater role in decision making. The questions on this assessment tool were adapted from the decision-making subscale of the *Early Childhood Work Environment Survey* (Jorde-Bloom, 1989a).

Directions:

Distribute the "Decision-Making Influence Questionnaire" and a blank envelope to all teaching staff who work at the center more than ten hours per week. Place a box labeled "Questionnaire Return Box" in your center's office or staff room and ask staff to put their completed questionnaires in this box.

Scoring:

Tally the results of Part I by assigning the following point value: very little influence = 0, some influence = 5, considerable influence = 10. To determine a discrepancy score between current and desired levels of decision-making influence, make the following calculations:

a. Total the amount of current decision-making influence for each person (scores will range from 0 to 50).

b. Total the amount of desired decision-making influence for each person (scores will range from 0 to 50).

----

c. Add together all the staff's current decision-making influence scores and divide by the total number of staff to get an average current decision-making influence score. Do the same thing for the desired decision-making influence to get an average desired decision-making influence score.

d. Subtract the average current decision-making influence score from the average desireddecision-making influence score to determine the discrepancy between current and desired levels of decision-making influence. If the desired decision-making influence score is larger than the current decision-making influence score, this discrepancy score will range from 0 to 50. Most often staff will express that they desire more decision-making influence than they currently have. The strength of this discrepancy will help you understand how strongly staff feel about wanting greater input into the decision-making processes at the center. A discrepancy score of greater than 25 would indicate that there are strong feelings about their perceived current and desired levels of influence. Occasionally teachers will voice concern that they desire less decision-making influence than they currently have. In this case the desired decision-making influence score will be lower than the current decision-making influence score.

e. To discern the areas where there is the greatest discrepancy between current and desired levels, follow the same procedure for each of the five decision-making areas listed. In this calculation, the scores will range from 0 to 10 for both the current and desired scales.

For Part II, tally the number of checks for each item and divide by the total number of questionnaires completed. This will yield a percentage of staff who feel that the statement characterizes decision-making processes at the center.

Decision-Making Influence Questionnaire

This questionnaire has two parts. Part I assesses your perceptions about your current and desired levels of decision-making influence. Part II assesses your perceptions about the way decisions are made at this center. Your honest and candid responses to these questions are appreciated. When you have completed your questionnaire, please put it in the envelope provided and place it in the "Questionnaire Return Box" in the office. There is no need to include your name.

PART I. Listed below are some common organizational decisions and actions. How much influence do you currently have in each of the areas below?

	very little influence	some influence	considerable influence
Ordering materials/supplies	_____	_____	_____
Interviewing/hiring new staff	_____	_____	_____
Determining program objectives	_____	_____	_____
Training new aides/teachers	_____	_____	_____
Planning daily schedule of activities	_____	_____	_____

How much influence would you like to have in each of these areas?

	very little influence	some influence	considerable influence
Ordering materials/supplies	_____	_____	_____
Interviewing/hiring new staff	_____	_____	_____
Determining program objectives	_____	_____	_____
Training new aides/teachers	_____	_____	_____
Planning daily schedule of activities	_____	_____	_____

PART II. Check (✓) all that describe how decisions are made at this center/school most of the time:

_____ teachers are asked their opinions on important issues
_____ the director/principal likes to make most of the decisions
_____ people don't feel free to express their opinions
_____ everyone provides input on the content of staff meetings
_____ people provide input, but decisions have already been made
_____ teachers make decisions about things that directly affect them
_____ decisions are made by those who know most about the problem or issue

What suggestions do you have for promoting shared decision making at this center/school?

Supervision and Evaluation Processes

Rationale:

It is customary in child care work settings for staff to be evaluated by their supervisors. Seldom, however, are teachers and support staff provided the opportunity to give feedback to their supervisors about the quality of the supervision and evaluation they receive. This is unfortunate, because a teacher's ability, interest, and desire to improve often rests on the quality of the relationship that the teacher has established with his/her supervisor. Without solid supervisory and evaluation processes in place, individual and collective change simply cannot take place.

Assessment Tool #8 measures staff's perceptions of the extent to which the supervisory and evaluation processes of the center pose restraints or opportunities for professional growth. This assessment focuses on the individual employee's relationship with his/her immediate supervisor. This could be a head teacher, master teacher, or assistant director. It could also be the director if he/she has immediate supervisory responsibility for the employees. It is important to remember that this assessment measures perceptions and these perceptions may or may not mirror "objective reality." Objective reality is not as important, however, as how people perceive any given situation or working relationship because it is their perception of reality that guides their behavior. The questions on this instrument were adapted from the work of Bean and Clemes (1978), Jorde-Bloom (1989a), and Neugebauer (1990).

Directions:

Distribute the two-page "Supervisory Behavior Questionnaire" and a blank envelope to each individual who works at the center more than ten hours per week. For non-teaching staff, it may be necessary to revise sections of this questionnaire to accurately reflect the nature of the different jobs. Before distributing the survey, indicate the name of the supervisor you want the employee to evaluate. This may be the head teacher of a single classroom or a teacher who supervises several classrooms. In centers where the director is the primary supervisor of staff, the same name will appear on all surveys. To get accurate feedback from the staff, you should stress the importance of providing honest, candid responses to all questions on this assessment. Assure them of the confidential nature of their responses.

Scoring:

Since the nature of this evaluation is very sensitive, the director may want to designate an outside person to tabulate the results and summarize the findings. This summary can then be given to the individual supervisors and the director. The results of this assessment will need to be coded separately for each supervisor involved.

To score Part I, merely add up the total number of items checked on each completed survey. The scores will range from 0 to 25. Sum all scores for each supervisor and divide by the number of respondents. This will yield an average supervisory behavior score for each individual. Scores over 20 indicate that the respondents have very positive attitudes about the opportunities for professional growth that are available, the fairness of evaluation procedures used at the center, and the support and helpful encouragement they receive from their supervisor. Scores lower than 10 would indicate that respondents have generally unfavorable perceptions about the supervisory and evaluation processes employed at the center.

It may be helpful to do an item analysis for this section of the instrument. This can be done by simply tallying the total number of individuals who checked each item. This number can be divided by the total number of respondents to get a percentage of those who responded affirmatively to the statement.

Part II of this assessment tool focuses on the supervisor's listening behavior. To derive a supervisory listening quotient, score each questionnaire in the following manner.

a. Add the number of checks next to items #1, 4, 7, 8, 11, 12, 13, 15, 19, 20

   total _____ (a)

b. Add the number of checks for items #2, 3, 5, 6, 9, 10, 14, 16, 17, 18

   total _____ (b)

c. The supervisor's listening quotient on each survey (c) equals (a) – (b) + 10

   total _____ (c) (scores will range from 0 to 20)

d. Sum all the individual respondents' (c) scores for each supervisor and divide by the total number of respondents to yield an average listening quotient for the supervisor.

Scores between 15 and 20 indicate that respondents feel their supervisor is attentive, genuinely interested, and supportive when engaged in conversation. Scores lower than 5 would signal the need for supervisors to build stronger listening and communication skills. This same instrument could be used as a posttest measure at a later date to determine if the staff's perceptions of the supervisor's listening skills had improved.

Supervisory Behavior Questionnaire

The purpose of this questionnaire is to give you an opportunity to provide feedback about the supervisory and evaluation processes at this center. In answering the questions that refer to a specific person, please provide feedback regarding the individual noted at the beginning of the section. When you have completed all three parts of this questionnaire, please put it in the envelope provided and give it to your staff representative. The results of this survey will be tabulated and a written summary will be given to your supervisor and center director.

Name of supervisor _____

PART I. Check (✓) all those statements with which you agree.

_____ At this center, I have many opportunities to learn new things.

_____ Evaluation of my teaching is used to help me improve.

_____ The standards by which my teaching is evaluated are clear and well specified.

_____ The methods used in evaluating my teaching are objective and fair.

_____ I know what I'm being evaluated on at this center.

My supervisor...

_____ provides suggestions to help me become the best possible teacher.

_____ encourages me to try out new ideas.

_____ encourages me to be independent and self-reliant.

_____ spends enough time in my classroom observing my teaching.

_____ sets high but realistic expectations.

_____ takes a strong interest in my professional development.

_____ displays a strong interest in improving the quality of our program.

_____ helps me understand the sources of important problems I face.

_____ provides the resources I need to help me improve my performance.

_____ provides constructive suggestions that help me deal with problems I encounter.

_____ uses praise appropriately.

_____ communicates effectively.

_____ is dependable and reliable.

_____ is friendly and sociable.

_____ is ethical, honest, and trustworthy.

_____ is patient and supportive.

_____ is knowledgeable about early childhood education.

_____ uses time wisely.

_____ is available when I need him/her.

_____ stays calm in difficult situations.

PART II. Check (✓) the following statements that reflect your appraisal of your supervisor's listening behavior.

When you and I are talking together...

1. _____ you make me feel as if this is the most important thing you could be doing right now.

2. _____ your attention is often divided; you interrupt our conversation by answering the phone or addressing the needs of others.

3. _____ you sometimes begin shaking your head or saying "no" before I finish my thought.

4. _____ you refer to our previous conversations; there is a history to our communication.

5. _____ you fidget and squirm and look at the clock as though you can't wait to get on to other more important projects and conversations.

6. _____ you begin asking questions before I finish my message.

7. _____ you look me in the eye and really focus attention on me.

8. _____ you ask thoughtful questions that let me know you were really listening.

9. _____ you finish my sentences for me as though nothing I have to say could be new to you.

10. _____ you change the agenda by taking over and changing the content of the conversation.

11. _____ you follow up on what we discussed and keep me posted on what is happening.

12. _____ you are sensitive to the tone of what I have to say and respond respectfully.

13. _____ you give me credit for ideas and projects that grow out of our communications.

14. _____ you try to speed things up and leap ahead with conclusions as though we're in a rush.

15. _____ you smile at me and make me feel comfortable and valued.

16. _____ you make jokes about things that are serious to me and thereby belittle my concerns.

17. _____ you get defensive and argue before I can fully explain my point.

18. _____ you often make me feel I have nothing worthwhile to say.

19. _____ you ask questions which demonstrate your efforts to understand what I have to say.

20. _____ whether or not you agree with me, you make me feel my opinions and feelings are respected.

Part II adapted from Neugebauer, B. (1990, September/October). Are you listening? *Child Care Information Exchange*, p. 62. Reprinted with permission.

Organizational Norms

Rationale:

Norms are standards or codes of expected behavior — shared assumptions about the way things are done at the center. Most norms are seldom verbalized or made explicit in writing, yet they still serve as powerful regulators of behavior. When an individual violates a norm, others in the group will probably respond with some kind of sanction or subtle reminder that the behavior is out of bounds. Such enforcement can be in the form of joking or kidding, ignoring the individual, or taking the person aside to give a cautionary warning. Some norms are useful; they provide staff with implicit guidelines about what to do in different situations. Other norms, though, may be counterproductive, obsolete, irrelevant, or actually prevent the center from achieving its stated goals.

Periodically assessing staff's perceptions of the dominant norms that exist can provide useful data about the degree to which certain norms are shared by members of the staff. Such an inventory also helps staff identify those norms that may need to be altered if center improvement efforts are to take hold. Assessment Tool #9 was adapted from the work of Fox and Schmuck (1973), Jorde-Bloom (1986a), and Schmuck and Runkel (1985).

Directions:

Distribute a blank envelope and the two-page assessment "The Way Things Are Done Around Here..." to all teaching and support staff who work at the center more than ten hours per week. Place a box labeled "Questionnaire Return Box" in the center's office or staff room and ask staff to place their completed surveys in the box. Let the staff know that although they will be handwriting their responses, their anonymity will be maintained because an outside third party will be summarizing the data.

Scoring:

Because of the potentially sensitive nature of some of the responses to this assessment, it is advisable that an outside third party summarize the data. Summarizing the responses is a fairly straightforward process. Create a separate summary page for each of the seven categories included on the assessment. On each page, list all the norms that were mentioned by respondents along with the corresponding +, −, or o. If a norm is mentioned by more than one individual, do not list it twice, merely indicate an additional +, −, or o next to the norm already listed. Those norms that are mentioned by several people indicate they are fairly established, shared norms. Those mentioned by only one person may indicate a misperception by that individual of center expectations.

The director will need to decide how to use the data generated from the results of this assessment. If a climate of trust has been established at the center, the summarized results can serve as a wonderful springboard for a discussion at a staff meeting. Sharing the results of this assessment can serve to free individuals to examine those norms that are beneficial and those that may need to be changed.

While acknowledging that the director has a significant role in both creating and sustaining norms, changing some norms will need the collaborative support of the whole staff. The entire group must have a shared perception of the value of change; otherwise, the effort to change will be fruitless. Changing a norm usually means changing the way people behave. This means consensus not only about what the new behavior will be but also how that new behavior will be reinforced. The value of doing this extends beyond the specific norm being changed; for in the process the staff will become conscious of their own group dynamic and grow together in structuring collaborative change.

"The Way Things are Done Around Here..."

When individuals work together in a work setting, implicit agreement develops about the way in which things are supposed to be done. Over time, these shared patterns of behavior become standard and define the appropriate range of acceptable behavior in a wide range of situations. The term "norm" is used to describe these shared assumptions and expectations. Norms include things we are expected to do and things we should not do. Every center varies in the kinds of norms it has and in the intensity in which they are felt.

This assessment asks you to think about some of the do's and don'ts of your center. It is divided into seven different areas. Under each category, think of some of the norms (the do's and don'ts) that you feel are shared expectations.

Everyday Demeanor (Includes expectations about appropriate dress, whether or not smoking is allowed, the amount of noise tolerated, and the degree of formality in everyday manners)

_____   _____

_____   _____

_____   _____

Use of Space and Materials (Includes such things as expectations for sharing of supplies, who cleans up and how often, and the amount of clutter tolerated)

_____   _____

_____   _____

_____   _____

Time and Task Orientation (Includes such things as assumptions about workload, expectations for promptness in beginning meetings, and the degree of participation expected)

_____   _____

_____   _____

_____   _____

Professional Conduct with Children and Parents (Expectations about the kind of discipline used with children, the teacher's classroom behavior, and the degree of parental involvement)

_____   _____

_____   _____

_____   _____

Collegiality (Includes assumptions that govern social interaction among staff such as the degree to which staff are open or reserved in displaying emotions, the extent to which people talk about their personal lives, or how new teachers and substitutes are treated)

_____   _____

_____   _____

_____   _____

Communication and Decision Making (Includes expectations about the kinds of topics that staff feel free to discuss, taboo subjects, how much griping is allowed, how decisions are made, and the degree to which people are frank, open, and free to disagree with one another)

_____   _____

_____   _____

_____   _____

Change and Experimentation (Includes expectations for individual and group improvement, the degree of risktaking tolerated, and openness to new ideas and ways of doing things)

_____   _____

_____   _____

_____   _____

Now go back through each category of norms and in front of each norm you have written, indicate whether or not you think this is a useful norm. In other words, does it support the goals of the school and enhance the staff's ability to carry out its work? If you feel it is a positive norm, indicate so by putting a + in front of the norm. If you feel the norm detracts in any way from the center achieving its goals, indicate so by putting a – in front of the norm. If the norm is neutral, neither positive nor negative, put an o in front of the norm.

When you have completed this assessment, put your survey in the blank envelope provided and place it in the "Questionnaire Return Box" in the office.

**Thank you**

Group Meeting Processes

Rationale:

Because staff meetings are the primary vehicle for decision making and problem solving in our child care centers, it is imperative that we regularly assess staff perceptions about their effectiveness. Assessment Tool #10 assesses staff's perceptions about the organization, content, and flow of a staff meeting. It also asks for feedback about the roles that individuals played during the meeting. While the ostensible purpose of this assessment is to elicit information that will help you plan and conduct future meetings more effectively, it is also a useful staff development tool in helping staff begin to understand the important role they play as part of a group in ensuring successful meetings. Included with this assessment is a handout that can be distributed to staff. This handout, "The Roles People Play" will help staff tune into the many facilitating and blocking roles that individuals assume in group meetings. This assessment tool was adapted from the work of Jorde-Bloom (1982), and Schmuck and Runkel (1985).

Directions:

It is probably sufficient to do this assessment twice a year. The day following a typical staff meeting, distribute a blank envelope and the two-page "Checklist for Effective Staff Meetings" to all staff who attended the meeting. Place a box labeled "Questionnaire Return Box" in the office or staff room and ask all staff to place the envelopes containing their completed surveys in the box.

Scoring:

Tabulate the results of Part I by simply adding the total number of checks in the "yes" column. Scores will range from 0 to 20. Add together all respondents' scores and divide by the number of individuals returning surveys. This will yield an average staff score. A score higher than 15 indicates that staff were generally quite pleased with the organization, content, and flow of the meeting. Scores lower than 10 indicate there are some areas in the planning and conducting of the meeting that could be improved. It is important on this type of assessment to also note the range of scores (the highest and lowest score).

It is possible that the group average will mask a strong variation in responses. In other words, it is possible that a number of people were extremely happy with the meeting, while a number of others were quite dissatisfied. It would also be helpful to do an item analysis noting the two or three items that consistently achieved a "yes" rating by staff and those that were consistently rated "no." This will help you know what areas need improvement in the future.

Part II will provide some insights into the staff's perceptions of the different roles that people played during the meeting. This section is perhaps most useful as a check against your own perceptions of how supportive individuals were in guiding the flow of the meeting in a positive way.

Checklist for Effective Staff Meetings

PART I. Check (✓) yes or no to indicate your reaction to the following questions:

	yes	no
1. Were all participants informed ahead of time with an agenda?	___	___
2. Did the meeting start on time?	___	___
3. Did the meeting begin on a positive note?	___	___
4. Was the room arranged to facilitate good interaction between staff?	___	___
5. Was the content of the meeting relevant to all participants?	___	___
6. Did the group have enough background, information, and expertise to make necessary decisions?	___	___
7. Did all participants have a chance to express their opinions and offer suggestions if they wanted to?	___	___
8. Was the facilitator successful in keeping the discussion focused and on track?	___	___
9. Did the facilitator restate and summarize issues when necessary?	___	___
10. Was an understanding or consensus achieved on one issue before moving on to the next issue?	___	___
11. Was there sufficient time allotted for each item scheduled?	___	___
12. Did the facilitator allow enough room and flexibility to adapt the agenda to the needs of the group?	___	___
13. Was the facilitator able to guide discussion so that it did not get bogged down in trivia or turn to petty gossip?	___	___
14. Did most participants listen carefully to each other?	___	___
15. Did most participants express themselves openly, honestly, and directly?	___	___
16. Were differences of opinion on issues openly explored and constructively managed?	___	___
17. When a decision was made, was it clear who would carry it out and when?	___	___
18. Did the meeting end on a positive note?	___	___
19. Did the meeting end on time?	___	___
20. Overall, did you feel your time was well spent at this meeting?	___	___

PART II. In your judgment, which members of our staff contributed most to meeting effectiveness by: *(list names)*

Helping to get the meeting started on time?

_____   _____   _____

Sticking to the agenda?

_____   _____   _____

Performing acts of encouragement, warmth, friendly interest, and support?

_____   _____   _____

Bringing in ideas, information, and suggestions?

_____   _____   _____

Helping us stay on track, summarizing, and checking to make sure we understood one another?

_____   _____   _____

What suggestions do you have for improving our staff meetings in the future?

Part I adapted from Jorde-Bloom, P. (1982). *Avoiding burnout.* Lake Forest, IL: New Horizons, p. 273.
Part II adapted from Schmuck, R, & Runkel, P. (1985). *The handbook of organizational development in schools.* Prospect Heights, IL: Waveland, p. 170. Reprinted with permission.

The Roles People Play in Meetings and Groups

Group Building Roles

The Initiator	Begins the discussion and suggests new or different ideas for discussion
The Opinion Giver	States pertinent opinions and beliefs in discussion
The Elaborator	Builds on the suggestions of others
The Clarifier	Provides examples, offers rationales, probes for meaning and understanding
The Tester	Raises questions to test out ideas; sees if group is ready to make a decision
The Summarizer	Reviews the discussion and pulls it all together

Group Maintenance Roles

The Compromiser	Willing to yield when necessary for progress
The Tension Reliever	Uses humor appropriately; calls for breaks when necessary to re-energize
The Harmonizer	Mediates differences and reconciles points of view
The Encourager	Praises, supports others, and is friendly and encouraging
The Gatekeeper	Pays attention to the clock, is task-oriented, keeps communication flowing, and encourages participation

Group Blocking Roles

The Aggressor	Criticizes; deflates status and suggestions of others; disagrees aggressively
The Blocker	Rejects others' points of view; stubbornly disagrees; returns to previous topics
The Withdrawer	Won't participate; often converses privately
The Recognition Seeker	Boastful and engages in excessive talking; conscious of status
The Topic Jumper	Continually changes the subject and detours discussion
The Dominator	Tries to take over; will manipulate and assert authority
Special Interest Pleader	Uses the group's time to plead his/her own case
Playboy/Playgirl	Show-off and story teller; is nonchalant and cynical
The Self-Confessor	Talks irrelevantly about his/her own feelings
The Devil's Advocate	More devil than advocate

---

* Adapted from Wedgwood, H.C. (1967, July-August). Where committees go wrong. *Personnel*, p. 64-65. Reprinted with permission of the publisher, American Management Association, New York. All rights reserved.

Parent Satisfaction

Rationale:

Parents are an integral part of the overall organization of a center. How the parental role is understood and accepted by the director and staff is related to how well the center functions. Open, trusting relationships with parents are built on respecting parents' positive and negative views of the center's program and including parents in assessment. Assessment Tool #11 was designed to provide a vehicle for parents to provide feedback about center policies, procedures, and the overall quality of program services.

Directions:

To ensure that the questionnaire does not get lost among the soggy art work and miscellaneous treasures that make their way home in every child's tote bag, it is probably best to mail it directly to each child's home. A stamped return envelope addressed to the center should be included. You may want to even include a separate cover letter letting parents know the importance of providing accurate, candid feedback to the center and the date by which you would like the questionnaire returned. It is advisable to send out this kind of questionnaire annually. More often than that can create a burden for parents and unnecessary paperwork for you. Most directors find that late spring is a good time to conduct this kind of assessment.

Scoring:

You will probably find it useful to do an item analysis and note the percentage of parents that either strongly agree or strongly disagree with each individual item. The results of this summary (both positive and negative) should be shared with the parents in your center's newsletter. In the summary you provide, you needn't overwhelm parents with too many details, but be sure and note the total percentage of parents returning questionnaires and those three or four items that had a noteworthy percentage of parents that either strongly agreed or strongly disagreed.

Without revealing the identity of respondents, it is also good to include a few quotes in your summary about how their children have benefitted from the program and areas in need of improvement. Such a published summary will convey a strong message to parents about your earnest interest in their feedback, both positive and negative. Such information can only help enhance your center's overall reputation.

To determine how parent perceptions of your program improve over time, you may want to derive a total mean score for the assessment. The numerical scores will range from a low of 8 to a high of 40, with a high score indicating positive perceptions. Add together the parents' total scores and divide by the number of respondents to yield a mean score.

Parent Feedback Survey

Dear Parents,

This questionnaire is designed to find out how we are meeting the needs of families in our program. Your candid and honest responses will enable us to improve communication and services for you and your child. It is not necessary to put your name on this form. Circle the numeral from 1 (strongly disagree) to 5 (strongly agree) that best represents your feelings regarding each of the statements below.

		strongly disagree				strongly agree
1.	I have received adequate information about program policies and procedures.	1	2	3	4	5
2.	My child received a warm introduction into the program.	1	2	3	4	5
3.	Teachers encourage me to be actively involved in my child's learning.	1	2	3	4	5
4.	I am regularly informed about my child's development.	1	2	3	4	5
5.	Classroom newsletters and teachers' written notes keep me well informed.	1	2	3	4	5
6.	I have had sufficient opportunity for informal conversations with the teaching and administrative staff.	1	2	3	4	5
7.	My parent-teacher conferences have provided me with useful insights about my child.	1	2	3	4	5
8.	I have been invited to participate in classroom activities and field trips.	1	2	3	4	5

How has your child benefitted from his/her experience at this center?

In what ways could we improve the program to better meet your child's needs?

Teaching Practices
Interactions Among Staff and Children

Rationale:

Optimal development of a child in all areas — social, emotional, cognitive, and physical — depends on positive, supportive, and individualized relationships with adults. Young children also develop socially and intellectually through peer interaction (NAEYC, 1984). Taking the time to periodically observe classroom interactions among staff and children is one way to monitor the quality of program services. Assessment Tool #12 was adapted from the center accreditation guidelines developed by the National Association for the Education of Young Children. For a more detailed description of specific behaviors that are indicative of the items included on this scale, see *Accreditation Criteria and Procedures* (NAEYC, 1984, pp. 8-10) and *Guide to Accreditation* (NAEYC, 1985a, pp. 23-25).

Directions:

Separate forms should be used for each classroom observed. The director or supervisor completing the observation will probably want to observe these items over three or four days and at different times during the day. This is important because any slice of a day's activities will probably not accurately reflect all the teaching practices included on these forms. After observing each item noted on the following observation scale, indicate your rating by circling the appropriate numeral from 1 (little evidence) to 5 (a great deal of evidence).

Scoring:

After completing the observation, tally your total score for this scale at the bottom of the observation sheet. The range of scores on this observation tool will vary from a low of 15 to a high of 75. The results of this observation will be useful in identifying those teaching practices related to interactions in the classroom in which a particular teacher or group of teachers may need improvement. This information should prove useful in modifying supervisory practices to support more positive teacher-child and child-child interactions.

This instrument is particularly useful as a pre and post measure of change in teaching practices as they relate to classroom interactions among staff and children. The observed score on the first observation can serve as baseline data from which to measure change in the way an individual or group of individuals teach. If the instrument is used in this way, it will be important that both the pre and post assessments be conducted by the same observer.

Classroom Observations – Teaching Practices

Interactions Among Staff and Children

	little evidence		some evidence		a great deal of evidence
1. Staff interact frequently with children showing affection and respect.	1	2	3	4	5
2. Staff are available and responsive to children.	1	2	3	4	5
3. Staff speak with children in a friendly, courteous manner. Tone of voice is pleasant.	1	2	3	4	5
4. Staff talk with individual children, and encourage children of all ages to use language.	1	2	3	4	5
5. Staff treat children of all races, religions, and cultures equally with respect and consideration.	1	2	3	4	5
6. Staff provide children of both sexes with equal opportunity to take part in all activities.	1	2	3	4	5
7. Staff encourage independence in children as they are ready.	1	2	3	4	5
8. Staff use positive approaches to help children behave constructively.	1	2	3	4	5
9. Staff do not use physical punishment or negative forms of discipline.	1	2	3	4	5
10. Overall sound of the group is pleasant most of the time.	1	2	3	4	5
11. Children are generally comfortable, relaxed, and happy.	1	2	3	4	5
12. Staff help children deal with anger, sadness, and frustration.	1	2	3	4	5
13. Staff encourage prosocial behaviors in children such as cooperating, helping, and taking turns.	1	2	3	4	5
14. Staff expectations of children's social behavior are developmentally appropriate.	1	2	3	4	5
15. Children are encouraged to talk about feelings instead of solving problems with force.	1	2	3	4	5

Comments:

Total score _____

Adapted from NAEYC. (1984). *Accreditation criteria and procedures*, Washington, D.C., pp. 8-10. Reprinted with permission.

Teaching Practices
Curriculum

Rationale:

The curriculum of an early childhood program consists of the program goals, the daily schedule of planned activities, the availability and use of materials, transitions between activities, and the way in which routine tasks of classroom life are implemented. The curriculum should support the knowledge that young children learn through active manipulation of the environment and concrete experiences which contribute to the development of important concepts (NAEYC, 1984). Assessment Tool #13 was adapted from the center accreditation guidelines developed by the National Association for the Education of Young Children. For a more detailed description of specific behaviors that are indicative of the items included on this scale, see *Accreditation Criteria and Procedures* (NAEYC, 1984, pp. 11-14) and *Guide to Accreditation* (NAEYC, 1985a, pp. 26-33, 48).

Directions:

Separate forms should be used for each classroom observed. In completing the observation you will probably want to observe these items over several days and at different times during the day. This is important because any slice of a day's activities will probably not accurately reflect all the teaching practices included on this form. After observing each item noted on the following observation scale, indicate your rating by circling the appropriate numeral from 1 (little evidence) to 5 (a great deal of evidence).

Scoring:

After completing the observation, tally the total score for this scale at the bottom of the observation sheet. The range of scores on this observation tool will vary from a low of 20 to a high of 100. The results of this observation should prove useful in identifying those areas of the curriculum where a particular teacher or group of teachers may need improvement. This information can then be used to structure staff development opportunities that will support more developmentally appropriate curricular practices.

This instrument is particularly useful as a pre and post measure of change in teaching practices as they relate to the classroom curriculum. The score on the first observation can serve as baseline data from which to measure change in the way an individual or group of individuals teach. If the instrument is used in this way, it will be important that both the pre and post assessments be conducted by the same observer.

Classroom Observation – Teaching Practices

The Curriculum

		little evidence		some evidence		a great deal of evidence
1.	There is a balance of activities indoors and outdoors.	1	2	3	4	5
2.	There is a balance of quiet and active activities.	1	2	3	4	5
3.	There is a balance of individual/small group/large group activities.	1	2	3	4	5
4.	There is a balance of large muscle and small muscle activities.	1	2	3	4	5
5.	There is a balance of child-initiated and staff-initiated activities.	1	2	3	4	5
6.	Multiracial, nonsexist, nonstereotypic pictures, dolls, books, and materials are available.	1	2	3	4	5
7.	Developmentally appropriate materials and equipment are available for this age group of children.	1	2	3	4	5
8.	Staff provide developmentally appropriate hands-on activities that foster a positive self-concept in children.	1	2	3	4	5
9.	Staff provide hands-on activities that develop social skills.	1	2	3	4	5
10.	Staff provide developmentally appropriate hands-on activities that encourage children to think, reason, question, and experiment.	1	2	3	4	5
11.	Staff provide activities that encourage language development.	1	2	3	4	5
12.	Staff provide activities that enhance physical development.	1	2	3	4	5
13.	Staff provide developmentally appropriate hands-on activities that demonstrate sound health, safety, and nutritional practices.	1	2	3	4	5
14.	Staff provide developmentally appropriate hands-on activities that encourage creative expression and appreciation of the arts.	1	2	3	4	5
15.	Staff provide hands-on activities that respect cultural diversity.	1	2	3	4	5
16.	Staff provide materials and time for children to select their own activities during the day.	1	2	3	4	5
17.	Staff conduct smooth, unregimented transitions between activities.	1	2	3	4	5
18.	Staff are flexible enough to change planned or routine activities.	1	2	3	4	5
19.	Routine tasks such as diapering, toileting, eating, dressing, and sleeping are handled in a relaxed and individual manner.	1	2	3	4	5
20.	The staff's curriculum plan details goals for children that are based on assessment of individual needs and interests.	1	2	3	4	5

Comments:

Total score _____

Adapted from: NAEYC. (1984). *Accreditation criteria and procedures.* Washington, D.C. pp. 11-14. Reprinted with permission.

Teaching Practices
Health, Safety, and Nutrition

Rationale:

A safe and healthy environment is essential in the provision of quality early childhood program-ming. High quality programs act to prevent illness and accidents, are prepared to deal with emergencies as they occur, meet the nutritional needs of children with appetizing and healthful foods, and educate children concerning safe and healthy practices (NAEYC, 1984). Assessment Tool #14 is adapted from the center accreditation criteria developed by the National Association for the Education of Young Children. While many of the items on this assessment are beyond the indi-vidual teacher's control, they will alert center personnel about health, safety, and nutritional areas of the program that may need to be improved. For a more detailed description of what to look for with respect to the items included on this scale, see *Accreditation Criteria and Procedures* (NAEYC, 1984, pp. 28-36) and *Guide to Accreditation* (NAEYC, 1985a, pp. 36-40, 89-91).

Directions:

Separate forms should be used for each classroom observed. You will probably want to observe these items over three or four days and at different times during the day. After observing each item noted on the observation scale, indicate your rating by circling the appropriate numeral from 1 (little evidence) to 5 (a great deal of evidence).

Scoring:

After completing the observation, tally the ratings of individual items to generate a total score for this scale at the bottom of the observation sheet. The range of scores on this observa-tion tool will vary from a low of 20 to a high of 100. The results of this observation may be useful in identifying those health, safety, and nutritional practices in a classroom in which a particular teacher or group of teachers may need help improving. This information can then be used to structure staff development opportunities that will support more desired practices.

This instrument is particularly useful as a pre and post measure of change in teaching prac-tices as they relate to health, safety, and nutritional issues. The observed score on the first observation can serve as baseline data from which to measure change in the way an individual or group of individuals teach. If the instrument is used in this way, it will be important that both the pre and post assessments be conducted by the same observer.

Classroom Observation – Teaching Practices

Health, Safety, and Nutrition

		little evidence		some evidence		a great deal of evidence
1.	Children are under adult supervision at all times.	1	2	3	4	5
2.	Children are dressed appropriately for indoor and outdoor play.	1	2	3	4	5
3.	Staff and children keep areas reasonably clean.	1	2	3	4	5
4.	Toileting and diapering areas are sanitary.	1	2	3	4	5
5.	Staff wash their hands with soap and water before feeding, preparing or serving food, and after assisting children with toileting.	1	2	3	4	5
6.	A sink with running hot and cold water is very close to the diapering and toileting areas.	1	2	3	4	5
7.	The building, play yard, and all equipment are maintained in safe, clean condition and in good repair.	1	2	3	4	5
8.	Equipment/materials are safe for the age of children (e.g. infants' toys are large enough to prevent swallowing or choking).	1	2	3	4	5
9.	Toilets, drinking water, and handwashing facilities are safe and easily accessible to children.	1	2	3	4	5
10.	Soap and disposable towels are provided.	1	2	3	4	5
11.	Children wash hands after toileting and before meals.	1	2	3	4	5
12.	Areas used by children are well-lighted, ventilated, and kept at a comfortable temperature.	1	2	3	4	5
13.	Electrical outlets are covered with protective caps.	1	2	3	4	5
14.	Adequate first-aid supplies are readily available.	1	2	3	4	5
15.	Floor coverings are attached to the floor or backed with non-slip materials.	1	2	3	4	5
16.	Cushioning materials such as mats, wood chips, or sand are used under climbing equipment, slides and swings.	1	2	3	4	5
17.	Climbing equipment, swings, and large pieces of furniture are secure.	1	2	3	4	5
18.	All chemicals and potentially dangerous products such as medicines or cleaning supplies are stored out of the reach of children.	1	2	3	4	5
19.	Mealtime is a pleasant social and learning experience for children.	1	2	3	4	5
20.	Mealtimes encourage independence in children.	1	2	3	4	5

Comments:

Total score _____

Adapted from NAEYC. (1984). *Accreditation criteria and procedures*, Washington, D. C. pp. 28-36. Reprinted with permission.

Teaching Practices
Physical Environment

Rationale:

Considerable research exists documenting that the physical environment of child care centers affects the attitudes and behavior of both children and adults. The quality of the arrangement of the physical space and the adequacy of equipment and materials affects the level of involvement of the children and the quality of interactions between adults and children. Given the importance of the physical environment, the amount, arrangement, and use of space should be evaluated on a regular basis.

The items that comprise Assessment Tool #15 were drawn from *Accreditation Criteria and Procedures* (NAEYC, 1984, pp. 25-27). While several items on this instrument may be beyond the immediate control of individual classroom teachers, the results of the observation will provide center personnel with information on how the physical environment might be improved. This assessment can be supplemented by the use of other instruments such as *The High/Scope Curriculum: Room Arrangement Checklist* available from the High/Scope Educational Research Foundation.

Directions:

Separate forms should be used for each classroom observed. After observing each item noted on the observation scale, indicate your rating by circling the appropriate numeral from 1 (little evidence) to 5 (a great deal of evidence).

Scoring:

After completing the observation, tally the individual items to generate a total score for this scale at the bottom of the observation sheet. The range of scores on this observation tool will vary from a low of 15 to a high of 75. The results of this observation will be useful in identifying those aspects of the physical environment that may need improvement. It is also a useful observation to use as a pretest and posttest measure to discern differences in the quality of the physical environment after staff development.

Classroom Observation – Teaching Practices

Physical Environment

		little evidence		some evidence		a great deal of evidence
1.	There is enough usable space indoors so children are not crowded.	1	2	3	4	5
2.	There is enough usable space for outdoor play for each age group.	1	2	3	4	5
3.	Space is arranged to accommodate individual children, small groups, and large groups.	1	2	3	4	5
4.	A variety of age-appropriate materials and equipment are available for children indoors and outdoors.	1	2	3	4	5
5.	Individual space is provided for each child's belongings.	1	2	3	4	5
6.	Private areas where children can play or work alone or with a friend are available indoors and outdoors.	1	2	3	4	5
7.	The environment includes soft elements.	1	2	3	4	5
8.	Sound-absorbing materials such as ceiling tile and rugs are used to cut down noise.	1	2	3	4	5
9.	A variety of activities can go on outdoors throughout the year.	1	2	3	4	5
10.	The outdoor play area is protected from access to streets and other dangers.	1	2	3	4	5
11.	There is a sense of order and organization to the environment.	1	2	3	4	5
12.	Overall, the classroom is aesthetically pleasing.	1	2	3	4	5
13.	There is a place where staff can get away from the children.	1	2	3	4	5
14.	There is an adult-sized bathroom conveniently located for staff.	1	2	3	4	5
15.	There is a workspace for staff to store their belongings and prepare materials and teaching aids.	1	2	3	4	5

Comments:

Total score _____

Adapted from NAEYC. (1984). *Accreditation criteria and procedures.* Washington, D. C. pp. 25-27. Reprinted with permission.

Learning Style

Rationale:

Styles of thinking and approaches to learning vary among any group of individuals. These differences determine why some learning experiences are so stimulating and interesting to some people while downright boring to others. Understanding differences in learning styles is important for the director who is concerned about tailoring modes of presentation and staff development activities to the needs of the individuals on the staff. Assessment Tool #16 draws on the work of several researchers whose approach to assessing learning styles has been particularly useful in educational settings. Part I of this assessment tool looks at styles of thinking from a right brain/left brain perspective. This portion of the instrument was adapted from the work of Wonder and Donovan (1984), McCarthy (1980), and Torrance (1979). Part II of Assessment Tool #16 looks at the environmental, emotional, sociological, and physical elements of one's preferred learning style. This portion of the assessment was adapted from the work of Dunn and Dunn (1978).

Directions:

This learning styles assessment tool is particularly useful to administer to new employees as you prepare their staff development profile for the first time. Since learning style is a fairly stable construct (it doesn't change from day to day), it will not be necessary to administer the assessment tool again for two or three years. The individual should be allowed to take the assessment tool home and spend as much time to complete it as necessary. The directions preceding Part I and Part II are self-explanatory.

Scoring:

It is suggested you do the scoring of this assessment together with the individual teacher. This will provide a good opportunity for the two of you to talk about the meaning of different learning styles as they relate to your work setting. For Part I, count the number of times the individual circled an (a) response to a question. These answers are associated with left-brain thinking. The (b) responses are associated with a right-brain orientation. More than a 10-point difference between the (a) and (b) totals would indicate that the individual probably has a strong preference for that orientation. If the results of the scoring show a balance between both orientations, the individual has an integrated style. Use the summary chart in the section labeled "Interpreting Part I" to review the characteristics of left-brain and right-brain dominance.

There are no specific scoring directions for Part II. This section provides a wealth of data, however, that will provide a comprehensive picture of an individual teacher's preferred learning style. This can be particularly useful as you design and implement staff development opportunities for that person. You may want to make some of the references noted earlier available to staff who express an interest in learning more about their learning style. Also recommended is an article by Patricia Scallan that appeared in October, 1988 issue of *Child Care Information Exchange*.

Appreciating Individual Differences

The purpose of this assessment is to help you gain greater insight into your style of thinking and your preferred learning style. This assessment will take about 30 minutes to complete. Set aside some quiet time for yourself where you won't be interrupted or distracted. For Part I, answer the questions quickly; don't try to over-analyze yourself. Simply circle the answer (a or b) that seems to characterize the way you approach different situations. There are no right or wrong answers. In Part II, take your time and write down your answers to each of the questions in as much detail as possible.

Part I. Styles of Thinking

1. In a problem situation do you...
    a. write down and consider all alternatives, and then pick the best?
    b. wait to see if the situation will right itself?

2. Do you think daydreaming is...
    a. a waste of time?
    b. a viable tool for planning your future?

3. In making decisions, are you more apt to...
    a. rely on facts, information, and logic?
    b. gut feelings and intuition?

4. In planning a typical day, do you...
    a. make a list of all the things you need to do?
    b. just let it happen?

5. With respect to organization, do you...
    a. have a place for everything and a system to keep things organized?
    b. feel comfortable with clutter — organization can stifle spontaneity?

6. Do you learn new sports and athletic skills by...
    a. learning the sequence and repeating the steps mentally?
    b. imitating, getting the feel of the sport?

7. Do you express yourself well verbally?
    a. yes
    b. no

8. Are you goal-oriented?
    a. yes
    b. no

9. When you want to remember directions, a name, or a news item, do you?
    a. write down notes to help you remember?
    b. visualize the information?

10. Do you remember faces easily?
    a. no
    b. yes

11. In attending meetings and keeping appointments, are you...
    a. on time?
    b. often late?

12. In an argument, do you tend to...
    a. find an authority to support your point?
    b. become animated, talk louder, even pound the table?

13. Do you have a sense of how much time has passed without looking at your watch?
    a. yes
    b. no

14. Do you gesture to...
    a. make a point?
    b. express your feelings?

15. In preparing yourself for a new or difficult task, do you...
    a. prepare notes and gather data regarding the task?
    b. visualize yourself accomplishing the task effectively?

16. Which handwriting position do you prefer?
    a. right handed
    b. left handed

17. When you sit and clasp your hands comfortably in your lap, which thumb is on top?
    a. left
    b. right

18. With respect to mood shifts, do you...
    a. experience almost no mood changes?
    b. experience frequent mood changes?

19. In a conversation with another person, do you...
    a. focus on what people say?
    b. interpret their body language?

20. Do you enjoy taking risks?
    a. no
    b. yes

Part I adapted from Wonder, J., & Donovan, P. (1984). *Whole brain thinking*. New York: W. W. Morrow & Co., pp. 31-39.

Interpreting Part I.

This assessment provides a profile of your cognitive style or brain dominance. We sometimes refer to this as left-brain or right-brain thinking. To determine your orientation, count the number of times you circled the (a) response to a question. These answers are associated with left-brain thinking. The (b) responses are associated with a right-brain orientation. If you had a 10 point difference between your (a) and (b) totals, you probably have a strong preference for that orientation. If you have a balance between both orientations, you have an integrated style. This means that your orientation draws on both the left-brain and right-brain in terms of your preference in cognitive style. Below is a summary of the characteristics of left-brain and right-brain dominance.*

LEFT (analytic)	*RIGHT (global)*
* trusts logic	* trusts intuition
* remembers names	* remembers faces
* responds to verbal instructions and explanations	* responds to demonstrated, illustrated or symbolic instructions
* systematic/sequential	* random
* solves problems by breaking them down into parts using logic	* solves problems by looking at the whole, looking for patterns, relying on hunches
* makes objective judgments	* makes subjective judgments
* planned and structured	* fluid and spontaneous
* prefers established, certain information	* prefers elusive, uncertain information
* analyzer	* synthesizer
* relies on language in thinking and remembering	* relies on images in thinking and remembering
* prefers talking and writing	* prefers drawing and manipulating objects
* prefers multiple choice tests	* prefers open-ended questions
* prefers carefully planned work and study	* prefers open-ended work and study
* prefers hierarchical (ranked) authority structures	* prefers collegial (participative) authority structures
* controls feelings (reflective)	* free with feelings (impulsive)
* plans ahead	* spontaneous
* speaks with few gestures	* gestures when speaking
* punctual	* less punctual
* responds to facts and dates	* recalls images and patterns
* appears tidy and organized	* appears disorganized

* Adapted from McCarthy, B. (1980). *The 4 MAT system.* Oak Brook, IL: EXCEL, Inc., p.79. Reprinted with permission.

Part II. Diagnosing Learning Style

Environmental Elements

* ***Sound*** — Do you learn best with music playing in the background, or do you need it absolutely quiet to concentrate? Are you able to screen out people's conversations and other extraneous environmental noise when you read and concentrate on a task?

* ***Light*** — Do you find either bright or dim lights distracting? Do you work best in natural filtered daylight? Describe your preference.

* ***Temperature*** — Are you affected by extremes in ambient temperature? Do you prefer cool, warm, or moderate temperatures in which to learn?

* ***Design*** — When you read something that requires your full attention, do you prefer to sit in an easy chair, a hard back chair, or do you like to stretch out on the carpet? Do you prefer formal or informal room arrangements when you attend a workshop or lecture?

Emotional Elements

* ***Motivation*** — Under what learning conditions do your sources of motivation differ? When do you need extrinsic reinforcement to encourage you to tackle new knowledge and skill areas (praise, grades, pay bonus)? Under what conditions are you intrinsically motivated to learn something new?

* ***Persistence*** — How would you describe yourself with respect to your level of persistence in learning new things? Do you prefer to set short, achievable goals or do you have a level of persistence that allows you to tackle long-range goals and objectives?

* ***Responsibility*** — Under what conditions are you most likely to take responsibility for your own learning?

* ***Structure*** — Do you like to have new areas of learning highly structured and tightly supervised or do you prefer to set your own goals and monitor your own progress?

Sociological Elements

* ***Grouping*** — What types of things do you learn best on your own, in small groups, or in large groups? What kinds of collegial staff development experiences do you find most rewarding?

Physical Elements

* ***Perceptual Preference*** — If you rely on a **visual** perceptual style when you learn new things, you learn best when information is written out, when there are ample diagrams, charts, and tables, and when visual media such as films, videos, and pictures are used. If you have an **auditory** preference, you learn best by hearing things spoken. You like discussions and lectures and have a facility for phonetically sounding out words you do not know. If you are primarily **kinesthetic** in your perceptual preference, you learn best by touching, moving, and feeling. You like to be active and involved in learning new things. Describe your perceptual preferences.

* ***Intake*** — How important is it to you to have something to eat or nibble on when you focus on a new task? Do you like to chew gum or drink something when you master something new?

* ***Time*** — Some people are more alert in the morning; others prefer to tackle new learning tasks in the afternoon or evening. Describe your preference.

* ***Mobility*** — When you attend a staff development workshop, do you need to get up and move around at regular intervals? When you work at a computer or when you read, do you like to take frequent breaks to stretch you muscles, or can you sit and concentrate for long periods?

Part II adapted from Dunn, R., & Dunn, K. (1978). *Teaching students through their individual learning styles.* Reston, VA: Reston Publishing, pp. 18-24. Reprinted with permission.

Temperament/Psychological Type

Rationale:

People differ in fundamental ways; they have distinct preferences for how they take in information and reach conclusions about the world. These different preferences for how we "function" are important because they govern both behavior (how we act in different situations) and beliefs (how we feel about different situations). A theory to explain these personality differences was first proposed by Carl Jung. Jung believed that individuals could be typed by their preference for a certain function. Jung's theory was popularized by the work of Isabel Briggs Myers who developed the Myers-Briggs Type Indicator (MBTI). The work of Jung and Myers is important because an understanding of the different psychological types can elicit a deeper appreciation for those who function differently than we do.

Assessment Tool #17 was designed as a self-assessment of psychological type along four dimensions: extraversion/introversion; sensing/intuition; thinking/feeling; and judging/perceiving. While the theoretical framework for this assessment tool is drawn from the work of Jung (1923) and Myers (1980), several other sources were useful in clarifying the concepts associated with temperament and psychological type (Champagne & Hogan, 1981; Keirsey & Bates, 1978; Kroeger & Thuesen, 1988; Lawrence, 1982). Assessment Tool #17 is not meant to substitute for the kind of thorough analysis of psychological type that can come from the administration of the Myers-Briggs Type Indicator. Rather, it is designed as a brief introduction to the concept and terminology. Directors interested in a more precise assessment of psychological type are encouraged to contact a psychologist or counselor who is professionally qualified to administer the MBTI.

Directions:

Administering the "Tuning Into Your Psychological Type" will probably be most useful shortly after you have hired a new staff member and are preparing his/her staff development profile for the first time. Since one's temperament or psychological type is a fairly stable construct and does not change from month to month, it will probably not be necessary to use this assessment tool more than once every three or four years. When you distribute the assessment to your staff, ask them to take it home and complete it where they have no distractions. Emphasize that there are no right or wrong answers. The information gleaned from this assessment will assist you in identifying and understanding the different psychological types represented by the center staff. It can also help you appreciate the importance of hiring a diverse staff that represents different psychological typologies.

Scoring:

Directions for scoring this assessment are included on the instrument itself. Also included is a handout that describes the effects of combinations of different preferences. In addition to the interpretation of temperament/psychological type that is provided here, it is highly recommended that you obtain copies of two or three of the following resources for a more complete description of the different psychological typologies.

Myers, I. B. (1980). *Introduction to type.* Palo Alto, CA: Consulting Psychologists Press.

Myers, I. B. (1980). *Gifts differing.* Palo Alto, CA: Consulting Psychologists Press.

Lawrence, G. (1982). *People types and tiger stripes.* Gainsville, FL: Center for Applications of Psychological Type, Inc.

Keirsey, D., & Bates, M. (1978). *Please understand me.* Del Mar, CA: Prometheus Nemesis.

Kroeger, O., & Thuesen, J. (1988). *Typetalk.* New York: Dell Publishing.

Kurtz R. (1991, Jan/Feb). Stabilizer, catalyst, troubleshooter, or visionary — Which are you? *Child Care Information Exchange*, 27-31.

Champagne, D., & Hogan, C. (1981). *Consultant supervision: Theory and skill development.* Wheaton, IL: CH Publications.

Tuning Into Your Psychological Type

Just as each of us has distinctive fingerprints, so too, do we have different preferences for how we perceive the world and make decisions that guide our everyday behavior. These preferences, in large part, shape our personality. The purpose of this survey is to provide a brief profile of your personality preferences with respect to four different dimensions: extraversion/introversion; sensing/intuition; thinking/feeling; and judging/perceiving. The labels associated with each of these dimensions are value free. In other words, a preference for a pattern of behavior associated with one end of a continuum is not necessarily better than the other. Likewise in some dimensions, you may exhibit a strong preference, while in other dimensions you may be more evenly balanced in your preferences. The most important thing to keep in mind is that there are no right or wrong answers.

As you read each statement, use the following coding system to indicate your responses. A description and interpretation of each dimension follows each section.

0 = not like me at all   *1 = somewhat like me*   *2 = exactly like me*

Extraversion

_____ Most of my social activities occur in the context of a group.
_____ I readily offer my opinion on issues.
_____ I feel comfortable initiating conversations with people.
_____ I enjoy working with others on projects and tasks.
_____ I find listening more difficult than talking.
_____ I feel energized when I am with a lot of people.
_____ I thrive on action and variety.
_____ I'd like to have a telephone answering machine so I wouldn't miss a call.
_____ I get impatient when things aren't happening.
_____ I don't mind interruptions when I am working.

_____ **Total Extraversion (E) score**

Introversion

_____ I am perceived as a good listener.
_____ I prefer a few close friends to a large number of casual acquaintances.
_____ I usually wait until I am approached before engaging in conversation.
_____ I often rehearse things before I say them.
_____ I relish having quiet time during the day to reflect and think.
_____ I'd like to have a telephone answering machine so I could screen my calls.
_____ In school I preferred written assignments to oral presentations.
_____ I dislike interruptions.
_____ I prefer to work alone on projects and tasks.
_____ I can concentrate for a long time on a single task.

_____ **Total Introversion (I) score**

The Extraversion/Introversion dimension has to do with the source, direction, and focus of one's energy. Extraverts are energized by the outer world. They are actively involved with people and things around them. For introverts, reflection, introspection, and solitude produce energy, focus, and attention. Introverts are more involved with concepts and ideas. They turn to the inner world of ideas and private thoughts.

Write the letter of the pattern that best describes you, (E) Extraversion or (I) Introversion? _____
(If your scores on the Extraversion and Introversion scales are the same, put an X in the space above)

Sensing   _____   I am good at recalling facts and details.
    _____   I carry out directions by completing each task in the order given.
    _____   I avoid conversations having to do with global ideas or abstractions.
    _____   I am a keen observer.
    _____   I am a realist — a practical sort of person.
    _____   I prefer the known to the unknown.
    _____   I like jobs that produce tangible results.
    _____   I get frustrated when people don't give clear instructions.
    _____   I do my job without worrying about how it fits into the larger scheme of things.
    _____   I like utilizing and refining the skills I have rather than learning new ones.

_____   ***Total Sensing (S) score***

Intuition   _____   I enjoy discussing conceptual schemes, ideas, and theories.
    _____   When I read a report, I look for the implications of the ideas presented.
    _____   I get impatient with routine tasks.
    _____   I have a vivid imagination.
    _____   When I read a magazine, I jump randomly from article to article.
    _____   I dislike reading directions; precise details bother me.
    _____   I enjoy trying to solve problems.
    _____   I've never enjoyed balancing my checkbook.
    _____   I'd rather learn a new skill than refine an old one.
    _____   I like to see the interconnections between things and come up with new possibilities.

_____   ***Total Intuition (N) score***

The Sensing/Intuition dimension has to do with how we gather information and perceive reality. Sensing types look at facts and details. They tend to be down-to-earth, very literal, and realistic. Sensing types are sequential in their thinking and rely on their five senses as a means of gathering information. They prefer the practical and enjoy hands-on tangible experiences. Intuition types, on the other hand, are concerned with the "big picture," the grand scheme of things. They are more abstract in the way they process information. Intuition types tend to look at the relationships between things. They strive to understand the meaning of situations to order to achieve insight and solve problems.

Write the letter of the pattern that best describes you, (S) Sensing or (N) Intuition? _____
(If your scores on the Sensing and Intuition scales are the same, put an X in the space above)

Thinking   _____   I am very rational in my decision making.
    _____   I rank and weight factors before making a decision.
    _____   I am comfortable with orderly rules.
    _____   I believe it is more important to be fair-minded than warm-hearted.
    _____   I can remain cool and calm in almost any situation.
    _____   I am very logical in the way I approach issues.
    _____   I keep my feelings to myself.
    _____   My style is brief and businesslike.
    _____   You can count on me to give constructive criticism.
    _____   I base decisions on what is fair and equitable and not what makes people happy.

_____   ***Total Thinking (T) score***

Feeling   _____ I believe good decisions always consider other people's feelings.

_____ I get impatient with people who plod through logical processes.

_____ Harmonious interpersonal relations are a high priority for me.

_____ In conversations, I tend to focus on the "who" rather than the "what."

_____ I am a very empathetic person.

_____ I go out of my way to accommodate other people.

_____ My heart guides my decision making.

_____ People sometimes take advantage of me.

_____ I show my feelings freely.

_____ I can usually predict how others will feel.

_____ ***Total Feeling (F) score***

The Thinking/Feeling dimension relates to how we make decisions about the information we've gathered. Thinking types tend to be very objective and analytical. They are logical in their decision-making processes and purposefully impersonal. Thinking types weigh facts objectively considering all sides of an issue, including the consequences of a decision. Feeling types are more subjective, using their personal value system for making decisions. Understanding people, achieving harmony, and feeling compassion are important to feeling types. They tend to need approval and personal support more than they need to achieve in intellectual tasks. Don't let the labels for this dimension mislead you. Thinking types certainly have feelings and feeling types surely have a capacity to think. When making decisions, however, their preferences for how to arrive at a decision are very different.

Write the letter of the pattern that best describes you, (T) Thinking or (F) Feeling? _____
(If your scores on the Thinking and Feeling scales are the same, put an X in the space above)

Judging   _____ I make decisions easily and quickly.

_____ Most of my daily activities are planned.

_____ Sometimes I make decisions too hastily.

_____ I work well with deadlines.

_____ I like to finish one project before starting another.

_____ I like things settled and decided.

_____ I am methodical and organized.

_____ It bothers me when people are not on time.

_____ I am more planned than spontaneous.

_____ I love the feeling that comes with completing a project.

_____ ***Total Judging (J) score***

Perceiving   _____ I like to examine an issue from all sides before making a decision.

_____ Sometimes I put off making decisions.

_____ I need little structure in my daily activities.

_____ I take life at a leisurely pace.

_____ I am able to adapt to almost any situation.

_____ I do just fine without a "to do" list.

_____ I am easily distracted.

_____ Some people think of me as being disorganized.

_____ I pride myself on being flexible.

_____ I sometimes have a problem finishing tasks.

_____ ***Total Perceiving (P) score***

The final dimension, Judging/Perceiving, has do with how we structure our lives — it is our lifestyle orientation. Judging types tend to have rather structured, scheduled, and organized personal and professional lives. They tend to see a "right way" to do things and proceed accordingly. Judging types are also decisive and deliberate when making decisions. Perceiving types, on the other hand, need variety, novelty, and change. They prefer to stand back and use a "wait and see" style when confronted with the need to make a decision. They often have a poor concept of time and feel comfortable with "a go with the flow" attitude toward life. They are more flexible, spontaneous, and adaptive than judging types.

Write the letter of the pattern that best describes you, (J) Judging or (P) Perceiving? _____
(If your scores on the Judging and Perceiving scales are the same, put an X in the space above)

Determining Your Typology

Write the four letters that make up your typology:

_____	_____	_____	_____
E or I	S or N	T or F	J or P

With the four pairs of preferences, there are 16 different possible combinations. Each typology is different from the others. There is no one "best" typology.

Circle your typology:

ISTJ	ISFJ	INFJ	INTJ
ISTP	ISFP	INFP	INTP
ESTP	ESFP	ENFP	ENTP
ESTJ	ESFJ	ENFJ	ENTJ

If your scores were the same on any one of the dimensions and you indicated an X for your preference, then circle the two typologies for that dimension. (For example if your type was EXTP, then you would circle ENTP and ESTP.)

The following table provides a brief description of the effects of combinations of different preferences. Remember, however, that condensing a description into a table involves considerable oversimplification and possibly even distortion of the richness and complexity of each typology. It should be underscored, therefore, that these brief descriptions should be used with caution. For a more complete description of each typology, several references are noted in the cover sheet to this assessment. These references will provide a fuller treatment of temperament and psychological types.

Description of Different Typologies

ISTJ	ISFJ	INFJ	INTJ
Serious, quiet, earn success by concentration and thoroughness. Practical, orderly, matter-of-fact, logical, realistic, and dependable. See to it that everything is well organized. Take responsibility. Make up their own minds as to what should be accomplished and work toward it steadily, regardless of distractions.	Quiet, friendly, responsible and conscientious. Work devotedly to meet obligations and serve their friends and school. Thorough, painstaking, accurate. May need time to master technical subjects, as their interests are not often technical. Patient with detail and routine. Loyal, considerate, concerned with how people feel.	Succeed by perseverance, originality and desire to do whatever is needed or wanted. Put their best efforts into their work. Quietly forceful, conscientious, concerned for others. Respected for their firm principles. Likely to be honored and followed for their clear convictions as to how best to serve the common good.	Have original minds and great drive which they use only for their own purposes. In fields that appeal, they have ability to organize a job and carry it through with or without help. Skeptical, critical, independent, often stubborn. Must learn to yield less important points in order to win the most important.
ISTP	**ISFP**	**INFP**	**INTP**
Cool onlookers, quiet, reserved, observing, analyzing life with detached curiosity and unexpected flashes of original humor. Usually interested in impersonal principles, cause and effect, or how and why mechanical things work. Exert themselves no more than necessary, because waste of energy would be inefficient.	Retiring, quietly friendly, sensitive, and modest about abilities. Shun disagreements, do not force opinions or values on others. Usually do not care to lead but are loyal followers. May be rather relaxed about assignments or getting things done because they enjoy the present moment and do not want to spoil it by undue haste.	Full of enthusiasm but seldom talk of ideas until they know you well. Care about learning, ideas, language, and independent projects of their own. Tend to undertake too much, then somehow get it done. Friendly, but often too absorbed in what they are doing to be sociable or notice much.	Quiet, reserved, brilliant in exams, especially in theoretical or scientific subjects. Logical to the point of hair-splitting. Interested mainly in ideas, with little liking for parties or small talk. Tend to have very sharply defined interests. Need career where strong interests can be used.
ESTP	**ESFP**	**ENFP**	**ENTP**
Matter-of-fact, do not worry or hurry, enjoy whatever comes along. Tend to like mechanical things and sports, with friends on the side. May be blunt or insensitive. Can do math or science when they see the need. Dislike long explanations. Are best with real things that can be worked, handled, taken apart or put back together.	Outgoing, easygoing, accepting, friendly, fond of a good time. Like sports and making things. Know what's going on and join in eagerly. Find remembering facts easier than mastering theories. Are best in situations that need sound common sense and practical ability with people as well as with things.	Warmly enthusiastic, high-spirited, ingenious, imaginative. Able to do almost anything that interests them. Quick with a solution for any difficulty and ready to help anyone with a problem. Often rely on their ability to improvise instead of preparing in advance. Can always find compelling reasons for whatever they want.	Quick, ingenious, good at many things. Stimulating company, alert, outspoken, argue for fun on either side of a question. Resourceful in solving new challenging problems, but may neglect routine assignments. Turn to one new interest after another. Can always find logical reason for whatever they want.
ESTJ	**ESFJ**	**ENFJ**	**ENTJ**
Practical realists, matter-of-fact, with a natural head for business. Not interested in subjects see no use for, but can apply themselves when necessary. Like to organize and run activities. Tend to run things well, especially if they remember to consider other people's feelings and points of view when making decisions.	Warm-hearted, talkative, popular, conscientious, cooperative, active committee members. Always doing something nice for someone. Work best with plenty of encouragement and praise. Little interest in abstract thinking or technical subjects. Main interest is in things that directly and visibly affect people's lives.	Responsive and responsible. Feel real concern for what others think and want, and try to handle things with due regard for other people's feelings. Can present a proposal or lead a group discussion with ease and tact. Sociable, popular, active in school affairs, but put time enough on their work to do good job.	Hearty, frank, able in studies. Leaders in activities. Usually good in anything that requires reasoning and intelligent talk, such as public speaking. Well-informed and keep adding to their fund of knowledge. May sometimes be more positive and confident than their experience in an area warrants.

Beliefs and Values

Rationale:

Teachers' attitudes and beliefs about children provide the foundation for their philosophy of teaching. Because beliefs are grounded in one's values, they have a strong impact on shaping behavior. Teachers' values also govern how they will react when confronted with the inevitable ethical dilemmas that occur from time to time. The director's role is one of assuring that the beliefs and values of individual teachers is consonant with the shared beliefs and stated philosophy of the center. Assessment Tool #18 asks teachers to reflect on their attitudes and beliefs about children, parents, and their own teaching role in the classroom. The information gleaned from this self-assessment will help you to better understand the undergirding values and beliefs that drive the teaching practices you observe in the classroom. Without clarification of these values, it is difficult to set goals for changing attitudes and behaviors.

Directions:

Since a teacher's attitudes and feelings about her teaching role change over time with experience, it is important to administer this kind of self assessment annually. It will provide you with valuable insights as you compile your staff development profile for each teacher. Assure your teachers of the confidentiality of their responses. You may even want to let them take the assessment home to complete it when they have more time and fewer distractions. Emphasize that there are no right or wrong answers to this assessment.

Scoring:

No quantitative score is generated by this instrument. Rather, the answers themselves should be used to generate discussion between you and your teachers about how attitudes and beliefs undergird one's philosophy of teaching.

Values Clarification

Values are enduring beliefs — ideas that we cherish and regard highly. Values influence the decisions we make and the course of action we follow. Some values we prize more deeply than others; they become standards by which we live. The purpose of this assessment is to help you assess the values and beliefs that guide your teaching attitudes and behaviors.

PART I. Complete the following sentences.

1. I think children are generally _____

2. When children are unhappy, it's usually because _____

3. I get angry when children _____

4. The most important thing a teacher can do is _____

5. Children should not _____

6. All children are _____

7. I wish parents would _____

8. When parents _____ I feel _____

PART II. Circle the five traits or characteristics you would like children to be or have as a result of their preschool experience with you.

adventurous	open-minded	determined
affectionate	inquisitive	energetic
polite	respectful	friendly
altruistic	self-starter	obedient
caring	sense of humor	spontaneous
honest	industrious	persistent
assertive	creative	proud
confident	independent thinker	risk-taker
cheerful	desire to excel	appreciate beauty

Job Satisfaction

Rationale:

Job satisfaction may be defined as an individual's evaluation of his/her job. It is a kind of "psychological contract" between the worker and demands of the workplace that is influenced by personal needs, values, and expectations (Jones & James, 1979; Jorde-Bloom, 1989a; Mumford, 1972). Put more simply, job satisfaction is the discrepancy between real conditions and ideal conditions. When job satisfaction is high, the discrepancy between existing and ideal conditions will be small. But job satisfaction is more than just a global feeling that things are going well or not so well. Indeed, many aspects of our work contribute to our feelings of professional fulfillment; and it is possible to be quite content in one facet of our work and discouraged and frustrated in another. Assessment Tool #19 is a modified version of the *Early Childhood Job Satisfaction Survey* (Jorde-Bloom, 1989a) which assesses five facets of job satisfaction: co-worker relations, supervisor relations, nature of the work itself, working conditions, and pay and promotion opportunities. The following page includes a fuller description of each facet.

Directions:

It is important to convey to staff that the "Work Attitudes Questionnaire" is a self-assessment designed to help each employee explore those areas of his/her job that are most satisfying and those that may need improvement. The employee is responsible for scoring the assessment and developing his/her own personal profile. This profile may then be brought to the goal setting conference and used as a springboard for discussing the individual's feelings about his/her job.

Examining the interaction between the nature of the work setting and individual attitudes may facilitate effective job restructuring. The goal, of course, is to implement organizational practices that facilitate a good fit. Sometimes, however, the analysis may lead to the realization that the fit is not right — that the individual and the center have differing goals and expectations. Many new teachers, for example, have unrealistic expectations about their jobs. Directors can specifically ask questions that relate to workers' conceptions of their ideal job with respect to each job facet. Such information may help reduce the incidence of mismatch in perceptions of what the role and work setting can offer and thus promote greater professional fulfillment.

Scoring:

The directions for scoring the "Work Attitudes Questionnaire" are included on the assessment.

Facets of Job Satisfaction

Satisfaction with...	Definition
Co-worker relations	The extent to which a worker has formed close relationships with colleagues. The degree of mutual trust and respect.
Supervisor relations	Perceived quality and quantity of feedback, encouragement, and helpful support from supervisor. The worker's assessment of supervisor's overall competence.
The nature of the work itself	Includes various job components as they relate to the nature of the work experience (degree of challenge, variety, autonomy, and control) as well as the sheer quantity of tasks to be done and the time frame in which to do them. Extent to which job provides intrinsic enjoyment and fulfills one's needs for recognition, creativity, and skill building. Also includes task identity (the perceived importance of the work).
Working conditions	Includes both the structure of the work experience (flexibility of hours, teacher-child ratio, adequacy of breaks, substitutes, and teaching materials) as well as the context in which the work is performed (the aesthetic quality of the physical environment, overall noise level, heat, ventilation, light, and spatial arrangement).
Pay and promotion opportunities	Concerns the adequacy of pay as well as the perceived equity and fairness of policies regarding the distribution of pay, fringe benefits, and opportunities for advancement. Also includes the worker's perceived job security.

From Jorde-Bloom, P. (1988c). Factors influencing overall job satisfaction and organizational commitment in early childhood work environments. *Journal of Research in Childhood Education*, 3(2), 110.

Work Attitudes Questionnaire

This survey is designed to find out how you feel about different facets of your job. The purpose of this assessment is to help you become more aware of those aspects of your work that contribute most to your job satisfaction, and those which you would like to improve. Clearly, the success of this assessment depends on your candid and honest responses. After you have scored your survey, you will develop a personal job satisfaction profile. This summary profile will be useful when you meet with your supervisor or director to plan your professional goals.

PART I. Check (✓) the corresponding space (strongly disagree to strongly agree) to indicate how you feel about each of the statements in the categories below:

My Co-workers...

	strongly disagree				strongly agree
1. care about me	___	___	___	___	___
2. encourage and support me	___	___	___	___	___
3. share their personal concerns with me	___	___	___	___	___
4. are hard to get to know	___	___	___	___	___
5. are critical of my performance	___	___	___	___	___
6. are competitive	___	___	___	___	___
7. are not very helpful	___	___	___	___	___
8. share ideas and resources with me	___	___	___	___	___
9. can't be trusted	___	___	___	___	___
10. are enjoyable to work with	___	___	___	___	___

My Supervisor...

11. respects my work	___	___	___	___	___
12. is too busy to know how I'm doing	___	___	___	___	___
13. supervises me too closely	___	___	___	___	___
14. gives me helpful feedback	___	___	___	___	___
15. asks for my opinion	___	___	___	___	___
16. is tactful	___	___	___	___	___
17. is not very dependable	___	___	___	___	___
18. encourages me to try new ideas	___	___	___	___	___
19. makes me feel inadequate	___	___	___	___	___
20. is unpredictable	___	___	___	___	___
21. is stimulating and challenging	___	___	___	___	___

My Work...   *strongly*   *strongly*
                                                           disagree   *agree*

22. is respected by the parents of my students   ___   ___   ___   ___   ___

23. involves too much paperwork and record keeping   ___   ___   ___   ___   ___

24. does not have enough variety   ___   ___   ___   ___   ___

25. is not very creative   ___   ___   ___   ___   ___

26. makes an important difference in my students' lives   ___   ___   ___   ___   ___

27. does not match my training and skills   ___   ___   ___   ___   ___

28. gives me a sense of accomplishment   ___   ___   ___   ___   ___

29. there is too little time to do all there is to do   ___   ___   ___   ___   ___

30. I have control over most things that affect my satisfaction   ___   ___   ___   ___   ___

Working Conditions...

31. my work schedule is flexible   ___   ___   ___   ___   ___

32. the teacher/child ratio is adequate   ___   ___   ___   ___   ___

33. I always know where to find the things I need   ___   ___   ___   ___   ___

34. I feel too cramped   ___   ___   ___   ___   ___

35. I need some new equipment/materials to do my job well   ___   ___   ___   ___   ___

36. the decor of my center is drab   ___   ___   ___   ___   ___

37. this center meets my standards of cleanliness   ___   ___   ___   ___   ___

38. I can't find a place to carry on a private conversation   ___   ___   ___   ___   ___

39. this place is too noisy   ___   ___   ___   ___   ___

40. the center's policies and procedures are clear   ___   ___   ___   ___   ___

My Pay and Promotion Opportunities...

41. my pay is adequate   ___   ___   ___   ___   ___

42. my pay is fair considering my background and skills   ___   ___   ___   ___   ___

43. my pay is fair considering what my co-workers make   ___   ___   ___   ___   ___

44. I'm in a deadend job   ___   ___   ___   ___   ___

45. my fringe benefits are inadequate   ___   ___   ___   ___   ___

46. I feel I could be replaced tomorrow   ___   ___   ___   ___   ___

47. I have enough time off for holidays and vacations   ___   ___   ___   ___   ___

48. I'm being paid less than I deserve   ___   ___   ___   ___   ___

49. opportunities for me to advance are limited   ___   ___   ___   ___   ___

50. I expect to receive a raise during the next year   ___   ___   ___   ___   ___

PART II. If you could design your ideal job, how close would your present position resemble your ideal job with respect to the following:

	not like my ideal at all		somewhat resembles my ideal		is my ideal
	1	2	3	4	5
relationship with co-workers	_____	_____	_____	_____	_____
relationship with supervisor	_____	_____	_____	_____	_____
the work itself	_____	_____	_____	_____	_____
working conditions	_____	_____	_____	_____	_____
pay and promotion opportunities	_____	_____	_____	_____	_____

PART III. Different people value different aspects of their work. In other words, we gain fulfillment in our jobs by meeting certain needs. Below is a list of some of the ways that our jobs can be rewarding. Put a check (✔) next to the three job characteristics that you value the most.

_____ Colleagues — working with people you like
_____ Altruism — helping others
_____ Achievement — that feeling of accomplishment of doing a job well
_____ Pay — earning a good living to buy the things you need
_____ Intellectual stimulation — learning new things
_____ Variety — the opportunity to do different kinds of things
_____ Challenge — the opportunity to master new skills
_____ Security — the assurance that your position is secure
_____ Creativity — developing new ideas, creating new things
_____ Autonomy — being independent in making decisions
_____ Prestige — gaining respect from others
_____ Environment — pleasant surroundings in which to work
_____ Leadership — the opportunity to guide and influence the work of others
_____ Other: _____

PART IV. What are the two most satisfying things about your present job? What are to two most frustrating things about your present job?

satisfactions	**frustrations**
1. _____	1. _____
2. _____	2. _____

Developing Your Job Satisfaction Profile

Step #1 Assign points (1, 2, 3, 4, or 5) to each statement in Part I according to the following formula:

Co-worker Relations
Score questions #1, 2, 3, 8, 10: 1 (strongly disagree) to 5 (strongly agree)
Score questions #4, 5, 6, 7, 9: 5 (strongly disagree) to 1 (strongly agree)

Supervisor Relations
Score questions #11, 14, 15, 16, 18: 1 (strongly disagree) to 5 (strongly agree)
Score questions #12, 13, 17, 19, 20: 5 (strongly disagree) to 1 (strongly agree)

Nature of the Work Itself
Score questions #21, 22, 26, 28, 30: 1 (strongly disagree) to 5 (strongly agree)
Score questions #23, 24, 25, 27, 29: 5 (strongly disagree) to 1 (strongly agree)

Working Conditions
Score questions #31, 32, 33, 37, 40: 1 (strongly disagree) to 5 (strongly agree)
Score questions #34, 35, 36, 38, 39: 5 (strongly disagree) to 1 (strongly agree)

Pay and Promotion Opportunities
Score questions #41, 42, 43, 47, 50: 1 (strongly disagree) to 5 (strongly agree)
Score questions #44, 45, 46, 48, 49: 5 (strongly disagree) to 1 (strongly agree)

Step #2 Now add together the scores within each category. These scores will range from 10 to 50.

Co-worker Relations   total score = _____

Supervisor Relations   total score = _____

The Nature of the Work Itself   total score = _____

Working Conditions   total score = _____

Pay and Promotion Opportunities   total score = _____

Step #3 Add together the total number of points for Part II:

Total congruence with ideal = _____ (score will range from 5 to 25)

Step #4 Plot your job satisfaction facet scores and your congruence with ideal score on the profile on the following page.

Step #5 Transfer the information from Part III and Part IV to the profile on the next page.

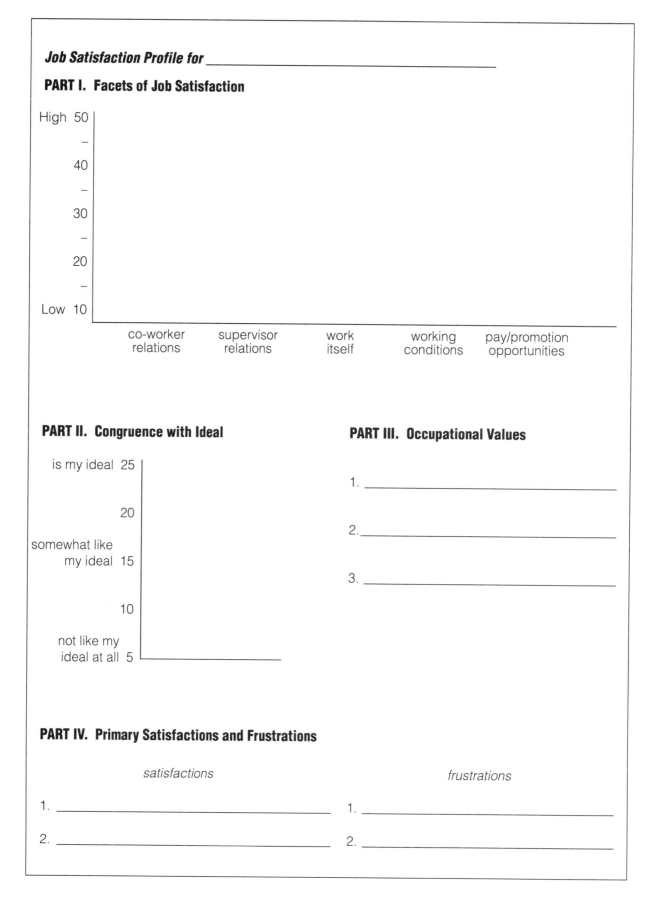

Job Satisfaction Profile for _____

PART I. Facets of Job Satisfaction

High 50
—
40
—
30
—
20
—
Low 10

co-worker   supervisor   work   working   pay/promotion
relations   relations   itself   conditions   opportunities

PART II. Congruence with Ideal

is my ideal 25

20

somewhat like
my ideal 15

10

not like my
ideal at all 5

PART III. Occupational Values

1. _____

2. _____

3. _____

PART IV. Primary Satisfactions and Frustrations

satisfactions

1. _____

2. _____

frustrations

1. _____

2. _____

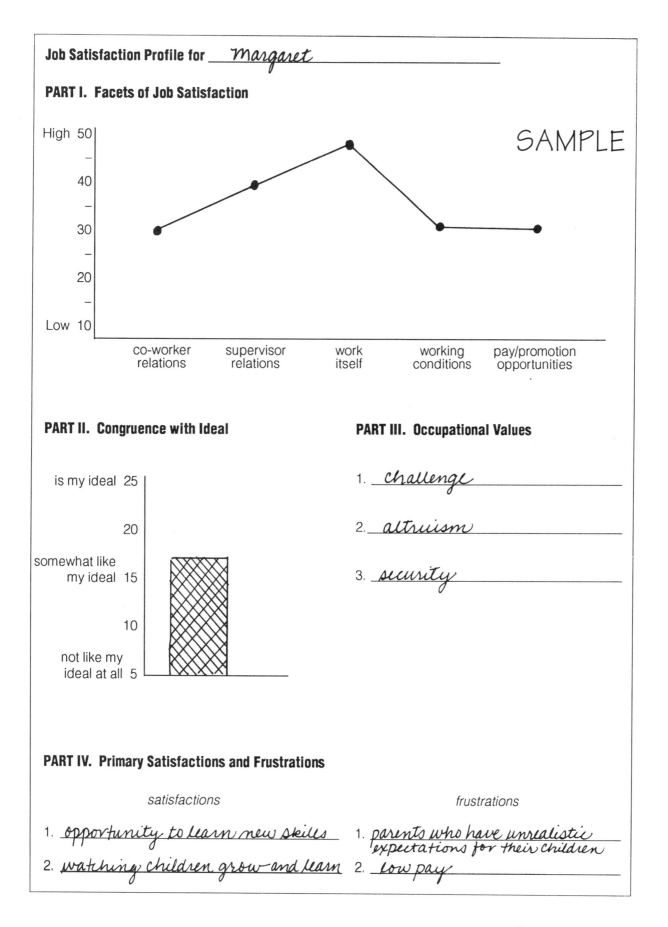

Job Satisfaction Profile for *Margaret*

PART I. Facets of Job Satisfaction

SAMPLE

High 50
40
30
20
Low 10

co-worker relations | supervisor relations | work itself | working conditions | pay/promotion opportunities

PART II. Congruence with Ideal

is my ideal 25

20

somewhat like my ideal 15

10

not like my ideal at all 5

PART III. Occupational Values

1. *challenge*

2. *altruism*

3. *security*

PART IV. Primary Satisfactions and Frustrations

satisfactions

1. *opportunity to learn new skills*
2. *watching children grow and learn*

frustrations

1. *parents who have unrealistic expectations for their children*
2. *low pay*

Professional Orientation

Rationale:

Professional involvement of teachers and administrators promotes growth and change, knowledge-based skill, reference-group orientation, and achievement of goals. Individuals who have a strong professional orientation also tend to have a stronger commitment to the center and demonstrate more enthusiasm about their work. Assessment Tool #20 assesses the type and variety of activities an individual engages in that promote professionalism. Reliability and validity data and a comparison to national norms are provided elsewhere (Jorde-Bloom, 1989a, 1989b).

Directions:

The kind of information elicited on the "Professional Activities Questionnaire" will provide important background data on prospective candidates for employment at your center. Once the teachers are employed, you will probably want to administer this assessment annually to see how they are progressing in their level of professional orientation. Staff should be instructed to answer the 13 questions as honestly as possible.

Scoring:

The scores on this instrument range from a low of 0 to a high of 20. The following may be used as a guide for scoring the 13 questions included on this assessment tool:

1. "just a job" = 0, a career = 1
2. no = 0, yes = 1
3. no = 0, yes = 1
4. 0 to 5 hrs = 0, 6 to 10 hrs = 1, more than 10 hrs = 2
5. give 1 point for each different organization noted up to 2 points (note, NAEYC and its affiliates ILAEYC, CAEYC, HAEYC, etc. are considered as only one organization)
6. give 1 point for each educational magazine or journal noted up to 2 points
7. none = 0, 1-3 = 1, 4 or more = 2
8. none = 0, 1 = 1, 2 or more = 2
9. none = 0, 1-3 = 1, 4 or more = 2
10. none = 0, 1 = 1, 2 or more = 2
11. 1 point if title and publisher noted
12. no = 0, yes = 1
13. no = 0, yes = 1

Professional Activities Questionnaire

1. Do you consider your work _____ "just a job" or _____ a career?

2. Did you enroll in any college courses for credit last year?   no _____   yes _____

3. Are you currently working toward a degree or CDA credential?   no _____   yes _____

4. On the average, how many hours per week do you spend over and above what you are paid for in activities related to early childhood?   _____ hours

5. What professional organizations do you currently pay dues to?

   _____   _____

6. What professional journals and/or magazines do you currently subscribe to?

   _____   _____

7. How many professional books did you read last year?

   _____ none   _____ 1 to 3   _____ 4 or more

8. How many advocacy letters to elected representatives or to the editor of your local newspaper have you written during the past year?

   _____ none   _____ 1   _____ 2 or more

9. How many professional conferences/workshops did you attend last year?

   _____ none   _____ 1 to 3   _____ 4 or more

10. How many workshops or lectures to professional groups did you give during the past year (not counting your own staff)?

    _____ none   _____ 1   _____ 2 or more

11. Have you published any articles or books on early childhood education?

    Title/publisher_____

12. Do you expect to be working in the field of early childhood three years from now?

    _____ no _____ yes   If no, why?_____

13. If you could do it all over again, would you choose a career in early childhood education?

    _____ no _____ yes   Why? _____

From Jorde-Bloom, P. (1989a). *Measuring work attitudes: Technical manual for the Early Childhood Job Satisfaction Survey and the Early Childhood Work Environment Survey.* Brandon, VT: Psychology Press.

Role Clarity

Rationale:

Central to program effectiveness is a clear understanding about who does what, when, and where. While job descriptions provide the broad framework for organizational functioning, everyday issues about the scope and nature of responsibilities often get blurred. Conflict between individuals at a center often arises when their definition of their own role responsibilities differs from the way in which others look upon their role. In addition, the way in which others perform their roles affects one's ability to perform at optimal levels. Role conflict occurs when one's formal position has conflicting organizational expectations. Role ambiguity results when there are vague or ambiguous job descriptions and operating policies and procedures.

Assessment Tool #21 assesses staff's perceptions about their jobs. It is adapted from the work of Dyer (1984), Fox and Schmuck (1973), Rizzo, House, and Lirtzman (1970), and Seashore, Lawler, Mirvis, and Cammann (1983).

Directions:

Distribute the "Role Perception Questionnaire" to all staff who have worked at the center for more than three months. Be sure and give each staff person a blank envelope. Ensure staff of the confidentiality of their responses. Place a box labeled "Questionnaire Return Box" in your center's office or staff room and ask respondents to deposit their completed questionnaires in this box. If you feel that staff will not be as honest and candid in their responses to the open-ended questions if they know you are tabulating the results, you may want an outside person to tally the results and summarize the responses.

Scoring:

Tally the individual scores for respondents. To do this add the numerals circled for all items except #5, 7, and 11. These three items are worded negatively and have to be reversed scored (seldom = 5, always = 1). The respondent's total score on this assessment tool will range from 12 to 60. Next add all the staff's scores together and divide by the total number of respondents to get an average role clarity score. A high score (48 - 60) indicates that staff perceive their jobs are clearly defined and they seldom experience conflicting demands and role expectations. A low score (12 - 24) indicates that confusion exists about lines of authority and in role assignments.

Role Perception Questionnaire

Please circle the response that most nearly describes your feelings about your present job.

		seldom		*sometimes*		*always*
1. I am clear about what my responsibilities are.		1	2	3	4	5
2. I am certain about how much authority I have.		1	2	3	4	5
3. I am given a chance to do the things I do best.		1	2	3	4	5
4. I have an opportunity to develop my own special abilities.		1	2	3	4	5
5. I spend time on unnecessary, irrelevant tasks.		1	2	3	4	5
6. Clear planned goals and objectives exist for my job.		1	2	3	4	5
7. I receive conflicting expectations from people about my job.		1	2	3	4	5
8. I have the knowledge and skills to do my job well.		1	2	3	4	5
9. I have enough resources to do my job well.		1	2	3	4	5
10. There is enough time to do my job well.		1	2	3	4	5
11. I ignore certain policies in order to carry out my job.		1	2	3	4	5
12. I get the support I need to do my job well.		1	2	3	4	5

What keeps you from being as effective as you would like to be in your position?

If you had the power to change anything about your job, what would you change? Why would this be an improvement over existing conditions?

What suggestions do you have for improving schedules, routines, and procedures so staff can function as a more effective team?

Role Clarity
(New Staff)

Rationale:

Confusion about roles and expectations often begins in the first days (even the first hours) that an employee starts a new job. Tapping into staff's perceptions about their new positions can create the beginnings of a relationship based on mutual trust and respect. It can also circumvent potential problems before they have a chance to grow into full-blown job grievances. Assessment Tool #22 is designed for new staff employed at a center. Ideally, it should be given to staff approximately four weeks after they have begun a new position.

Directions:

Distribute the "Staff Orientation Assessment" to all new staff approximately four to six weeks after they have begun working for your program. It is advised that the individual have the opportunity to take the assessment home and complete it without the distractions of the classroom.

Scoring:

Since the responses on this assessment tool are open-ended, they will vary from individual to individual. The results of this assessment should help alert the director to potential misunderstandings about the scope and nature of the position assumed. The results can also prove helpful in modifying orientation policies for new staff in the future.

Staff Orientation Assessment

Please take a few minutes to answer the questions below. Your honest, candid responses will help us continue to meet the needs of new staff in our center.

1. Were you made to feel comfortable and welcome at the center on your first day on the job? Did other staff know you were coming?

2. Were you given enough familiarity with the particulars of our school environment to help you through those first difficult days (parking, supplies, storage, lunch routines, schedules, etc.)?

3. Were you given sufficient background on the center's policies, goals, and philosophy?

4. Were you made to feel that others had a personal interest in your progress? Have staff made you feel like you are part of a team?

5. Are there any policies or procedures you would like to know more about?

Organizational Commitment

Rationale:

The level of commitment of child care workers relates to their acceptance of the center's goals and values. It will directly affect their willingness to exert effort on behalf of the program, and their desire to remain working at the center. Assessment Tool #23 was designed to help you tap into your staff's level of commitment. It was adapted from the work of Mowday, Steers, & Porter (1979) and Jorde-Bloom (1989a).

Directions:

Because the nature of the questions included on the "How Committed Am I?" questionnaire are quite sensitive, it is recommended that individuals use it as a self-assessment to reflect on their level of commitment to the center. Please emphasize to staff that you are not interested in their answers to specific questions, but rather their overall total score. For this reason, staff should be responsible for scoring the instrument themselves. Reassure them of the confidential nature of their score and that your interest in knowing their total score is to help you get a sense of the collective commitment of the staff and if that commitment has fluctuated over time. It is recommended that this assessment tool be administered annually, prior to the teacher's goal setting conference.

Scoring:

The total scores for this instrument will range from a low of 0 to a high of 90. A score ranging between 75 and 90 would indicate that the individual has quite positive feelings about the center as a place to work. From the employee's perspective, the match between what he/she brings to the center and what the center can offer is obviously quite good. A score lower than 30 would indicate that there are strong feelings on the part of the individual that this may not be the most appropriate place for him/her to work.

From the other data you have collected on this person, you will be able to discern if the individual is a candidate for burnout and needs to be re-energized, or if the possibility exists that there is a mismatch between the needs and expectations of this person and what the program can offer. This kind of situation may necessitate the person leaving the center to find a more satisfying and fulfilling place to work.

How Committed Am I?

Below are a series of statements that represent possible feelings that individuals may have about the early childhood center for which they work. With respect to your own feelings about your center, please indicate your degree of agreement or disagreement with each statement using the scale below:

strongly disagree						strongly agree
0	1	2	3	4	5	6

_____ I am willing to put in a great deal of effort beyond that normally expected in order to help this center be successful.

_____ I talk about this center to my friends as a great place to work.

_____ I feel a great deal of loyalty to this center.

_____ I would accept almost any type of job assignment in order to keep working for this center.

_____ I find that my values and this center's values are very similar.

_____ I am proud to tell others that I work for this center.

_____ It would not be the same working for another center even if the type of work I did was similar.

_____ This center really inspires the very best in me in the way of job performance.

_____ It would take a big change in my present circumstances to cause me to leave this center.

_____ I am extremely glad that I chose to work at this center over other options I was considering at the time I started.

_____ Most of the time I agree with this center's policies on important matters relating to its employees.

_____ I really care about the fate of this center.

_____ For me this is the best of all possible centers for which to work.

_____ Even if I had a slightly higher paying job offer, I wouldn't leave this job.

_____ I intend to work here at least two more years.

Perceived Problems

Rationale:

One approach to providing meaningful, individualized staff development is based on identifying the day-to-day problems which staff experience as they go about their work. If we can identify what teachers feel their problems are, then we have accomplished the first step in helping them manage or solve those problems. The director will then be better able to design staff development activities which address these problems. Assessment Tool #24 was developed by John M. Johnston (1984).

Directions:

Distribute the "Prekindergarten Teacher Problem Checklist" to those teachers or assistant teachers for whom you feel the issues addressed are appropriate. Ask the teacher to read through the 60 problems carefully. This will take some time and reflection, so you may advise them to take the assessment tool home with them for a day or two. Be sure and tell them that these problems were generated by teachers. This may help reduce their level of anxiety about identifying their most problematic areas. Ask your staff to put a check by the problems that are troublesome for them. Then ask them to put a star in front of the 10 problems they seem to experience most frequently. These can then be discussed at the annual planning conference as you develop new goals for the following year.

Scoring:

The 60 problems can be grouped into seven major problems areas: subordinate staff relations; control and nurturance of children; remediation; relations with supervisors; parent cooperation; management of time; and management of routines. The 10 problems selected by the teacher can be reviewed in light of these seven areas to determine if they tend to focus more on one particular area. Such analysis can lead to a discussion of staff development strategies for improvement in that area.

Assessment Tool #24 may also be used as a basis for staff development plans for the center. Using a scale of 1 (not a problem) to 5 (this is a serious problem), have the staff assign a rating to each item. Tally all the staff's ratings for each item and divide by the number of staff. This will yield an average score for each item. The items with the highest average score represent problems of importance to the staff as a whole. Several teachers may share the same problem; these can form the basis for a small group staff development activity. Other problems shared by most staff members can form the basis for center-wide staff development activities.

Prekindergarten Teacher Problems Checklist

Read through the following list of 60 problems that prekindergarten teachers have identified as troublesome. As you read through the list, preface each problem statement with the phrase, "I have a problem..." Put a check next to those that seem to be troublesome for you. When you are finished, go back through your list and put a star next to the 10 most troublesome problems you experience.

_____ 1. Getting children to do what I ask them to do.

_____ 2. Controlling the noise or energy level in the room.

_____ 3. Understanding the reason for children's problem behavior.

_____ 4. Getting parents to supply accurate, up-to-date information for our files.

_____ 5. Getting children to share or take turns.

_____ 6. Providing for communication among staff.

_____ 7. Getting parent cooperation in solving their children's preschool/center-related problems.

_____ 8. Orienting new staff to all aspects of the program and their job.

_____ 9. Knowing how to handle children's aggressive behavior.

_____ 10. Getting parents to drop off or pick up their children on time.

_____ 11. Dealing with a child who cries or whines frequently.

_____ 12. Promoting effective mutual communication between home and center/preschool.

_____ 13. Getting staff to follow through on assigned responsibilities.

_____ 14. Getting parents to keep their children home when they are sick.

_____ 15. Getting children to clean up.

_____ 16. Motivating myself to be involved in outside professional activities.

_____ 17. Dealing with parents who say their child is toilet-trained when he/she is not.

_____ 18. Providing adequate staff to meet all program needs.

_____ 19. Knowing how to help the special or atypical child.

_____ 20. Spending personal time doing necessary classroom tasks or administrative tasks.

_____ 21. Contending with interruptions while I am working.

_____ 22. Meeting the required staff-child ratios at all times during the day.

_____ 23. Getting children to learn and follow room rules and routines.

_____ 24. Finding time away from children for planning and preparation.

_____ 25. Getting children to use words and not hit others when they are angry.

_____ 26. Getting parents to follow policies on enrollment or fee payments.

_____ 27. Keeping children's attention during group time.

_____ 28. Getting parent cooperation with toilet training.

_____ 29. Getting children to sleep or rest quietly without disturbing others at nap time.

_____ 30. Working with an ineffective supervisor.

_____ 31. Getting parents to provide appropriate clothing from home.

_____ 32. Finding effective substitute staff.

_____ 33. Feeling positive toward a child who frequently misbehaves.

_____ 34. Getting my supervisor to respect my professional judgment.

_____ 35. Being able to stay home when I am sick.

_____ 36. Keeping one child's problem behavior from affecting other children.

_____ 37. Finding workshops that are appropriate to my level of skill and knowledge.

_____ 38. Meeting an individual child's needs without neglecting the group.

_____ 39. Getting children who are toilet trained not to wet their pants.

_____ 40. Helping parents understand and deal appropriately with their child's behavior.

_____ 41. Getting staff to model appropriate behavior for children.

_____ 42. Getting staff to work in a cooperative fashion.

_____ 43. Helping parents of special or atypical children recognize and adjust to their child's needs.

_____ 44. Getting parents to come to scheduled events or conferences.

_____ 45. Getting my supervisor to give me feedback about my job performance.

_____ 46. Getting my supervisor to include me in the decision-making process for my classroom.

_____ 47. Knowing how to counteract a child's negative home environment.

_____ 48. Meeting the needs of the children when the room is short staffed.

_____ 49. Working with equipment or facilities which are in poor condition.

_____ 50. Getting all children to participate in group activities.

_____ 51. Knowing if parents are abusing or neglecting their children.

_____ 52. Finding time for cleaning and other non-teaching tasks.

_____ 53. Involving the passive child in activities.

_____ 54. Getting staff to recognize and act on children's needs.

_____ 55. Dealing with unfair criticism from my supervisor.

_____ 56. Meeting the needs of all children in a multi-age group.

_____ 57. Giving adequate attention to the special or atypical child without neglecting other children.

_____ 58. Getting staff to understand and deal appropriately with young children's behavior.

_____ 59. Dressing and undressing children for cold weather outdoor play.

_____ 60. Understanding the public attitude that day care or preschools are just babysitting.

From Johnston, J. (1984, March). Assessing staff problems: Key to effective staff development. _Child Care Information Exchange,_ pp. 1-4. Reprinted with permission from Exchange Press.

Flexibility and Openness to Change

Rationale:

Gaining insight into one's attitudes and behaviors relative to change is an important first step in identifying potential resistance to new and innovative ideals. When we think about attitudes toward change, it is possible to think of a continuum from a flexible (typically more open-minded) approach to a more conservative (typically more cautious) approach. Knowing a teacher's orientation on this continuum can help directors to structure the pace and timing of staff development experiences to accommodate individual needs. Assessment Tool #25 is a modified version of an instrument developed by the Public Management Institute (1980).

Directions:

You will probably want to administer the "Flexibility Index" to your staff about once every two or three years. This instrument is designed to be self-administered and self-scored by the individual staff member. Using the scoring directions below, a flexibility profile can be generated. This profile can then be brought to the planning conference and used to stimulate discussion about the individual's openness to change.

Scoring:

Instruct teachers how to use the grid on the page following the questionnaire to chart their "yes" and "no" answers to create an individual profile regarding their orientation toward change. To analyze the results, consider that a flexibility profile with fewer than 6 "yes" answers indicates a dynamic, change-oriented approach to work. The higher the number of "yes" answers, the more conservative (and possibly resistant) the person may be to change.

Flexibility Index

Answer "yes" or "no" to the 20 questions below using the introductory words, "I generally...," before each phrase. There are no right or wrong answers to this questionnaire. Instead, the responses should reflect your preferred orientation with respect to change.

I generally...   *yes*   *no*

1. try to cope with things as they are.   _____   _____

2. feel there is a right way and a wrong way to teach young children.   _____   _____

3. think change often just interrupts the efficiency of my classroom routine. _____   _____

4. must believe I will succeed before I try something new in my classroom.   _____   _____

5. believe that changes in routine will only make teaching more difficult.   _____   _____

6. believe a rational approach to problem solving is best.   _____   _____

7. choose alternatives according to their risk factors.   _____   _____

8. believe I'm not particularly creative in my teaching.   _____   _____

9. believe if I fail to manage my classroom well, I'll probably lose my job.   _____   _____

10. tend to set short term rather than long term goals for my children and
    the classroom.   _____   _____

11. have trouble evaluating alternatives quickly.   _____   _____

12. am skeptical of plans that will change the basic routine of my classroom. _____   _____

13. believe that change happens so slowly that in the end it is ineffective.   _____   _____

14. like my job for security reasons.   _____   _____

15. believe that routine is an important element of teaching.   _____   _____

16. feel the old way of doing things works just as well or better.   _____   _____

17. feel that many changes don't make any real difference.   _____   _____

18. believe that most people are quite satisfied with the way things are.   _____   _____

19. see most risks as win/lose situations.   _____   _____

20. must understand every facet of the problem before I make a decision.   _____   _____

Chart Your Flexibility Profile

Using your responses to the statements on the previous page, circle your "yes" answers and your "no" answers on the profile below.

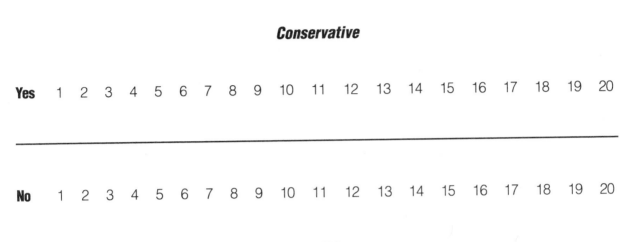

Conservative

Yes 1 2 3 4 5 6 7 8 9 10 11 12 13 14 15 16 17 18 19 20

No 1 2 3 4 5 6 7 8 9 10 11 12 13 14 15 16 17 18 19 20

Flexible

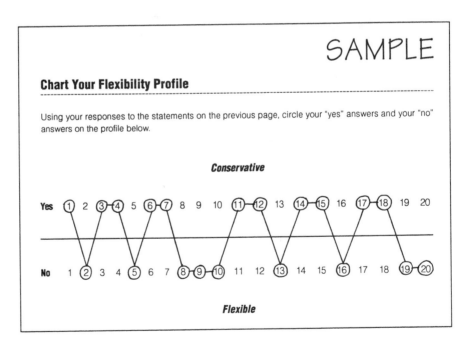

SAMPLE

Chart Your Flexibility Profile

Using your responses to the statements on the previous page, circle your "yes" answers and your "no" answers on the profile below.

Conservative

Yes 1 2 3 4 5 6 7 8 9 10 11 12 13 14 15 16 17 18 19 20

No 1 2 3 4 5 6 7 8 9 10 11 12 13 14 15 16 17 18 19 20

Flexible

Adapted from Public Management Institute. (1980). *Non-profit management skills for women managers.* San Francisco, CA: PMI, pp. 173-175. Reprinted with permisison.

Supervisory Beliefs

Rationale:

Before choosing a supervisory approach to use with a teacher, it is important for the director to assess her own beliefs about teacher supervision and staff development. Although supervisors probably use directive, collaborative, and non-directive styles at one time or another, one style usually dominates. The director will benefit from being aware of her strongest orientation. Other staff who serve in supervisory roles such as Master Teachers may also enjoy taking this self assessment. Assessment Tool #26 was developed by Carl Glickman (1981). For a full discussion of the three different supervisory styles assessed by this instrument, readers are encouraged to read Glickman's book, *Supervision of Instruction: A Developmental Approach* (1985).

Directions:

This inventory is designed to be self-administered and self-scored. As you read the questions, circle one of two options: A or B for each item. You may not completely agree with either choice, but choose the one that is closest to how you feel.

Scoring:

Step #1. Circle your answers from the inventory in the following columns:

Column I	Column II	Column III
1B	1A	
	2B	2A
3A	3B	
4B		4A
	5B	5A
6A		6B
	7A	7B
8A		8B
9A	9B	
10B		10A
11A		11B
12A	12B	
	13B	13A
14B	14A	
	15A	15B

Step #2. Tally the number of circled items in each column and multiply by 6.7.

2.1 Total response in Column I _____ x 6.7 = _____

2.2 Total response in Column II _____ x 6.7 = _____

2.3 Total response in Column III _____ x 6.7 = _____

Interpretation:

The product you obtained in step 2.1 is an approximate percentage of how often you take a directive approach to supervision. The product you obtained in step 2.2 is an approximate percentage of how often you take a collaborative approach, and that in step 2.3 an approximate percentage of how often you take a nondirective approach.

The Supervisory Beliefs Inventory

Circle either A or B for each item. You may not completely agree with either choice, but choose the one that is closest to how you feel.

1. A. Supervisors should give teachers a large degree of autonomy within broadly defined limits.

    B. Supervisors should give teachers directions about methods that help them improve teaching.

2. A. It is important for teachers to set their own goals and objectives for professional growth.

    B. It is important for supervisors to help teachers reconcile their personalities and teaching styles with the philosophy and direction of the school.

3. A. Teachers are likely to feel uncomfortable and anxious if the objectives on which they will be evaluated are not clearly defined by the supervisor.

    B. Evaluations of teachers are meaningless if teachers are not able to define with their supervisors the objectives for evaluation.

4. A. An open, trusting, warm, and personal relationship with teachers is the most important ingredient in supervising teachers.

    B. A supervisor who is too intimate with teachers risks being less effective and less respected than a supervisor who keeps a certain degree of professional distance from teachers.

5. A. My role during supervisory conferences is to make the interaction positive, to share realistic information, and to help teachers plan their own solutions to problems.

    B. The methods and strategies I use with teachers in a conference are aimed at our reaching agreement over the needs for future improvement.

6. In the initial phase of working with a teacher

    A. I develop objectives with each teacher that will help accomplish school goals.

    B. I try to identify the talents and goals of teachers so they can work on their own improvement.

7. When several teachers have a similar classroom problem, I prefer to:

    A. Have the teachers form an ad hoc group and help them work together to solve the problem.

    B. Help teachers on an individual basis find their strengths, abilities, and resources so that each one finds his or her own solution to the problem.

8. The most important clue that an inservice workshop is needed occurs when:

    A. The supervisor perceives that several teachers lack knowledge or skill in a specific area, which is resulting in low morale, undue stress, and less effective teaching.

    B. Several teachers perceive the need to strengthen their abilities in the same area.

9. A. The supervisory staff should decide the objectives of an inservice workshop since they have a broad perspective on the teachers' abilities and the school's needs.

   B. Teachers and supervisory staff should reach consensus about the objectives of an inservice workshop before the workshop is held.

10. A. Teachers who feel they are growing personally will be more effective than teachers who are not experiencing personal growth.

    B. The knowledge and ability of teaching strategies and methods that have been proved over the years should be taught and practiced by all teachers to be effective in their classrooms.

11. When I perceive that a teacher might be scolding a student unnecessarily:

    A. I explain during a conference with the teacher why the scolding was excessive.

    B. I ask the teacher about the incident, but do not interject my judgments.

12. A. One effective way to improve teacher performance is to formulate clear behavioral objectives and create meaningful incentives for achieving them.

    B. Behavioral objectives are rewarding and helpful to some teachers but stifling to others; some teachers benefit from behavioral objectives in some situations but not in others.

13. During a preobservation conference:

    A. I suggest to the teacher what I could observe, but I let the teacher make the final decision about the objectives and methods of observation.

    B. The teacher and I mutually decide the objectives and methods of observation.

14. A. Improvement occurs very slowly if teachers are left on their own, but when a group of teachers work together on a specific problem, they learn rapidly and their morale remains high.

    B. Group activities may be enjoyable, but I find that individual, open discussion with a teacher about a problem and its possible solutions leads to more sustained results.

15. When an inservice or staff development workshop is scheduled:

    A. All teachers who participated in the decision to hold the workshop should be expected to attend.

    B. Teachers, regardless of their role in forming a workshop, should be able to decide if the workshop is relevant to their personal or professional growth and, if not, should not be expected to attend.

From Glickman, C. (1981). *Developmental supervision: Alternative practices for helping teachers improve instruction.* Alexandria, VA: Association for Supervision and Curriculum Development, pp. 13-15. Reprinted with permission.

Goal Setting Motivation

Rationale:

Whether it's a New Year's resolution to lose 10 pounds or a promise to our grandmother that we'll call more often, we have all set goals and made promises to change our behavior. But too often our goals go unfulfilled; our promises go unkept. Somewhere along the way we lost our will power to see them through. Often this is because we do not take the time to accurately assess our true motivation in reaching our goals. Setting goals for oneself is only the first step to changing behavior. We also need to determine what reasons might affect our motivation to achieve the goal. Otherwise, goal setting and action plans may become merely a paper exercise. Assessment Tool #27 was designed to help you assist staff in assessing their level of motivation for achieving the goals they have set as part of their staff development action plan. This assessment is a modified version of a goal-setting motivation questionnaire developed by Dyer (1984).

Directions:

After you have met with your staff at their annual planning conference to target new professional goals for the coming year, distribute the "How Motivated Am I" questionnaire to them and ask them to complete it. This questionnaire is designed to provoke reflection on their part about the level of commitment they have for achieving the goals that have been drawn up on the action plan. It is designed to be self-administered. There is no need to collect it after the staff member has completed it.

Scoring:

This questionnaire is designed to be self-scored by the individual teacher or staff member completing it. The most important part of this assessment is the goal motivation continuum at the bottom of the page. The individual should determine his/her overall level of motivation for achieving the goals on the staff development action plan that has been drawn up. Let teachers know that if they have rated their overall motivation a 3 or lower on this scale, it will be important for them to meet with you again to revise the action plan to more accurately reflect those areas that they are sincerely motivated to accomplish.

"How Motivated Am I?"

The two lists below show some of the reasons people make a change (payoffs) or don't make a change (blocks). As you set your goals and write your action plan, identify those reasons that might affect your motivation to achieve your goals.

"Blocks"	**"Payoffs"**
Fear of the unknown	Greater recognition
Complacency	More freedom/autonomy
Lack of skill	More productive
Takes too much time	More efficient
Don't want more responsibility	More responsibility
Don't see a need for change	Increased feelings of self-worth
Too much effort required	Opportunity to be of help to others
Fear of rejection	Better interpersonal relationships
Forced to make the change	More control over what I am doing

other_____   other_____

Which of the "blocks" affects you the most?

_____

In what ways can you reduce the impact of these blocks?

_____

_____

What is the "payoff" for you for taking on this goal?

_____

_____

On a scale of 1 – 7, assess the strength of your motivation to achieve the goal you have set.

(low)   1   2   3   4   5   6   7   (high)

Adapted from Dyer, W. (1984). *Strategies for managing change.* Reading, MA: Addison-Wesley, pp. 101-102. Reprinted with permission.

Sample Forms

The sample forms included in this appendix are available for purchase from the publisher as a separate packet. The masters included in the packet may be freely reproduced for professional development activities at your center. Permission for systematic large-scale reproduction for other training and research purposes, or for inclusion in other publications must be obtained from the copyright holder. The authors would appreciate any feedback from individuals using the forms included in this book. This appendix includes the following sample forms:

1. Individual Profile

2. Observations

3. Preparing for the Planning Conference

4. Goals Blueprint

5. Staff Development Action Plan

6. Peer Observation

7. Performance Appraisal

8. Working Together Toward a Common Vision

Individual Profile

Name _____ Age _____

Education/training _____

Teaching experience _____

_____

_____

Professional orientation _____

_____

_____

Special interests/skills/talents _____

_____

_____

Relevant personal history _____

_____

_____

Concomitant roles _____

_____

_____

Stage of adult development/ego development _____

_____

_____

_____

Career stage _____

_____

_____

Personal traits and characteristics

Energy level _____

_____

Level of abstract thinking _____

_____

Temperament/psychological type _____

_____

Learning style _____

_____

General dispositions _____

_____

Self-confidence/self-efficacy _____

_____

Degree of flexibility/openness to change _____

_____

Commitment/motivation _____

_____

_____

Beliefs and values _____

_____

_____

Expectations/needs _____

_____

_____

Observations

Name _____

Date: _____

_____

_____

_____

_____

_____

Date: _____

_____

_____

_____

_____

_____

Date: _____

_____

_____

_____

_____

_____

Preparing for the Planning Conference

Dear staff member:

As you prepare for our planning conference, think about the following:

▶ What aspect of your job gives you the greatest personal satisfaction?

▶ What aspect of your job is most frustrating?

▶ What keeps you from being as effective as you would like to be in your position?

▶ If you had the power to change anything about your job, what would you change? Why would this be an improvement over existing conditions?

▶ What do you see yourself doing five years from now?

▶ What new skills or knowledge would you like to learn this next year?

▶ How can I or other staff help you achieve your personal and professional goals?

Goals Blueprint

Teacher's name _____ Date _____

Strengths as a teacher

1. _____

2. _____

3. _____

Areas in need of improvement/growth

1. _____

2. _____

3. _____

Goal _____

_____

Objectives

1. _____

2. _____

3. _____

Staff Development Action Plan

Name _____ Date_____

Objective #1_____

Activities	Time Needed	Resources Needed
1.		
2.		

Evaluation (how/when) _____

Objective #2_____

Activities	Time Needed	Resources Needed
1.		
2.		

Evaluation (how/when) _____

Objective #3_____

Activities	Time Needed	Resources Needed
1.		
2.		

Evaluation (how/when) _____

Peer Observation

Name of colleague observed _____ Date _____

As you observe, please note comments about the following aspects of the classroom environment: interactions between the teacher and children; interactions between the teacher and other co-teachers or volunteers; interactions between the teacher and parents; the physical arrangement of space; the curriculum; and health, nutrition, and safety aspects of the program.

Aspects of this classroom I was impressed with include ...

1. _____

_____

2. _____

_____

3. _____

_____

Aspects of this classroom that might be improved include . . .

1. _____

_____

2. _____

_____

3. _____

_____

Signed _____

Performance Appraisal – Preschool Teacher

Name: _____

Date _____

	seldom	sometimes	frequently	always	Comments

To establish and maintain a safe and healthy learning environment

1. Designs appropriate room arrangement

2. Plans and implements a nutritious snack program

3. Promotes healthy eating practices

4. Maintains a safe environment

5. Posts necessary health and safety information

6. Maintains an orderly learning environment

To advance physical and intellectual competence

1. Provides balance between child-/teacher-initiated activities

2. Provides a balance between quiet/active learning activities

3. Uses equipment/materials to promote physical development

4. Involves children in planning and implementing activities

5. Provides an integrated curriculum that meets the needs of individual children

6. Plans and implements experiences that promote language and literacy development

7. Plans and implements activities that promote the acquisition of number concepts

To support social and emotional development and provide positive guidance

	seldom	sometimes	frequently	always	Comments
1. Plans and implements hands-on activities that develop positive self-esteem					
2. Plans and implements hands-on activities that develop social skills					
3. Plans and implements culturally diverse experiences					
4. Uses and promotes positive guidance techniques					
5. Provides a wide variety of creative/expressive activities					
6. Establishes routines with smooth transition periods					
7. Communicates with children at their developmental level					
8. Encourages children to be independent					

To establish positive and productive relationships with families

	seldom	sometimes	frequently	always	Comments
1. Relates assessment information to parents and offers support for dealing with children at different stages					
2. Plans and conducts home visits					
3. Promotes communication with parents through progress notes, monthly newsletter, and parent conferences					
4. Provides a variety of ways that families can participate in the program					
5. Encourages parents to participate in the program					

To ensure a well-run, purposeful program responsive to participant needs

	seldom	sometimes	frequently	always	Comments
1. Assesses program supplies and materials needed prior to implementing activities	—	—	—	—	
2. Coordinates and helps supervise aides, assistants, and volunteers working in the classroom	—	—	—	—	
3. Maintains written plans on a weekly basis	—	—	—	—	
4. Assesses children's needs and developmental progress on an ongoing basis	—	—	—	—	
5. Uses the results of assessment to plan activities	—	—	—	—	

To maintain a commitment to professionalism

	seldom	sometimes	frequently	always	Comments
1. Promotes the center's philosophy and objectives	—	—	—	—	
2. Supports the center's code of ethical conduct	—	—	—	—	
3. Engages in ongoing staff development to improve personal and professional skills	—	—	—	—	
4. Supports the professional growth and development of colleagues by sharing materials and information	—	—	—	—	
5. Attends staff meetings, workshops, and inservice training provided by the center	—	—	—	—	

Additional Comments:

Name of Supervisor _____

Working Together Toward a Common Vision

Date:_____

Center Goal

Name:_____

_____

_____

_____

Name:_____

_____

_____

Objectives

_____

_____

Name:_____

_____

_____

_____

_____

Name:_____

_____

_____

_____

Name:_____

_____

_____

_____

Name:_____

_____

_____

_____

Index

Blueprint for Action

Assessment Tools and Sample Forms
Order Form

Packet includes the 27 assessment tools and 8 sample forms included in this book. One-sided, 104 pages total. Reproducible for staff development purposes at your center. Cost: $11.95 per packet.

- -

Name _____ Date _____

Address_____

City _____ State _____ Zip _____

Please send _____ Packet(s) of **Blueprint for Action** Assessment Tools and Sample Forms @ $11.95 each

Subtotal	_____
Sales tax*	_____
Postage/handling**	_____
Total Enclosed	_____

*   *Illinois residents add 6% sales tax*

**   *Postage/handling: $3.50 for the first packet and 50 cents for each additional packet*

- -

Please make checks payable to: **New Horizons**
and send to: P.O. Box 863
Lake Forest, Illinois 60045